I0061512

AP
Advanced Placement

United States Government and Politics

Duane L. Ostler, PhD
Nancy McCaslin, JD
Sujata Millick, PhD

XAMonline

Copyright © 2017 XAMonline, Inc.

All rights reserved. No part of the material protected by this copyright notice may be reproduced or utilized in any form or by any means, electronic or mechanical, including photocopying, recording or by any information storage and retrievable system, without written permission from the copyright holder.

To obtain permission(s) to use the material from this work for any purpose including workshops or seminars, please submit a written request to

XAMonline, Inc.
21 Orient Avenue
Melrose, MA 02176
Toll Free 1-800-301-4647
Email: info@xamonline.com
Web: www.xamonline.com
Fax: 1-617-583-5552

Library of Congress Cataloging-in-Publication Data
Millick, Sujata

AP United States Government and Politics / Sujata Millick
ISBN: 978-1-60787-635-9

1. Advanced Placement   2. Study Guides   3. Government   4. Politics

Disclaimer:
The opinions expressed in this publication are the sole works of XAMonline and were created independently from The College Board, or any State Department of Education, National Evaluation Systems or other testing affiliates. Between the time of publication and printing, state specific standards as well as testing formats and website information may change that are not included in part or in whole within this product. XAMonline develops sample test questions, and they reflect similar content as on real tests; however, they are not former tests. XAMonline assembles content that aligns with state standards but makes no claims nor guarantees candidates a passing score. Numerical scores are determined by testing companies such as The College Board.

Cover photo provided by © Can Stock Photo Inc./ArtImages; © Can Stock Photo Inc./billperry; © Can Stock Photo Inc./Marcopolo; © Can Stock Photo Inc./PixelRobot; © Can Stock Photo Inc./gary718

Printed in the United States of America

AP United States Government and Politics
ISBN: 978-1-60787-635-9

Table of Contents

SECTION I: About the Advanced Placement
U.S. Government and Politics Examination 3

    About the Exam 5
    Why Take the Exam 7
    College Board Websites 8

SECTION II: How this Study Guide is Organized 9

    What To Expect In This Book 11
    Introduction To Topical Areas 11

SECTION III: Strategies for the AP U.S. Government and Politics Examination . . . 15

    Study Techniques 17
    How to Attack the Multiple-Choice Questions 17
    How to Attack the Free Response Questions 17
    Test-taking Strategies 18

SECTION IV: Topic Summaries 25

  Chapter 1: Constitutional Underpinnings of the U.S. Government 26
    What You Will Be Tested On 26
    Considerations that Influenced the Formulation and Adoption of the Constitution 27
    Separation of Powers 31
    Checks and Balances 33
    Federalism 35
    Theories of Democratic Government 37
    Summary 38
  Chapter 2: Political Beliefs and Behaviors 39
    What You Will Be Tested On 39
    Beliefs of Citizens 40
    Beliefs Citizens Hold About Their Government And Its Leaders 42
    Processes By Which Citizens Learn About Politics 42
    Public Opinion 43
    Voting And Other Methods Of Participation In Politics 47
    Summary 51
  Chapter 3: Political Parties, Interest Groups, and Mass Media 52
    What You Will Be Tested On 52
    Political Parties And Elections 52
    Interest Groups And Political Action Committees 61
    The Mass Media 64
    Summary 68
  Chapter 4: Institutions of National Government 69
    What You Will Be Tested On 69
    Congress 69

The Presidency **77**

The Bureaucracy **85**

The Courts **92**

Arrangements Of Institutions **97**

Relationships Within Government And With Groups **98**

Summary **108**

Chapter 5: Public Policy **109**

What You Will Be Tested On **109**

Policymaking in a Federal System. **110**

The Formation of Policy Agendas **111**

The Role of Institutions in the Enactment of Policy **112**

The Role of the Bureaucracy and the Courts
 in Policy Implementation and Interpretation **113**

Linkages Between Policy Processes **114**

Summary **116**

Chapter 6: Civil Rights and Civil Liberties. **117**

What You Will Be Tested On **118**

The Development of Civil Liberties and Civil Rights by Judicial Interpretation **118**

Knowledge of Substantive Rights and Liberties. **122**

The Impact of the Fourteenth Amendment on the Constitutional
 Development of Rights and Liberties **126**

Summary **127**

SECTION V: Practice Test One **129**

Multiple Choice Answer Sheet **153**

Multiple Choice Answer Key and Explanations **154**

Free Response Sample Answers **181**

SECTION VI: Practice Test Two **187**

Multiple Choice Answer Sheet **212**

Multiple Choice Answer Key and Explanations **213**

Free Response Sample Answers **241**

SECTION VII: Practice Test Three **247**

Multiple Choice Answer Sheet **270**

Multiple Choice Answer Key and Explanations **271**

Free Response Sample Answers **297**

SECTION VIII: Practice Test Four. **301**

Multiple Choice Answer Sheet **325**

Multiple Choice Answer Key and Explanations **326**

Free Response Sample Answers **352**

APPENDIX: US Government and Politics Time Line **357**

MEET THE AUTHORS

Duane L. Ostler

Duane L. Ostler has a BA (history), MPA and JD from BYU in Provo, Utah, and a PhD in legal history from Macquarie University in Sydney, Australia. He lives in Orem, Utah with his wife, five children and two cats.

Nancy McCaslin

Nancy McCaslin is an attorney in Elkhart, Indiana. She has as B.S. in Education from Indiana University (Bloomington) and an M.A. in American History from Ball State University. Her J.D. in Law is from Valparaiso University. Nancy has taught history, government, and business law and has developed curriculum in those areas. She loves to read and travel in her free time.

Sujata Millick

Dr. Sujata Millick works at the intersection of the technology, education, security and privacy domains. She has over two decades of public sector executive and programmatic experience in science, R&D, and STEM education portfolios in the defense, commerce, and maritime organizations. She pursues work in the areas of education, internet connectedness, and emerging technologies.

SECTION I:
About the Advanced Placement U.S. Government and Politics Examination

The Advanced Placement® program is designed to offer students college credit while still in high school. There are more than 30 AP courses that culminate in an intensive final exam given every year in May.

The Government and Politics Examination is one of two exams in the area of government and politics. The other examination is Comparative Government and Politics.

About the Exam

Students taking the Government and Politics Examination should be able to describe and compare facts, concepts, and theories relating to U.S. government; explain political processes and principals; explain the effects of political structures and procedures; interpret government and political data; and analyze political theories and concepts. Additionally, students need to apply those concepts and connect the concepts across the government-related curriculum.

The exam will cover six topics.

(a) Constitutional underpinnings of government that include the organization of government, federalism, checks and balances, and separation of powers as well as theoretical perspectives relating to the Constitution, the republican form of government, elitism, pluralism, and democratic theory.

(b) Political beliefs and behaviors of government leaders and the political system of the United States and how beliefs are changed by individuals and media. This includes the demographics of America, the differing viewpoints of Americans, and group differences in political beliefs.

(c) Political parties, interest groups, and mass media and the mechanisms that allow citizens to communicate interests and concerns. Subjects such as political parties, elections, interest groups, the role of the media, and political action committees are also covered. Elections, voting behavior, lobbying, and policy are part of this topic.

(d) National government institutions and their powers and organization. This includes a working knowledge of the organization of Congress, the presidency, and the courts. The topic includes information about the relationships between the institutions and the implications of the sharing of powers.

(e) Public policy. This includes the formation and enactment of policies as well as the implementation and interpretation of those policies. Policy-making in the federal context is the focus of this topic.

(f) Civil rights and civil liberties, which includes an understanding of the development of those rights and liberties and their corresponding impact on the citizenry. This topic also includes important U.S. Supreme Court decisions that resulted from the examination of issues involving civil rights and liberties and the role of the Supreme Court as a mechanism for social change.

The Make Up of the Exam

The Advanced Placement United States Government and Politics Exam is administered every May. It lasts 2 hours and 25 minutes. The exam has two sections—a multiple-choice section and a free-response section.

Part I: Multiple-Choice Section—45 minutes, 60 questions

Select the best answer among the five-answer choices.

The total score for this section is based on the number of correctly answered questions. Points are not deducted for incorrect or unanswered questions.

Part II: Free-Response Section—100 minutes, 4 questions

Most questions have multiple parts. You will need to answer each sub-part, and should allocate 25 minutes to read, draft an outline, and write the response for each question.

Exam Scoring

The multiple-choice part of the test is scored by machine and the free response portion is scored by hand. Every summer hundreds of professors, content specialists, and AP Government teachers meet to grade the 250,000+ exams that are taken. Once both scores have been tallied, they are combined and then scaled. This raw score is then changed into a composite score ranging from 1–5.

The College Board proposes the following qualifications for each score:

Exam Grade	Recommendation
1	Extremely Well Qualified
2	Well Qualified
3	Qualified
4	Possibly Qualified
5	No recommendation

The minimum score required for college credit to be granted is a 3. As mentioned above, many schools require scores of 4 or 5 in order to grant credit.

For comparison, the College Board makes the equivalents of the AP Exam scores at follows:

AP Exam Grade	Letter Grade Equivalent
5	A
4	A-, B+, B
3	B-, C+, C
2	None
1	None

For reference, the 2015 administration of the AP U.S. Government and Politics Exam had this score distribution:[1]

Exam Score	Percentage of Students
5	9.
4	13.6
3	24.7
2	25
1	26.9

You can see that almost 75% of the students scored 3 or below. This shows that most students didn't do as well on this examination. Remember only a score of 3 or above on the exam, will get you college credits. So, roughly 50% of the 2015 exam-takers got a score below a 3.

Why Take the Exam

The AP exam is an opportunity to show the colleges you are applying to, that you know and understand a specific subject area. It is not required that you take this AP exam for admission to college, however, if you have taken History, Government, or Civics courses through your first three years of high school, and are comfortable with the subject matter, and did reasonably well in the coursework (at least a B in the classes), then, it might be an easy test to take to add to your achievements.

[1] http://www.totalregistration.net/AP-Exam-Registration-Service/2015-AP-Exam-Score-Distributions.php

High scores often translate into college credit after graduation. It's a good idea to ask colleges what their policy is regarding AP test credit and get any information they have on what scores they'll accept during college visits or through their website. You can re-take an AP test each year it's offered. If you're not happy with the score you got on an exam in 11th grade, you can always try again senior year.

College Board Websites

https://advancesinap.collegeboard.org/english-history-and-social-science/us-government-politics

https://secure-media.collegeboard.org/digitalServices/pdf/ap/ap-us-government-and-politics-course-description.pdf

SECTION II:
How this Study Guide
is Organized

This study guide will assist you in preparing for the AP examination that covers United States Government and Politics. The materials that are presented in the study guide have been included to bring together the general concepts and specific examples you have learned in your AP course.

The materials will present a review of the institutions that form the basis of our America government and theoretical and practical beliefs and concepts that have been instrumental in the development of American government.

What To Expect In This Book

As you move forward through the next pages, you will see a variety of information. The first section is a review of major concepts of government and politics that you should know, or at least that you should be familiar. You will see they are broken down by each of the six topics recommended by the College Board. As a reminder, the topics are:

- Constitutional underpinnings of the United States government
- Political beliefs and behaviors
- Political parties, interest groups, and mass media
- Institutions of national government
- Public policy
- Civil rights and civil liberties

You will also find two sample tests at the end of this book. These are designed to give you experience that simulates the actual exam you will be taking. Each question on these tests has a detailed answer as to why it is correct and why the incorrect answers are wrong. Use this information to help guide your learning.

Introduction To Topical Areas

The topics that are presented in this study guide are those topics that are suggested by the AP College Board for inclusion in the exam. After you have completed your high school course in U.S. government and politics and have reviewed the materials in this study guide, you should have an understanding and knowledge of the institutions of government so that you can analyze relevant concepts and apply those concepts to modern-day situations.

You will also be introduced to facts that are significant to the growth and development of U.S. government and politics. In order to understand their significance, it is important for you to be able to compare and contrast the facts and analyze them in relation to governmental processes and consequences.

The six topics that are presented in this study guide will assist you in analyzing important concepts in U.S. government and politics, applying facts to the concepts—and concepts to resulting events—and gaining a better, in-depth, understanding of the role of government and politics in American life.

Constitutional Underpinnings of United States Government

The Constitution established the framework for American government. The document created the organization of three separate branches of government, but it also identified the concepts of federalism and checks and balances. As you analyze the reasons for the need for the written Constitution, you will understand that there were ideological and philosophical concepts from the age of the Enlightenment that the drafters incorporated into their new framework for American government. You will also analyze why the framers of the Constitution feared too much power in a single branch of government and why some of the leaders feared factions and elitism. You will also understand why the ratification of the Constitution was not a foregone conclusion and why the Bill of Rights was added soon after the document's ratification. As you analyze the background of the Constitution and relate the document to modern times, you will be able to explain how the document has evolved over time and how the concepts that were debated more than two hundred years ago are applicable and relevant today.

Political Beliefs and Behaviors

What beliefs do you hold about the American government? How do you view political leaders in America? Your beliefs about government and the beliefs of others have a basis. This segment of the study guide will introduce the ways in which beliefs form, how beliefs evolve, and how the beliefs are shared and communicated.

Families, schools, religious institutions, the area of the country in which you live, and society in general influence ideas and beliefs about government and participating in the governmental process. Voting, of course, is one way to participate in the process but there are other types of participation, such as protests, campaigning, and participating in mass movements.

This segment also covers types of political beliefs, how they differ from and are similar to each other, and how they affect the political process and the political system.

Political Parties, Interest Groups, and Mass Media

The political process of selecting candidates to represent their political parties in the quest for the American presidency captured the interest, attention, and enthusiasm of people in ways that had not been evidenced for several years. This topic will help you understand more about political parties, interest groups, the media, and political action committees. You will learn about the history of third parties, issues that third parties have raised, and the impact third parties have on the political process. This topic will cover campaign financing, campaigning in the electronic age, and how the political parties play a major role in the choice of candidates and the election process.

You will also learn about interest groups and lobbying—how they are similar and how they are different—and how the media plays a role in American politics. The topic will present information for you to analyze how the role of media has changed over the years, how the media can influence voters, and the role of the media toward candidates.

Institutions of National Government

The institutions of national government that will be analyzed in this study guide include: Congress, the presidency, the federal courts, and the bureaucracy. Each institution has specific functions and powers. Some of the powers are shared, while others are not. You will learn about situations in which one branch or institution needs to assume power to place a check on the actions of the other branch or institution. The content will present examples of how conflicts arise between the branches and show how the conflicts may, or may not, be resolved through the system of checks and balances.

Public Policy

Government policies are formulated with the public in mind. The foundations of public policy stem from the Constitution, statutory and common law, and from regulations derived from the branches of government. Public policy is also the result of branches of government interacting, the concerns of the public, and the interaction between various leaders, interest groups, and political processes. Policy decisions are made at each level of government, and the federal policy involves decisions made about both foreign and domestic issues. The study guide will discuss various governmental policies, and you will be analyzing those government decisions in relation to their historical background, political heritage, and the needs and /or desires of the American public.

Civil Rights and Civil Liberties

The final topic in this study guide relates to civil rights and civil liberties. Individual rights and liberties have been a concern for the federal government since the creation of the Constitution. You will review U.S. Supreme Court decisions that involve civil rights and liberties. These decisions are significant and guide the behavior of government as to the specific issue involved in the case. As you read about the case decisions, you should analyze how these decisions have impacted society. You will read about liberties such as freedom of expression, freedom of assembly, and freedom of speech. You will also analyze cases involving rights of the accused and rights of minorities. The development of minority rights can be traced from events such as the ratification of the Civil War Amendments to the decision in *Plessy v. Ferguson* to the decision in *Brown v. Board of Education*, and further to the decisions involving the civil rights movement of the 1960s and the

Study Techniques

How should you study for the exam? Most of you will have taken the AP Government and Politics course in your high school. That will prepare you for much of the material. But, if you make the effort to create a list of key facts, examples, and events for each of the six topical areas, then you will have a great way of reviewing material at a glance.

Below you'll see some suggestions for the multiple-choice questions and the free response questions.

How to Attack the Multiple-Choice Questions

As you know by now, AP exams contain both multiple-choice questions and essay questions. The U.S. Government and Politics exam is no different.

Remember, the first section of the exam is the multiple-choice portion. Questions cover all six topical areas. There will be 60 questions on the section and you will have 45 minutes to complete it.

Multiple-choice questions can be tricky. A lot of times it is possible to eliminate one or two of the answers right away, but then get stuck with the others. On the AP United States Government and Politics Exam there is no penalty for incorrect answers, so be sure to record an answer for every question, even if it is a complete guess.

It is also very important to know what the question is asking of you. The College Board is notorious for saying things like, "All of the following are examples, EXCEPT..." or, "Which of these is NOT..." These words can change the entire meaning of the sentence. Be on alert for qualifiers like this.

You will be using a number 2 pencil to bubble in your answers on an answer sheet. At this stage of your academic career you have taken enough tests of this type, and hopefully know how to properly fill in the circles. If you need to erase an answer, be sure to do it completely.

Remember your timing. Sure, 60 questions in 45 minutes sounds easy enough. But remember, some of these questions are going to take longer to answer.

How to Attack the Free Response Questions

The second section of the exam is the free response or essay part. You will be asked to answer four questions, with multiple parts or sub-questions. You will have 100 minutes to do this part.

The free response questions are usually the items that give students the most difficulty. The score for each question accounts for 25% of the total score for the free-response section. Therefore, you should spend approximately 25 minutes answering each question.

It is important to practice writing for the free response questions under a timed situation, so, you get to know how you approach the questions.

You will need to integrate knowledge and use analytic and organizational skills in writing your answer. You will also need to incorporate specific examples in your responses. Therefore, read each question carefully and answer the question in the way it was asked. You may be expected to utilize provided charts, diagrams, and graphs to draw conclusions and relate those conclusions to general concepts and relationships.

The exam readers are not concerned about spelling, grammar, or penmanship because the answer is considered a draft. However, if a reader in unable to determine what is was you wrote, they cannot grade it, but they do their best to interpret a student's "chicken scratch."

Be certain your writing is in essay form (tell a story). Do NOT just list important concepts in an outline.

Also like the multiple-choice questions, the free response questions have key terms about which you should pay particular attention. These terms include, "Compare,' "Contrast," Describe,' and their favorite, "Explain." Pay particular attention to these terms and be sure to do what they ask.

Be aware of what you are writing. You do not want to say one thing in the first paragraph and then say the complete opposite in the second paragraph. If you do this, you will not get any credit, even if one of them is correct. This is because the reader does not know if you knew which was correct or just took a guess and got lucky.

Finally, the biggest piece of advice for answering the free response questions is to answer the question and then move on. Do not spend time going back over it (certainly reread it to make sure it makes sense) to edit it and turn it into a major piece of literature. You do not have time for this. Write what the question asks you to write and then move on. This will be the fastest 100 minutes you have ever seen and you have a lot, a REAL LOT, of information through which to get—so writing brief, but detailed, essays is essential.

Test-taking Strategies

Prepare your test day material, the day before. The tests usually starts in the morning so do not wait until the last minute to find your gear. Here's what you will need at a minimum:

1. A printed copy of your Admission Ticket
2. Photo identification
3. No. 2 pencils and an eraser
4. A watch, so you know how much time is remaining

You cannot bring the following into the testing room:

1. Any form of cellphone, tablet, or computer device
2. No ipods or music devices
3. No cameras or recording devices

Test-taking Tips

Finally, some test-taking tips gathered from our years of writing guides and teaching.

1. **Get smart, play dumb.** Sometimes a question is just a question. No one is out to trick you, so don't assume that the test writer is looking for something other than what was asked. Stick to the question as written and don't over-analyze.

2. **Do a double take.** Read test questions and answer choices at least twice because it's easy to miss something, to transpose a word or some letters. If you have no idea what the correct answer is, skip it and come back later if there's time.

3. **Turn it on its ear.** The syntax of a question can often provide a clue, so make things interesting and turn the question into a statement to see if it changes the meaning or relates better (or worse) to the answer choices.

4. **Get out your magnifying glass.** Look for hidden clues in the questions because it's difficult to write a multiple-choice question without giving away part of the answer in the options presented. In most questions you can readily eliminate one or two potential answers, increasing your chances of answering correctly to 50/50, which will help out if you've skipped a question and gone back to it.

5. **Call it intuition.** Often your first instinct is correct. If you've been studying the content you've likely absorbed something and have subconsciously retained the knowledge. On questions you're not sure about trust your instincts because a first impression is usually correct.

6. **Graffiti.** Sometimes it's a good idea to mark your answers directly on the test booklet and go back to fill in the optical scan sheet later. You don't get extra points for perfectly blackened ovals. If you choose to manage your test this way, be sure not to mismark your answers when you transcribe to the scan sheet AND be sure to leave time near the end to go back and fill in the scantron sheet.

Managing Time During the Exam

Become a clock-watcher. You have a set amount of time to answer the questions. Don't get bogged down laboring over a question you're not sure about when there are ten others you could answer more readily.

For example, if you cannot answer a multiple-choice or free response question, then don't stop there, MARK IT, and move on. Come back to it when you've finished the ones you can readily answer.

Do the practice tests, time yourself, and see how you do. The more practice you have on answering the multiple-choice questions and free-response questions, the less "stressed" or "strange" the actual test-day will seem.

Fact Versus Opinion

It is essential that answers to the Free Response Questions be based on facts rather than opinions, even if the question seems to call for an opinion. In your AP course in Government and Politics you have largely been learning facts. At the same time, you have been exposed to a wide range of opinions. Indeed, when dealing with politics it is impossible to avoid opinions—since opinions are the stuff from which politics is made! Distinguishing between the two can sometimes be somewhat challenging.

At the simplest level, a fact is a statement that can be established or proven by evidence as either false or true. An opinion cannot. Sometimes however, the lines can be blurred, so that what seems to be an uncontested factual conclusion based on evidence is in reality nothing more than an opinion which was supported by facts.

We will start with a simple example. Consider the following two statements, and how they distinguish between fact and opinion:

Abraham Lincoln was president during the American Civil War.

Abraham Lincoln was a great American president.

The first statement is clearly a fact, but what of the second? While few Americans today would say that Lincoln was not a great president, his "greatness" cannot be clearly or absolutely proven, since what constitutes "greatness" is a matter of opinion. That does not mean we cannot try to "prove" he was great, or conclude (in our opinion) that he must have been great for many reasons. Indeed, the reasons that lead us to believe he was great will usually be fact-based. However, the leap between fact and opinion occurs when people assume that a list of facts unavoidably results in proving an opinion to be uncontested and factual as well.

The Lincoln example is helpful in distinguishing between fact and opinion precisely because few people question his greatness. Therefore there is little tendency to question the reasoning that leads to the conclusion he was great. But as we shall now see, his greatness is not a proven fact—it is still just an opinion. To highlight this, we will look at Lincoln's greatness from two vastly different perspectives, each of which is based on the same facts—but with a slightly different emphasis on those facts.

A. Lincoln as Great.
   (a) Lincoln was president during a difficult and divisive war between the north and south.
   (b) Lincoln's Emancipation Proclamation freed slaves.

(c) Lincoln's policies toward the south at the end of the war tended to focus on conciliation, rather than punishment.

(d) Regarding secession, Lincoln interpreted the Constitution to mean that a state did not have the right or ability to secede and leave the Union.

(e) Lincoln was very insistent that the South would fire the first shots of the war, rather than the North.

(f) For all these reason, Lincoln was a great president.

B. Lincoln as Terrible.

(a) Lincoln was president during a divisive war between the North and South in which the South only sought to assert its rights.

(b) Lincoln's Emancipation Proclamation took what the constitution itself recognized as "property" without compensation contrary to the Fifth Amendment.

(c) While Lincoln's policies toward the South at the end of the Civil War had the appearance of conciliation, he had insisted on fighting the South in the first place, rather than let them peacefully leave the union.

(d) Lincoln's position regarding Southern secession from the Union was contrary to the Constitution, since nothing in the Constitution prohibits a state from leaving the union. Indeed, the Constitution says that if a state in the 1780's did not ratify the Constitution, it would not be forced to join the Union. Secession is nothing more than a state's rescission of a prior ratification.

(e) Lincoln provoked the South into firing the first shots of the war, when he intentionally sent supplies to the federal troops at Fort Sumter.

(f) For all these reasons, Lincoln was a terrible president.

The above narrative highlights how the same or similar facts can support vastly different opinions, leading each side to believe that the final conclusion must be factual as well. While the example deals with Lincoln's greatness, this process of amassing facts to support our opinions is something that all of us do all the time. For example, if you are with friends and someone suggests eating at restaurant "A," you are likely to hear some members of the group quickly agree, while others will want to go elsewhere. In the ensuing discussion over whether to go to restaurant "A," many in the group will present their list of facts followed by a final opinion as to whether the group should go there or not.

It is important to recognize that expressing opinions is not a bad thing. We are all entitled to our opinions, and as noted above, the expression of opinions is what politics is all about. Even in the context of writing answers to the Free

Response Questions on the AP exam, expression of opinions is not necessarily fatal or a bad thing, if it is done in the right way. But it is essential that you are able tell the difference between fact and opinion when writing your answers, and that you make it clear which of the two you are dealing with in your answer.

Most of the essay questions on the exam will be fact based, and will ask you to provide facts in your answer. Some of them however may call for an expression of opinion as well, or at least open the door to an expression of opinion. In answering any question that involves opinion, your main effort should be to identify and distinguish facts from opinions, and to put most of your emphasis on the facts.

Gun control is one of many hot topics that are heavily debated in America today, along with abortion, gay marriage, and marijuana usage. Each of these currently contested issues is a seedbed of differing opinions, with the differing opinions on each side of the question usually being presented by each side as if they were incontestable facts. The gun control question clearly opens the door for expression of an opinion. But in your answer, it is essential that you are as clear as possible about the difference between facts and opinions. For example, consider the question below on gun control. A short, sample answer is given, which identifies facts and opinions in brackets. The underlined words in the short answer are very important, and will be explained afterward.

Question: While a number of federal laws in respect to gun control have been passed, many state legislatures have decided to make independent laws on the subject. Some states have few gun laws and are quite liberal in allowing citizens to buy and carry guns. Other states have enacted very strict gun laws. Assume that you are a lobbyist in a state with lax gun laws, and have been hired to encourage the legislature to make stricter laws. What sorts of arguments would you make to support your position?

Answer: While the Second Amendment guarantees the right of the people to bear arms [fact], the Supreme Court has ruled that this right can be <u>legitimately limited</u> by government [fact]. For example, in the 2008 case of *DC v. Heller*, the court recognized that government <u>can restrict</u> mentally ill persons and convicted felons from buying guns, and that guns <u>can be</u> banned from public places [fact].

In modern America, there have been <u>a number of</u> shooting sprees in recent years in which innocent persons have been wounded or killed [fact]. <u>Sometimes</u> guns have been used in an attempt to kill persons in a prominent position [fact]. For example, President John F. Kennedy was assassinated in 1963, as was his brother Robert in 1968. Martin Luther King was also shot and killed in 1968 [fact]. In 1981, John Hinckley tried to kill President Ronald Reagan, and nearly succeeded [fact]. James Brady was also shot in this attempt, and not long thereafter Congress passed a gun control law that was commonly called the "Brady Bill," which <u>restricted</u> the purchase of handguns [fact].

Life in America today is not the same as it was in frontier days, when most people owned and used guns to hunt food for their families [fact and opinion mixed together]. Today we can buy our food at supermarkets [fact], and have less need for guns [opinion]. Meanwhile, population has grown greatly [fact], and I will argue in my lobbying [opinion] that with it has grown the number of people with mental illnesses and convicted felons who may use guns to hurt others [fact, but with clear opinion overtones]. I will argue that we should do what we can to prevent them from doing so [opinion].

The underlined portions are the parts of the answer in which the writer seeks to either clarify that he is dealing with a fact, or that he is dealing with an opinion. For example, the first underlined words in the second paragraph are "a number of," in respect to how many shooting sprees there have been in recent years. You must be very careful so that these types of descriptive words in your answer do not bridge from fact to opinion. The words "far too many" or "an incredible number of" would have bridged into the realm of opinion. But the words "a number of" is factually correct, since it did not imply either a large or small number.

The final paragraph of the short answer clearly departed from facts and entered the realm of opinion. The first sentence was rather vague, and mixed both facts and opinions. While it is best to avoid vague, mixed statements of this kind, to some extent these types of statements are expected when presenting the conclusion of an argument. Note that the remaining sentences of this last paragraph still sought to clarify fact from opinion. Use of the words "I will argue" show that you are aware of the distinction and make it clear you are jumping from fact to opinion.

Finally, it must be recognized that since the AP exam is timed, you may feel that do not have enough time to analyze every sentence for facts and opinions. Do not worry. The main goal of the exam is not to penalize you for expressing your opinion, but to see the extent to which you can support your opinions with facts. Simply concentrate as much as possible on the facts, and put most of your efforts into clearly articulating the facts that support your position.

SECTION IV:
Topic Summaries

Chapter 1: Constitutional Underpinnings of the U.S. Government

What You Will Be Tested On

When the United States Constitution was formed in 1787, it was a unique document. After all, each of the individual states had each crafted their own written constitutions a decade earlier, and the colonies had previously operated under various written charters, which acted as constitutions, for over 100 years. In particular, the truly unusual aspect of the U.S. Constitution was that it created a hybrid nation, in which the national government would co-exist with the state governments that would continue to maintain a great deal of power. This new arrangement was called "federalism."

The federal Constitution also contained other unique and unusual aspects, such as a series of checks and balances between the branches of government, and a clear separation of powers that many of the states lacked. This new Constitution was ingeniously crafted so that no single person or branch of government could gain too much power. Such a governmental structure was new and untried in the late eighteenth century. The success of this American governmental "experiment" has been proven over the last 200 years.

Because of its success the U.S. Constitution has been copied and used as a model many times by other nations in forming their own national governmental structure. However, these copied constitutions have not always worked as well as in the United States. Much of this has to do with unique societal aspects that go beyond the mere wording of a written constitution. The values, goals and political climate of societies in different locales have usually differed from those present in the U.S. when the Constitution was adopted. These underlying differences have often resulted in the decreased success of constitutional governance in other places.

In short, the political structure that evolved meshed well with the development of the Constitution in the United States to produce a system of participative governance. While many of the details of American political society will be addressed later in this book, the foundation on which the U.S. political framework has been built is the U.S. Constitution. It is therefore essential to gain an understanding of this most basic and important document.

This chapter focuses is on the philosophical roots and underpinnings of American government and the events and issues that led to the development of the United States Constitution, from the Enlightenment to Shays' Rebellion. You will need to understand the Constitution in-depth, focusing on its main components and the framework for how the American governmental system is designed to work. Early interpretations and debates about the Constitution are also important to know.

Considerations that Influenced the Formulation and Adoption of the Constitution

The Articles of Confederation

During the War for American Independence, most of the former colonies became self-governing and independent states. Relatedly, they crafted new constitutions for their state, and in many cases drafted a state bill of rights, which described the individual liberties of the people.

In forming these new state constitutions, the states assumed governmental powers previously held by the Parliament in England. These constitutions placed power primarily in the hands of the legislative branch, which consisted of two houses in most states (Pennsylvania was an exception, with only one legislative body). The executive branch (governor) and judicial branch in the state governments at this time were usually weaker. Most state constitutions included a property ownership requirement in order to vote.

The newly independent states were unwilling to yield too much control to a central government. While the states were forced to cooperate with each other in order to fight the British, they saw themselves as independent within their geographic boundary, and were very reluctant to yield any of their sovereign power to a centralized government. Therefore, during the Revolution, only a very loose and weak federal government structure was put in place, in the form of the Articles of Confederation. A first draft of the Articles was prepared in 1776, and was debated by the Continental Congress for a year. A final draft was sent to the states for ratification in 1777. Although not ratified by all of the states until 1783, the Continental Congress considered the intent of the Articles as binding from 1777 until they were replaced by the Constitution a decade later.

The Articles of Confederation unified the newly independent states, but specified that the federal government would have only very limited powers. In particular, the federal government under the Articles could not levy taxes, but could only request money from the states. Major decisions could only be made with the unanimous consent of all the states, which proved to be extremely difficult or impossible to attain. While the Continental Congress held some war and foreign affairs powers, it could not negotiate trade with foreign countries on behalf of all the states. Instead, each state regulated its own trade with foreign countries.

After the Revolution was officially ended by the Treaty of Paris of 1783, the states continued to largely go their separate ways. While the Articles of Confederation were still in operation during this period, they did not provide adequate federal control over international trade and foreign relations, taxation and finances, and interstate commerce. Lack of a coherent national policy led to economic hardship for many, and internal unrest.

Shays' Rebellion in Massachusetts in 1786-1787 was a prime example of such unrest. Daniel Shays was leader of a group of farmers who were unhappy with state supported seizures of land as a consequence of bankruptcy. They marched on the armory at Springfield, but were repelled by the state militia.

Because of the growing problems and unrest, many leaders felt there was a need for a stronger central government. A convention of delegates from five states met in Annapolis, Maryland, in September 1786 in an effort to resolve some of these problems. Little was accomplished other than reaching an agreement to call for another convention to be held the following May in Philadelphia, which they hoped would be better attended.

The Constitutional Convention

In late May 1787, delegates from twelve states gathered in Philadelphia for the convention, which was originally intended to "revise" the Articles of Confederation. Rhode Island sent no delegates, since it was skeptical of the entire affair. Over the ensuing hot Philadelphia summer the delegates met in secret. In the first few days, and due to the objections of many, the delegates agreed that it would be more fruitful to completely abandon the Articles of Confederation and create an entirely new federal government. The "Virginia Plan" of government was taken as the primary guide in the ensuing debates. Although a few alternate plans were presented during the convention, none were debated for long, and the convention continued coming back to the original Virginia Plan. The original draft of the Virginia Plan was written by James Madison, and was presented to the convention by Virginia Governor Edmund Randolph.

Through hard fought negotiation, collaboration, and compromise, the convention hammered out a proposed Constitution, which contained a great many checks and balances specifically designed to prevent any one person or governmental body among its three distinct branches from assuming too much power. The federal government was to have powers limited solely to what was stated in the Constitution itself, unlike the state governments which were presumed to possess all power in their domain, unless limited by their state

Constitution. Hence, the presumption of power in the federal government was opposite to that of the states. In spite of this, the new federal government was specifically given dynamic powers, including control over interstate commerce, foreign policy and foreign trade, and taxation/financial matters. One important aspect of the new constitutional arrangement was the concept of "federalism," in which the state governments and the federal government both hold extensive powers and would co-exist.

One of the most hotly debated compromises during the Constitutional Convention had to do with slavery. While the institution of slavery was repulsive to many northern delegates, the majority of southern states made it clear they would not support the convention's agreements, unless slavery was allowed to continue. A compromise was ultimately reached regarding how to count the population of slave states, since the number of Congressional representatives a state could have was based on its population. Under this compromise, slaves would count as three-fifths of a person. The importation of slaves was allowed through the end of 1808 but not thereafter. For many in the north, these concessions suggested that the federal government had authority to both regulate slavery and the slave trade. Many in the south disagreed with this however, viewing the regulation of slavery as solely within the decision making power of the states.

The Constitution

The proposed Constitution was completed and sent to the states in the fall of 1787 for ratification. In accordance with terms contained within the document, the Constitution would go into effect once it had been ratified by nine states, rather than requiring unanimous consent, a condition that had been required for the Articles of Confederation. This did not mean that a non-ratifying state would be bound by the new Constitution; rather, the Constitution would only apply to those nine states which ratified it, plus any other states that chose to ratify at a later date.

The draft Constitution was hotly debated by many who felt it was a dangerous document. In these debates, so-called "Anti-Federalists" expressed concern that the federal government had been given too much power, in spite of the significant limitations expressed within the Constitution. Rising in defense of the Constitution were the "Federalists," who argued that it should be adopted. Three Federalist leaders—James Madison, Alexander Hamilton and John Jay—wrote and published a series of articles about the Constitution designed to answer the numerous Anti-Federalist arguments circulating in the newspapers. These writings in favor of the Constitution were eventually compiled into book form which came to be known as "*The Federalist Papers.*" To this day, these essays are considered the best descriptive source regarding the meaning of the Constitution.

The Bill of Rights

One of the chief complaints against the Constitution was that it did not contain a bill of rights, which would describe individual rights and liberties, and restrict the powers of the federal government. Ultimately, Federalist supporters of the Constitution promised that a bill of rights would be quickly added to the Constitution if it were ratified. This promise was one of the key reasons some of the states voted for ratification. Indeed, either as part of their ratification vote or by way of a separate document produced thereafter, many states proposed a list of rights they felt should be included.

In the first session of Congress in 1789, James Madison made good on the promise of introducing a bill of rights, by proposing twelve new rights-based amendments, although many in the new Congress opposed him. They felt there were more pressing problems more worthy of attention than protecting rights that few people considered to be in danger. After all, bills of rights already existed in most of the states, and it was known that a federal bill of rights would only apply to the (then) small federal government. It would be 100 years before the federal Bill of Rights began to be "incorporated" through the Fourteenth Amendment as applicable directly to the states.

Madison pushed for adoption of a bill of rights in the opening session of Congress for very practical reasons. Like others, he was not overly concerned about protecting rights, and even expressed concern that by listing the rights to be protected, some people might assume that any rights not on the list could be taken over and abused by the federal government. However, Madison pressed strongly for adoption of the bill of rights for political reasons. He knew that there were still many opponents of the new Constitution who would not rest until they saw it either fail or undergo significant modifications. While the main complaint of these constitutional detractors was the lack of a bill of rights, in actuality their primary concerns related more to structural matters than rights. Madison believed that if he acted quickly and proposed the adoption of noncontroversial rights protections, the majority of the populace would be satisfied. Detractors of the Constitution would then be forced to admit the actual structural changes they wanted, and would no longer be able to use the lack of a bill of rights to build emotional support against the Constitution. Madison's foresight proved correct, and his effort largely avoided the more substantial constitutional revisions desired by its detractors.

Over the summer and fall of 1789 Madison continued to bring the proposed bill of rights to the fore. His twelve proposals were discussed in Congress, but the debates were relatively brief. As Madison had intended, most of the provisions were not controversial and were quickly agreed upon. Ten of the twelve proposals were ultimately adopted by Congress and sent to the states for approval, ultimately becoming the federal Bill of Rights when three-fourths of the states ratified them. They came into effect in 1791 upon the ratification of Virginia. One of the two proposed amendments, which failed at that time—regarding compensation of Congressmen—was ratified over 200 years later, and became a part of the Constitution in 1992 as the Twenty-seventh Amendment.

Separation of Powers

Montesquieu was one of several political philosophers heavily relied on by the founders in breaking from England and forming the new American government. One of Montesquieu's chief arguments in respect to the structure of government was that there should be a strict "separation of powers" between the executive, legislative and judicial branches. John Locke was also supportive of this view. In fashioning the unique structure of the U.S. Constitution, the founders drew heavily on these ideas and sought to create a format in which each branch would be truly unique and independent from the others, and would not rely on the others for its continuing existence or support.

Powers of the Congress

Under the system created by the U.S. Constitution in Article I, Congress possesses all legislative powers—the power to make laws. Unlike the other branches of government, Congress is divided into two separate houses, which sometimes cooperate with each other and sometimes fight with each other. The probable reason the founders diluted legislative powers between two houses was the view that the legislative branch was probably the most powerful, and therefore needed to be more carefully controlled. As James Madison said in the Federalist Number 51, "In republican government, the legislative authority necessarily predominates."

Article I, Section 8 specifically lists the powers of the federal Congress. Included is the power to tax, borrow money, provide for defense of the nation, regulate commerce, set rules for citizenship, provide for coining money, set measurement standards for the nation, establish post offices, protect intellectual property rights (by way of copyrights and patents), establish courts lower than the Supreme Court, declare war, provide for an army and navy, and regulate the militia. Under the constitutional scheme, the executive and judicial branches have no authority to do any of these things. The most important power of the legislature however is the power to enact new laws. This Congressional law-making power cannot be delegated to any other body.

In contrast, Article I, Section 9 sets limits on the powers of Congress. The federal Congress may not suspend the writ of habeas corpus (the right of prisoners to force a court to investigate why they are in jail), pass laws that punish past offenses (ex post facto laws), require a tax on goods transported from one state to another, give favors to one state over another in commercial matters, and create titles of nobility. Congress must also give an accounting of how government monies are spent.

One of the most significant prohibitions in Article I, Section 9—which is usually overlooked or misunderstood—is the prohibition of the legislature enacting "bills of attainder." This is directly connected with the concept of separation of powers, since a bill of attainder is essentially a legislative act of judging. For example, if Congress passes a law, which identifies an individual or a group as lawbreakers and punishes them without the benefit of a court trial—this is a bill of attainder. The Constitution strictly forbids such a thing, either by the federal Congress (Article 1, Section 9) or the state legislatures (Article 1, Section 10).

Powers of the Executive Branch

Article II of the Constitution pertains to the executive branch. Unlike a parliamentary system in which the Prime Minister is a Member of Parliament, the Executive branch in the U.S. under the Constitution is to be a completely separate and independent branch. The President is the main member of this branch, with a back-up person in the form of the Vice President in case the President dies or cannot fulfill his duties. The Twentieth and Twenty-fifth Amendments to the Constitution have expounded on what happens in case a President is incapacitated.

Article II, Sections 2 and 3 describe the powers of the President. He shall be the commander-in-chief of the Armed Forces, may grant pardons for crimes against the United States, is to periodically make a "State of the Union" address to Congress, may convene both houses of Congress on extraordinary occasions, and is to receive ambassadors and take care that the laws are faithfully executed. Some additional powers require cooperation of the Senate, such as making foreign treaties or appointing ambassadors or Supreme Court justices.

Powers of the Judicial Branch

The description of the judicial power in Article III of the Constitution is the shortest description of a branch of government. In Section 2, the Supreme Court is given authority to handle cases "in law and equity." In old England, through the process of many centuries of decisions in the English courts, a separation occurred between cases decided by some courts "at law"—that is, pursuant to statutes and laws written by the legislature—and cases decided by other courts "at equity"—that is, cases in which there was not a specific applicable law, but principles of fairness (equity) should apply in order to reach a just resolution. What the equity courts used in making their "fairness" decisions was what is known as the "common law"- court-made decisions over time about a variety of topics, which are not addressed by legislation. As the Constitution specifies, cases in law and equity in today's world are decided by the same court.

Checks and Balances

It is readily apparent from the structure in the Constitution that the President and Supreme Court have no authority to pass legislation; Congress and the Supreme Court cannot enforce laws; and Congress and the President cannot decide individual cases involving parties in dispute. This is the "brilliance" of the U.S. Constitution—no one branch can "do it all." If you have control of allocating money, you can't spend it. If you have control of passing law, you can't enforce it. This has kept any one branch from becoming too powerful.

Not surprisingly however, over the process of time situations and disputes have arisen as to whether one of the branches has overstepped its authority and ventured into the territory of another branch. For example, administrative agencies created by Congress (such as the IRS or the Department of the Interior) are generally considered to be part of the executive branch. However, these and other agencies include internal "tribunals" which try cases brought before them. This has the appearance of intruding on the judicial branch. Likewise, administrative agencies are also charged with making rules in their sphere of influence—such as tax rules enacted by the IRS. This has the appearance of intruding on Congress' power to enact laws that impact people.

Disputes over alleged intrusions by one branch into another have frequently been brought to the Supreme Court for resolution. For example, in the 1935 depression era case of *Schechter Poultry Corp. v. United States*, regulations of the poultry industry promulgated by the newly created National Recovery Administration (NRA) were declared unconstitutional as a violation of the separation of powers.

Checks and Balances

The essence of checks and balances is that different branches of government are given some authority to check or limit the power of another branch. By this method, no single branch can ever gain too much power.

Veto Power

For example, although Congress is given the exclusive authority to create new laws, Article I, Section 7 states that such new laws cannot become final and binding until they have been presented to the President for his review and approval. If he does not approve of a bill he can "veto" it. The bill is then returned to Congress for further review. If both houses re-pass the law by a two-thirds vote, it becomes a law in spite of the President's veto. If a two-thirds vote cannot be mustered in one or both houses, the bill will die. Hence, even though the principle of separation of powers specifies that the executive does not make laws, the check and balance of the veto power gives the executive a significant voice in the laws that are enacted.

Judicial Review

Another well-known example of a constitutional check and balance is judicial review. It is unique however because it is not clearly stated in the Constitution that the Judiciary has the power to declare the acts of other branches unconstitutional and therefore unenforceable. Certainly this power of review is implied by the mere existence of the Supreme Court and its right to hear a variety of cases, but the constitutional wording does not specifically provide for it. This power was clearly articulated in the 1803 case of *Marbury v. Madison*, in which the Supreme Court ruled that part of the Judiciary Act of 1789 passed by Congress was unconstitutional because it was in conflict with Article III of the Constitution. Ever since then, it has been generally recognized that the Supreme Court has the authority to decide on the constitutionality of actions taken by the other branches.

The Power to Impeach

Another example of checks and balances is the impeachment power. Article I, Section 2 of the Constitution gives the House of Representatives the "sole power of impeachment" of members of the executive and judiciary. Impeachment is defined in Article 1, Section 3 to be removal from office and disqualification from holding another office in the government. While the House of Representatives is given the power to initiate the process of such removal, Article I, Section 3 gives the Senate the sole power to "try all impeachments." This clearly sounds like a judicial power, and indeed Article I, Section 3 says that when the President is the one being impeached, the Chief Justice of the Supreme Court is to preside over the trial. Conviction and removal must be by two-thirds vote of the members present. Therefore the House can start the impeachment process, but cannot finish it. The Senate on the other hand has no power to start the process.

Only nineteen times in U.S. history have impeachment proceedings been approved by the House, and passed on to the Senate for trial. Two of these were in respect to presidents (Andrew Johnson and William Clinton). Most of the impeachment trials resulted in acquittal, since the required two-thirds vote was not achieved. However, there were five instances in which there was an impeachment conviction by the Senate, all of which were of lower federal court judges (lower than the Supreme Court).

The Power to Tax

Another example has to do with money or revenue bills, or in other words, the power to tax. Article I, Section 6 states that "all bills for raising revenue shall originate in the House of Representatives." The Senate lacks the power to initiate tax bills, although it can vote on them if the House gets them started. Because every member of the House of Representatives is subject to vote every two years, it was considered by the founders to be they were closer to the people.

Since the power to tax is considered one of the greatest powers of government, the founders wanted to make sure this power was located as close to the people as possible. In short, if the people did not like a new tax proposed by the House of Representatives, they could vote out the supporters of it in the next election.

Appointment of Supreme Court Justices

Finally, one of the most visible of the checks and balances in the Constitution has to do with appointment of Supreme Court justices. Article II, Section 2 gives the President the power to appoint new justices to the Supreme Court "with the advice and consent of the Senate." Confirmation hearings are usually held before the Senate Judiciary Committee, in which the nominee for justice has to respond to a series of questions by Committee members. This process tends to focus on the political views of individual justices. After the Senate Committee approves the nomination, it goes to a floor vote in the Senate. Usually a simple majority vote is sufficient for confirmation, although a filibuster can increase the vote needed to a "supermajority" of at least 60 votes.

Federalism

In 1789 the Constitution created a unique government in which a dual system of federal and state governments co-exist with each other, with each being considered co-equal in power and authority. Such a hybrid form of government was previously considered unworkable, since it was considered unclear how two competing governmental powers could coincide for long without destructive conflict.

One of the interesting and often overlooked aspects of federalism has to do with the degree to which the rights of the people are protected at the state level as compared to the federal level. In other words, the structure of federalism allows the potential for greater protection of the rights of the people. In this system, if the rights of the people are oppressed by one government (state or federal) they have the ability to turn to the other for redress.

Indeed, one of James Madison's main points in the Federalist Number 10 was that the rights of the people would be better preserved in a large republic made up of diverse groups of people, rather than in a small republic. The reason for this had to do with "factions." A faction is a group of like-minded people whose goals do not necessarily mesh with other groups. When a faction is a minority of the people, the majority holds it in check. But when the faction is a majority, as Madison said, then the minority has cause to fear for their rights.

Madison had seen how factions in his home state of Virginia had sometimes oppressed the rights of minorities. He believed that the ability of a faction to overcome a legislature was less likely on the large scale of the federal government than on the smaller scale of a state government, since it would be harder for a faction to gain sufficient control over the people in many states and thereby assert its power. Hence, for Madison the unique federalism structure created by the Constitution added an additional layer of protection for the rights of the people. If groups were oppressed within their respective states, they could bring their claims before the federal government where they would be more likely to be protected.

Prior to the Civil War the federal government was not considered as powerful as it later came to be. State governments in this "antebellum" period exerted great power, and sometimes openly defied the federal government. For example, this occurred in 1832-33 when a state convention in South Carolina "nullified" as "unconstitutional" a recent tariff law enacted by Congress. Before federal enforcement of the tariff in South Carolina could occur, a new and modified tariff was enacted, and South Carolina then repealed its prior nullification. 28 years later, similar efforts at nullification and secession by states due to dissatisfaction with federal policies led to the Civil War. The authority of the federal government to compel state compliance with federal law was tested to the fullest extent. The federal government won of course, and since that time federal power has been generally considered superior to that of the states. This has been bolstered by liberal interpretation by the Supreme Court of the "commerce power" in Article I, Section 8, Clause 3, whereby federal oversight of interstate commerce can be used to justify almost any intrusion by the federal government into state law.

Additionally, following the Civil War the Supreme Court began to "incorporate" many of the federal Bill of Rights, through the Fourteenth Amendment, as now being directly applicable to the states. With this "incorporation," a uniformity of rights across all the states was achieved. In addition, the equal protection clause of the Fourteenth Amendment was applied with greater vigor to the states. Hence, when the Supreme Court later decided in 1954 in *Brown v. Board of Education* that states could not segregate blacks from whites in public schools, the ruling applied to all 50 states and not just the State of Kansas where the case originated.

Few people today question the pre-eminent status of the federal government over the states. Notwithstanding this, however, the states continue to retain a great deal of power within their jurisdictions. For example, almost all aspects of family law (marriage, divorce, child support, etc.) are handled at the state level. State criminal laws also vary widely, as is demonstrated by the number of states that "legalize" gambling or marijuana use, as compared to states that do not.

Within the geographic boundaries of states another form of federalism is generally considered: the relationship between state and local governments, such as cities and counties. As with the federal/state model, in this lower form of federalism the local governments are generally considered inferior and subject to state government, and retain jurisdiction mostly over local matters. One primary distinction however between this type of "federalism" and that between the federal and state governments is that cities and towns within states are creatures of the states, deriving their very existence from the state. In the larger version of federalism applicable to the state and federal governments, states were understood by the founders to predate the federal government, and banded together to form the federal government.

Theories of Democratic Government

Elitism was the dominant political philosophy in Europe at the time of the American Revolution. Those with power in England were the king, lords, and members of the House of Commons. Most power in continental Europe, was concentrated among an elite aristocracy. Monarchy was the rule of the day, to be followed after the French Revolution, with dictatorship and other forms of authoritarian control.

Because the American colonies were relatively new and had only a short history, an elite colonial society had not developed. While there were men of wealth and influence, such as Virginia plantation owners, most white male colonists considered themselves to be largely equal in their rights and privileges. As common and simple as this concept is for us to understand, at that time, the very idea of such commonly held rights was somewhat shocking to all but the Americans.

One of the principle dividing lines in the early days of the American Republic had to do with property ownership. Most states in their state constitution specified that only white male property owners over the age of 21 could vote. The delegates to the constitutional convention and most leading political leaders in the new states were men of property who were a sort of American elite. This made their creation of the federal Constitution all the more remarkable, since that document does not distinguish or give special privileges to an American elite class. Indeed, the qualifications for office of President or Congress listed in the Constitution only deal with attainment of a certain age and residency at birth. In short, elitism was renounced as a guiding philosophy among the American people and founding fathers. All men (at least all white males) were considered as approximate equals. As the views of society have changed over time, this equality has been extended to women and persons of all colors and races.

The chief political theory adopted by the founding generation had to do with principles of democracy. James Madison and others decried the problems and weakness of a pure democracy in which every man would have an equal vote. They opted instead for a republican form of government in which the people would elect representatives who would act as their proxies in government. If these proxy representatives failed to vote in a way that pleased the majority, they would be voted out at the next election. From the very beginning therefore, the

United States was never intended to be a pure democracy. Rather, it is a Republic built on democratic ideals.

The chief ideals and aims of democratic theory in this era were liberty, equality and justice. These were the overriding themes of the Declaration of Independence, and served as the rallying cry during the Revolutionary War. The elite in Europe cringed at the way the American "riff raff" vaunted their rights and their equality. From those early days until today, Americans have been known as a rights-loving and highly independent people, who chaff at authoritarian forms of government.

The unique governmental structure created by the Constitution with its numerous checks and balances and its separation of powers tended to glorify concepts of pluralism. Under pluralistic theory, multiple layers of groups join together in society to achieve their common goals. Power and control is ever shifting among these pluralistic groups, with no single group gaining so much authority that it can set itself up as an elite controller of the others.

Whether characterized as republican or democratic in theory, the main essence of the American political view has been to highlight liberty, equality and freedom as the central rights of all mankind. Government is considered to be derived from the people, and is to be the servant of the people—not the other way around. Individual responsibility and accountability are enshrined as central, guiding concepts for all the people. It is the people who made the government, and it is the people who can change it. Ultimately, all authority and power came back to the people as a whole, acting through their duly authorized representatives.

Summary

Current American politics is primarily built on the foundation of federalism, with its Bill of Rights. You must have a strong understanding of the basic elements of the Constitution, including how it was written and how it was intended to function, and the powers it granted to government, all of which are essential to a complete understanding of American governance.

Chapter 2:
Political Beliefs and Behaviors

This chapter on political beliefs and behaviors deals with understanding and recognizing how individuals form their political beliefs and how an individual's political behaviors are influenced by their peers, groups, and government action. This section will cover beliefs that citizens hold about their governments and its leaders. It will cover the processes by which citizens learn about politics. It will cover the nature, sources, and consequences of public opinion. Lastly, it will cover the ways in which citizens vote and participate in political life, and how citizens decide on their vote.

What You Will Be Tested On

In the AP Government and Politics exam, 10 to 20 percent of the exam will contain questions about political beliefs and behaviors. The best way to prepare is to understand the different sub-topics and be able to tie them into a coherent picture of public opinion, voting, and opinion-forming.

The sub-topics include:
- beliefs of citizens
- beliefs citizens hold about their government and leaders
- processes by which citizens learn about politics
- public opinion
- voting and other methods of participation in politics
- factors that influence citizens to differ in their opinions about politics

The role of citizens is critical in the functioning of a representative democracy like the United States. Citizens vote for their local, state, and federal government representatives; they vote for the President and Vice-President, they vote on referendums and bonds, etc. in local elections. When they vote, they make a decision—this section deals with how they get to that decision, how they learn about the issue, how they form an opinion, who influences them, and how they participate in the democratic process.

Beliefs of Citizens _____

Every citizen has a set of values, ideals, and political beliefs, perhaps even a political ideology. They have been shaped through political socialization by an array of forces, including their parents and overall upbringing, the church, schools, and the everyday experiences that shape their daily lives.

Questions like: what are your political values, do you consider yourself liberal, moderate or conservative and to which political party, if any, would you belong, are the kinds of decisions that an engaged voter or citizen needs to make. Identifying where you place on the political spectrum and being aware of your own political identity is important not only in knowing the whats and whys of yourself even better, but also in understanding the how and why by which the political beliefs of others are formed.

This belief is called political ideology. Political ideology refers to a set of beliefs, doctrines, symbols, and group beliefs about the ways by which society should work, operate, and serve its citizens. Political ideologies are also identified across a political spectrum. For example, you have probably heard of someone being left of center or right of center. This means that their ideology is either liberal or conservative.

Ideologies

Let's look at the two main ideologies in the United States: Democratic or the liberal -"right" AND Republican or the conservative -"left". A third emerging political belief is that of an independent, where the citizen does not necessarily align with any one major party, but chooses sides on issues and candidates, based on the issue or election.

What does it mean to be democratic or "left of center"? There are some common aspects. First, it means that the person or citizen has said that they identify with democratic beliefs and maybe the Democratic Party. They might support democratic policies at the local, state, or federal government levels. Liberal ideologies often promote a strong central government and a wide scope for the central government.

What then does it mean to be conservative or to the "right of center"? Conservative ideologies promote a limited central government. The Republican Party in the United States is considered to be a conservative party and believes that the scope of American government has become too wide-ranging. Conservatives tend to support a small, centralized government. They tend to be pro-defense, pro-industry growth policies (like tax relief for businesses), anti-union, and more lax on environmental regulations than liberals.

Remember though, that while the two ideologies—democratic and conservative—have defined leanings on issues, it may not always be the case. Policy politics is complex and often has many forces that drive it, so, one might find a case where a conservative or Republican might support a predominantly Democratic stance as for example, on trade issues or the environment.

Voting Groups

Two key groups often courted by politicians are young voters and women voters. Both are considered important groups, and often vote politically—that is, they vote on issues and for specific candidates.

Over the past decade, there has been a pronounced age gap in American politics. Younger Americans have been the Democratic Party's strongest supporters in both vote preferences and partisanship, while older Americans have been the most reliably Republican.

It has been shown that young people are more apathetic towards the government. Young people are also just forming their political opinions, so they vote differently than another segment—the elderly voter. They tend not to have a large interest in foreign affairs and political issues. After the start of the Vietnam War and the Watergate incident, a general decline in the trust of the government grew among the younger citizens. Since college education tends to have a liberalizing effect younger people, in general, tend to identify themselves as liberals over conservatives.

A recent Pew Research Center report on partisan identification found that:
- 1% of Millennials (18-33 years old in 2014) identify with or lean toward the Democratic Party
- 5% identify as Republicans or lean Republican
- 7% of those in the Silent Generation (ages 69-86 in 2014) say they are Republican or lean Republican
- 3% affiliate with the Democratic Party or lean Democratic

Women and the Gender Gap

Women are more likely to support spending on social services and oppose higher levels of military spending. Women are significantly less conservative in voting trends then men, leading to a gender gap. The "gender gap" refers to the statistical fact that more women have voted in elections since 1980 than men. This makes women a very attractive group to pursue in terms of political beliefs. From 1964-2008, here's how the gender gap computes:
- The number of consecutive presidential elections in which a larger percentage of eligible women have voted than eligible men, back to 1980.
- The number of consecutive presidential elections in which the number of female voters has been greater than the number of male voters, back to 1964.

- The number of consecutive presidential elections in which the majority of women have voted for the Democratic candidate, from 1992 to 2008.
- The number of times since 1980 in which the majority of men have voted for the Democratic candidate, in 1992 and 2008.

Beliefs Citizens Hold About Their Government And Its Leaders

Government policies, elections, and the government's functioning are influenced by the beliefs that citizens hold about their government and its leaders. This is their political ideology or political leanings. Political ideology refers to a more or less consistent set of beliefs about what policies government ought to pursue.

Political ideology is measured in two ways: how frequently people use broad political categories to describe or justify their own views and preferences; and determining to what extent a citizen's policy preferences are consistent over time or are based on consistent principles. People may also have strong predispositions even if they do not satisfy the condition of being "ideological." One may be ideological by crossing the borders of traditional liberalism or conservatives in their issue affiliations.

What do "liberalism" and "conservatism" mean? Liberal and conservative labels have a complex history. In the early 1800's, liberals supported personal and economic liberty, while conservatives wanted to restore the power of the state, church, and aristocracy. The Progressive Era, followed by Roosevelt and the New Deal began to change this definition, so liberalism began to mean support for an activist government. Conservative reaction to the activism, especially during the Vietnam era, favored a free market, states' rights, and individual choice in economics. Today's meanings are imprecise, but still reflect important differences within and between the parties and form the basis of how citizens vote on governmental direction.

As described previously, two groups of citizens tend to have somewhat predictable views of government. The younger voter tends to distrust government and the older voter tends to support government.

Processes By Which Citizens Learn About Politics

Political socialization is the process, most notably in families and schools, by which we develop our political attitudes, values, and beliefs. Political socialization is a lifelong process by which people form their ideas about politics and acquire political values. The family, educational system, peer groups, and the mass media all play a role.

Most informal socialization is accidental. Children will pick up or absorb what they hear or see from their parents or adult figures, and side with those views. Children will then also usually identify with their parents party. The first small part of political socialization is done formally, or in a classroom setting.

Another factor is media, or the "new parent", as children increase the amount of time they spend watching television or YouTube, their primary source of information coming from the shows that they watch. For example, The Daily Show (previously hosted by Jon Stewart) became a source of information for the younger voter on political happenings. The Pew Research Center cites that 12% of online Americans cite The Daily Show as the source of their news. So, in terms of how the younger and future generations learn about politics, one can see a changing trend. As a result of increased television watching, attention to news broadcasts and newspapers have decreased.

Religion also plays a part in political socialization. Religious traditions impact political beliefs. For example, Catholic families tend to be more liberal on economic issues, Protestant families are more conservative and Jewish families are more liberal on economic and social issues. Again, this is not absolute, but a general trend. You already know how terrorist groups like Al Qaeda and others have used religion to further their agenda and make their citizens sympathetic to their cause.

Public Opinion _____

Politicians have long been interested in the moods and opinions of the people. After all, members of Congress and the President are elected to represent the people, a difficult task if one does not know and understand what the people want. Even George Washington employed his own "pollster," a friend from Virginia who would mingle with the "ordinary folks" to find out what they thought of the President. While the measurement of public opinion has become much more scientific and precise since Washington's day, the attitudes of the public have always played an important role in shaping public policy and the direction of the nation.

What is Public Opinion?

Public opinion refers to how people think or feel about a particular issue.

Individuals hold a wide variety of opinions. By measuring these opinions through polls or surveys at the individual level and aggregating them, the proportions of the population with particular beliefs and preferences can be determined.

When measuring public opinion, pollsters are not only concerned with the content of public opinion, i.e. what it is that people think and believe, but also with the stability of opinions over time. It is also useful to know how strongly the public holds particular opinions, and the direction in which those opinions seem to be moving. The content, stability, intensity and direction of public

1. Opinion saliency – some people care more about certain issues than other people do.
2. Opinion stability – the steadiness or volatility of opinion on an issue.
3. Opinion-policy congruence – the level of sameness between government action and majority sentiment on an issue.
4. Opinion differences – between the mass and political elites. Political elites know more about politics, they know the nuances, the different sides, and are generally more informed. Elites are more likely to hold a consistent set of opinions about the policies government ought to pursue.

Cleavages In Public Opinion

A cleavage in public opinion means that people are very much divided in their opinions. Cleavages in politics are seen in race, social class, and regional differences. The concept of political cleavages, and their role in structuring political conflict, is vital to understanding political behavior across political systems

A cleavage is a metaphorical line, which divides members of the community into sides. Cleavage lines are founded on values.

Social Class

In some political systems, class is the dividing line, with members of the working class at odds with members of the middle class over inequalities in wealth and the workings of the status system. Social class, mainly the province of sociologists is also called socioeconomic status and is typically thought of as a compound of education, occupation, and income.

Social class is poorly defined in U.S., though recognized in specific cases (e.g., truck drivers and investment bankers). It's not a strong factor in cleavage, but it exists and politicians are aware of it. Social class is less important in the U.S. than in Europe; and the extent of this cleavage has declined in both places. In general, some class differences remain; unskilled workers are more likely to be Democrats than affluent white-collar workers.

Race and Ethnicity

This is becoming more important even on nonracial matters. African Americans are most consistently the liberal group within Democratic Party; and there is little cleavage among blacks. Generational differences also surface among African Americans; younger blacks are less likely to believe that social and economic differences between the races are due to discrimination.

Hispanic and Asian Americans tend to be less liberal. Hispanics tend to identify as Democrats, though not as strongly as African Americans. Asians are even more identified with the Republican Party than are whites. Latinos are somewhat more liberal than Anglos or Asians, but less liberal than African Americans.

Finally, Caucasians are fairly evenly divided within the political spectrum, but lean slightly conservative

Regional Differences

First there is the cleavage between large cities and the rest of the region. Most large cities in the U.S. tend to vote democratic. Also, there is a recognized cleavage in the Southern states, which tend to be more conservative than other regions. Historically, the South is more accommodating to business interests (and less accommodating to organized labor) than the North.

Voting And Other Methods Of Participation In Politics _____

Political participation refers to those activities, which constitute citizen participation in the government.

Causes of Participation

Should citizens participate? Is participation in the democratic process a right? Is it a duty or is it optional? Many citizens do not participate in the democratic process or the selection of their government officials. They do not vote or participate in most of the other ways described in this chapter. Others believe that citizens have a responsibility to participate.

Deciding whether to participate and how much time to spend participating is important. To make good decisions, you must consider several factors:

- The purpose of our government
- How important your rights are to you
- How satisfied you are with the way the government is working

You are more likely to participate if you are more educated, more religious, or have a higher socio-economic status. Whites participate more than blacks, but not if socio-economic status is factored out. Men and women participate at almost same rate (women vote slightly more).

Methods of Participation

Generally there are two types of Political participation. Conventional forms of participation refer to accepted models of participating in government. For example, writing a letter, voting, holding public office, etc. Unconventional forms of participation refer to more dramatic forms of participation like protesting, boycotting, etc. Unconventional participation has been successful in influencing government decisions like the civil rights movement and the Vietnam War.

There are multiple ways that citizens can participate in political action.

- Judging the accuracy of information in newspapers, magazines, and reference materials
- Voting in local, state, and national elections

- Participating in a political discussion
- Trying to persuade someone to vote a certain way
- Signing a petition
- Wearing a button or putting a sticker on the car
- Writing letters to elected representatives
- Contributing money to a party or candidate
- Attending meetings to gain information, discuss issues, or lend support
- Campaigning for a candidate
- Lobbying for special interest laws
- Demonstrating through marches, boycotts, sit-ins, or other forms of protest
- Serving as a juror
- Running for office
- Holding public office
- Serving the country through military or other service
- Disobeying laws and suffering the consequences in an effort to demonstrate that a law or policy is unjust

Factors That Influence Citizens To Differ In Their Opinions

Not everyone goes through the same process to acquire their political knowledge and form their political opinion. This process of acquiring the knowledge and forming the opinion is called political socialization. It is the process by which personal and other background traits influence one's views about politics and government. We know some common outcomes of political socialization. For example, children tend to share their parents political orientations. Opinion seems to vary with social class, race, religion, and gender. But people with similar family histories, religious affiliations, formal educations, and job experiences do not think or vote exactly the same way.

The most common explanation as to why a voter votes a certain way is that the voter agrees with most of the candidate's views. Voters may also vote based on their party identification, i.e. along party lines. Voters may vote based on the candidates policies. Although, true policy voting rarely happens because the voter needs to be clear on the candidates and their own political beliefs, and know the differences of policies between candidates. Respective voting refers to the prospect of voting based on past actions. Basically the voter asks himself which candidate has done the most for them lately and whichever one has done the most will receive their vote.

Political Opinion Labels

Once you immerse yourself into political discourse with your friends, peers, or for school, you'll hear terms or labels that people apply to the two parties in the U.S. We briefly mentioned them earlier in this chapter, however it is important to become familiar with these terms, as they represent certain points of view.

The terms "left" and "right" define opposite ends of the political spectrum. In the United States, liberals are referred to as the left or left-wing and conservatives are referred to as the right or right-wing. On the U.S. political map, blue represents the Democratic Party (which generally upholds liberal principles) and red represents the Republican Party (which generally upholds conservative principles).

The table below shows the labels as related to the political spectrum.

LEFT	The Political Spectrum	RIGHT
Democrats	Moderate	Republicans
Liberal	Centrist	Conservative
Left of Center		Right of Center
Left-wing		Right-wing
Identified in Blue color		Identified in Red color
Symbol: Donkey		Symbol: Elephant

Divisive Political Issues

Also realize that non-economic issues now define who considers themselves as liberal or conservative. Several "hot-button" issues in recent elections include stem-cell research, the Iraq War, the War on Terror. Other "common" partisan issues include Social Security, abortion or the right to life, gay marriage, the environment, and social welfare.

Let's look briefly at issues where Democrats or liberals tend to demonstrate partisan views.

- They believe in government action to achieve equal opportunity. Liberal policies generally emphasize the need for the government to solve problems.
- Right to choose in the abortion debate
- Minorities face job and race discrimination, so federal affirmative action is necessary.
- The death penalty should be abolished. It is inhumane and is 'cruel and unusual' punishment.
- A market system in which government regulates the economy is best. Government must protect citizens from the greed of big business.
- Public schools are the best way to educate students. Vouchers take money away from public schools.

- The use of embryonic stem cells for research should be supported. It is necessary (and ethical) for the government to fund embryonic stem cell research, which will assist scientists in finding treatments and cures for diseases.
- Oil is a being depleted as a resource. Other sources of energy must be explored. The government must produce a national plan for all energy resources and subsidize alternative energy research and production.
- To combat global warming and climate change, proposed laws to reduce carbon emissions in the U.S. are urgently needed and should be enacted immediately to save the planet.
- The Second Amendment does not give citizens the right to keep and bear arms, but only allows for the state to keep a militia (National Guard). Additional gun control laws are necessary to stop gun violence and limit the ability of criminals to obtain guns.
- Free or low-cost government controlled health care should be supported.
- Legal immigration should be supported. Support amnesty for those who enter the U.S. illegally (undocumented immigrants). Also, undocumented immigrants have a right to the educational and health benefits that citizens receive.
- The Social Security system should be protected at all costs.
- Higher taxes for the wealthy and a larger government are necessary to address inequity/injustice in society. Government should help the poor and needy using tax dollars from the rich.
- Welfare, including long-term welfare, should be supported. Welfare is a safety net, which provides for the needs of the poor. Welfare is necessary to bring fairness to American economic life. It is a device for protecting the poor.

Similarly, Republican or conservative beliefs and partisan issues are listed below.
- A belief in personal responsibility, limited government, free markets, individual liberty, traditional American values and a strong national defense. Conservative policies generally emphasize empowerment of the individual to solve problems.
- Right to life in the abortion debate
- A belief that an individual should be hired based on their abilities. Affirmative action should not be supported.
- The death penalty is a punishment that fits the crime of murder; it is neither 'cruel' nor 'unusual.'
- Free markets produce more economic growth, more jobs and higher standards of living than those systems burdened by excessive government regulation.

- School vouchers create competition and therefore encourage schools to improve performance.
- The use of adult and umbilical cord stem cells should be supported only for research. It is morally and ethically wrong for the government to fund embryonic stem cell research.
- Oil, gas and coal are all good sources of energy and are abundant in the U.S. Support increased production of nuclear energy. Wind and solar sources will never provide plentiful, affordable sources of power.
- Proposed laws to reduce carbon emissions will do nothing to help the environment and will cause significant price increases for all.
- The Second Amendment gives citizens the right to keep and bear arms. There are too many gun control laws—additional laws will not lower gun crime rates. What is needed is enforcement of current laws. Gun control laws do not prevent criminals from obtaining guns.
- A competitive, free market health care system should be supported.
- Only legal immigration should be supported. Amnesty for those who enter the U.S. illegally should be opposed. Those who break the law by entering the U.S. illegally do not have the same rights as those who obey the law and enter legally.
- The Social Security system is in serious financial trouble. Major changes to the current system are urgently needed.
- Lower taxes and a smaller government with limited power will improve the standard of living for all.
- Long-term welfare should be opposed. Opportunities should be provided to make it possible for those in need to become self-reliant.

Summary

After reviewing this chapter, you should understand the political beliefs and the political landscape of the United States. You should be able to recognize key themes of American political culture, ideology, political beliefs, and behavior. You should understand the process of political socialization, what factors affect it, how different groups socialize and form political opinions. You should also know the beliefs that some groups hold about their government. Finally, you should place a particular emphasis on your understanding of polling: what constitutes a good poll, how accurate polls are and what constitute the cleavages in public opinion.

Chapter 3: Political Parties, Interest Groups, and Mass Media

The functions of and interrelations between political parties, interest groups, and mass media are important to the political process and the role of citizens in government. Each of these groups can be, and usually is, a major force in America's politics. Each group's actions have an impact on the general public because each group has goals and incentives that ultimately affect all citizens.

What You Will Be Tested On

This section on political parties, interest groups, and the mass media focus on how the processes of democratic governance are communicated and influenced. You must know the mechanisms that allow citizens to organize and communicate their interests and concerns. You will examine the significance of the historical evolution of the U.S. party system, the functions and structures of political parties, and the effects they have on the political process. An understanding of elections, election laws, and election systems at the national and state levels is also part of this unit.

Political Parties And Elections

A political party is a group of individuals who are organized in an effort to win elections, determine public policy, and operate the government. The U.S. Constitution does not create, or formally address political parties, and the early leaders believed that there should not be "factions" that would result in partisanship. The founding fathers did not support the formation of political parties, which were viewed as a divisive instrument at that time. When James Madison and Alexander Hamilton wrote the *Federalist Papers*, they wrote about reasons why political factions were dangerous for the new nation. George Washington was not a member of any political party, and he expressed his disfavor of political parties or "factions" in his farewell address. However, as the American government took shape in the years after the ratification of the Constitution, political parties and partisan politics entered the political dialogue of the time. Although Alexander Hamilton and James Madison expressed their beliefs about the dangers of political parties, they were both leaders in the political parties that were developed.

Evolution of the U.S. Party System

The first political parties in the United States were created in 1792 and consisted of the Federalists and the Democratic-Republicans. The Federalists believed in a strong central government, a central banking system, and continued ties with England. Alexander Hamilton was a Federalist. The appeal of the Federalists began to decline by the time James Monroe became president, beginning the Era of Good Feeling which focused on internal improvements such as canal building and road expansion after the country had been victorious in the War of 1812. James Madison and Thomas Jefferson founded the Democratic-Republican Party. This party consisted of men who were anti-federalists, or men who opposed a strong central government. The Democratic-Republicans believed the states should have more rights and opposed Alexander Hamilton's policies of a strong central government.

The two-party system began in the late 1820s when the Democratic-Republican Party split into the (Jacksonian) Democrats and the Whigs. Andrew Jackson's Democrats believed in a presidency that was stronger than other branches of government. The Democrats also opposed a national bank. The Whigs, led by Henry Clay, took the position that Congress should be the superior branch of government. They also wanted high tariffs to protect American products from imported goods. The two most-debated issues during this time period involved the central bank and the patronage system. The National Bank needed to be re-chartered in 1836 and President Jackson made the issue of the re-charter an issue in the political campaign. Jackson and the Democrats believed that a National Bank favored the elitists and violated state powers. Congress passed a bill to re-charter the bank but President Jackson vetoed the bill. He also had the funds in the bank transferred to state banks before the bank's charter expired. Patronage was also an issue during the second period of political parties. President Jackson appointed friends and loyal political supporters to positions in the federal government. This system of patronage was also referred to as the "spoils" system. This second age of political parties lasted about 30 years until some of the Whig Party's leaders died and the party experienced disunity over the issue of the spread of slavery.

The Republican Party came into existence in the 1850s and adopted some of the Whig policies. The Republicans favored high tariffs and a national bank. The party also focused on the anti-slavery issue. After the Civil War, many freed slaves became Republicans. The Democrats were conservatives and had many Catholic immigrants as members. This phase of political parties lasted about 40 years, from the 1850s to the 1890s.

The fourth period of political parties lasted from the mid-1890s to the early 1930s. The Republicans dominated the Progressive Era and attributed the Panic of 1893 to the Democrats. The Republicans were "trust busters" and focused efforts on raising tariffs and regulating big business. During this period, the issues of women's suffrage, child labor, direct election of senators, and immigration were debated by the political parties. The Northeast was an industrial area and became more Republican.

The fifth period of political parties began during the Great Depression and beginning of the New Deal when the Republicans lost favor with much of the country. This period ended, possibly in the 1960s. Beginning in the 1960s various Republican movements have taken place. The Moral Majority formed in the 1990s, and in the 1990s, the Democrats became more liberal while the Republicans became more conservative. The Democrats gained more African Americans, white progressives, and Hispanics. The Republicans have gained power in rural areas and in the South and suburban areas. Today, the Republican Party and the Democrat Party are the two major political parties in the United States.

Functions of Political Parties

Political parties serve several purposes. One of the most important jobs of political parties is to select candidates to run for political office and to serve in government. Parties also encourage people to serve as volunteers to work at election sites and register voters before elections. Before the election, volunteers distribute literature, help with candidates' campaigns, and help the candidates encourage people to register to vote. On Election Day, the volunteers may make telephone calls to encourage people to vote and offer to take people to the polling locations if they are otherwise unable to vote.

Parties establish platforms to express their views for the citizens. Platforms are usually determined before and during the national political conventions, before elections for president and other national leaders. In addition to selecting candidates and helping them win elections, political parties try to select candidates who favor and support their platform and policies. Government staff and people working in the bureaucracy implement policies that the elected officials establish. Political parties, whether winning elections or not, continue to promote their policies and agenda with their supporters. This allows the parties to continue to debate their positions and keep public momentum on their stances.

Structure of Political Parties

In order to carry out their functions, political parties exist on national, state, and local levels. The three levels overlap in some respects, but also have distinct regions of oversight.

Local members of a political party form the "grass roots" for the parties. The parties form committees at the city and county level and select leaders in each precinct or geographic voting area. Volunteers at the local level help organize party events, organize election details, and work at the polling locations on voting days. The local level of a political party has a great deal of influence in its specific area and often coordinates closely with the state level to promote the election of individuals to hold state office.

The state level of a political party organization has a committee to organize the party's events and hold state conventions to nominate candidates for state office. State congressional district committees are included in the state-level political party organization. Each of the 435 members of Congress represents one Congressional district. As a result, each state will have the same number of Congressional districts as it has Representatives in Congress.

The national level of a political party serves as an overseer of the state and local political party levels. The national committee is elected by state committees or at the party's national convention and coordinates that party's activities during the four years between elections. The committee selects a chairperson who is the speaker for the party. The committee for each party plans its respective national campaign and convention. It also writes the party's platform.

States also hold political conventions to elect party candidates to run against the opposing party's candidates on the state level. The state convention delegates elect the people who will serve as delegates at the national convention.

Ideological Differences Between Two Parties

Generally, Republicans tend to be conservative and can be described as "right of center" thinkers. They favor small government and believe that government best serves the people when there is less regulation. They believe wages should be set by the free market economy and that capitalism and the free market economy are hindered by government regulation. As a party, Republicans believe that taxes should not be increased for any economic group, and some republicans favor a "flat" tax rate that does not vary with income level. They favor increased spending for the military and believe that government regulation can slow job growth. Republicans are characterized as favoring the death penalty, opposing gay marriage, and opposing abortion. They take the position that private companies should provide healthcare services rather than the government. Republicans believe the U.S. immigration policy should not favor amnesty for undocumented immigrants, should not put a moratorium on deporting some types of workers, and favor stronger border policy and enforcement of laws banning undocumented immigrants. Republicans generally oppose gun control, strongly support the Second Amendment right to bear arms, and favor carrying concealed weapons.

Democrats are thought to be more liberal and "left of center" thinkers and favor the expansion of the role of government for the good of the people. They favor a progressive tax that has higher rates for wage earners with higher incomes and favor government funding through taxation. The party's policy supports government funding to protect consumers. Generally, they believe in more government regulation. They favor a higher minimum wage and less spending on the military. Democrats generally support gay marriage and favor abortions, believing that the Supreme Court's decision in *Roe v. Wade* is correct. They also, as a party, support the death penalty. Universal healthcare is important to the Democrats, and they generally support Obamacare. Democrats support instituting a process to provide certain undocumented immigrants with citizenship and favor a moratorium on deportation of some undocumented immigrants. They also favor gun-control laws and do not support the citizenry carrying concealed weapons.

Demographic Differences Between The Two Parties

You'll often hear of the blue states during presidential elections. These are states that are Democratic strongholds. Historically, the Democrats have been dominant in the southeastern part of the United States. More recently, the Democrats have gained more popularity in New England and other areas of the Northeast and the Middle Atlantic states. They are strong in the Midwest, particularly the Great Lakes states and are gaining strength in the Mountain states, such as Colorado and Montana. Democrats are strong in California, particularly along coastal areas and in urban areas throughout the United States.

In contrast to blue states, the reference to red states is to those states that are Republican strongholds. The Republican Party has generally been known as a party that attracts voters in rural areas and in smaller towns and cities in the Midwest. Since the Reagan area in the 1980s, the Republicans have played a major role in the South and the West, as well. They are also strong in the Great Plains states, such as Oklahoma, Kansas, Nebraska, and Texas. They have also been strong in western states, such as Wyoming and Idaho. Republicans have less strength in the Northeast and along the Pacific coast.

Effects of Parties on the Political Process

Political parties can affect the political process in various ways. Party members in Congress can prevent the success of the opposing party's agenda by joining together to keep their bills from passing. A party can also stop a nomination by not voting for a presidential appointment or, as in the case of the Republicans reaction to President Obama's nomination for a Supreme Court vacancy, by refusing to hold confirmation hearings.

Parties can also have an effect on the political process by presenting issues to the public and offering suggestions for resolving issues that are different from the opposing parties' suggestions for solution. The party can also run advertisements for members of their party running for office or against the opposition's candidate. The purpose of these advertisements is to affect the political process by suggesting to voters the names of individuals for whom the party believes the voter should cast a ballot. The effect of this action is to sway the outcome of an election in a direction favored by the party.

Third Parties and Elections

Third parties have played important roles in America's national politics even though third-party candidates have never been elected to the presidency. They have been successful in promoting issues, whether for reform or for recognition, that the two major political parties have later adopted.

The Populist Party, for which James Weaver ran for president in 1892, was influential from the 1890s through the first decade of the 1900s. It was an agrarian-based group of farmers in the American South and West that campaigned against big business, railroads, and the gold standard for currency.

The Progressive Party, called the Bull Moose Party, ran former president Theodore Roosevelt for president in 1912. The party was created as the result of a split in the Republican Party when its candidate was considered too conservative. The party supported women's suffrage; the registration of lobbyists; campaign contribution limits; insurance for the elderly, disabled, and unemployed; and other efforts to curb the corruption and abuse that the party believed existed in big business and government.

The Independent Party that nominated Ross Perot as a candidate for President in 1992 campaigned for a balanced budget, no gun control, and an end to the outsourcing of jobs.

Issues of Party Reform

The purpose of party reform is to meet the public's expectations and reduce and/or eliminate issues of manipulation and corruption. Issues of party reform can include a variety of subjects and may include anything from campaign money to eliminating or changing the method of electing the president. Some of the following could be issues for possible party reform:

- Does the primary election process treat the candidates fairly?
- Should states have a "winner take all" policy for primary elections or should the results of the primary elections be distributed to candidates on the basis of the percentage of votes that candidate received?
- Does the caucus system unduly influence voters?
- Should there be finance reform? If so, what reforms are necessary?
- Should candidates receive limited funding?
- Should Super Pac funding practices be changed?
- Should parties hold primary elections on a single day across the nation?

- Should the party organization have more control over the primary elections and caucuses for the nomination of candidates? For example, should there be "super delegate" votes? If so, when should the super delegate votes be announced to avoid persuading or influencing a voters selection of a candidate?
- Does the Electoral College meet the needs of today's society, if candidates receiving the most popular votes do not win the number of Electoral College votes required to be elected President?

Throughout the history of our country's political party system, reforms have corrected many issues that could have resulted in allegations of corruption. The registration of lobbyists is only one such example. Political parties have a stake in the public's interests because each party needs public support. As the result of active participation in a political party, necessary changes can be made that reform the party in order to meet the public's expectations and goals for the party.

Campaign Strategies

A candidate campaigns to persuade people to vote for him/her and to elect him/her to office. Strategies for a specific type of campaign are determined by the party, the public, the candidate, or the party and candidate together. A good campaign is one that is organized, has specific issues that will be presented, and knows how to present the issues. Once a strategy has been decided, the campaign's target groups should be identified and the strategy implemented. A candidate's resources (in people and money) should be a defining factor as to how the candidate proceeds to campaign. Usually, campaigns are focused on issues and a candidate's position on those issues; however, some campaigns implement a negative approach in order to discredit the opposing candidate's views. Regardless of the selected strategy or strategies, a candidate's focus is directed to winning the election and taking part in government.

Financing in an Electronic Age

Campaign financing regulations are intended to reduce corruption or the possibility of corruption. A candidate running for a federal election receives can receive funding from various sources. It may come from individuals who donate large or small amounts, a political action committee, or from the candidates themselves who self-finance. In the 2016 campaign for the office of the President, some of the candidates encouraged small contributions through Internet campaign sites or social media sites. The Internet is a significant source of small donations and has had an impact on the financing of campaigns in recent years. In the 2016 campaign, for example, Bernie Sanders, a Democratic candidate, encouraged small donations. He received huge sums as the result of supporters making small donations on the Internet.

Election Laws

The Federal Election Commission is the independent regulatory agency that administers the Federal Election Campaign Act. The Commission also issues regulations to implement the law and issues advisory opinions that apply the law. The Federal Election Campaign was enacted in the 1970s and has been amended several times by Congress. The Act focuses on the financing of campaigns, the disclosure of sources, and the amount of funding. This Act preempts, or takes priority over, state laws relating to federal elections and other federal laws involving elections. The Supreme Court has struck down some Congressional amendments of the laws and in other cases, has narrowed the meaning of the law.

State election laws vary by state and are written by the state legislatures to cover the procedure for electing officials, the qualifications the candidates must meet to be eligible to run for office and the requirements individuals must meet in order to vote. State election laws also provide rules for the processes of voting and counting votes; conducting primary elections or caucuses; recounting of votes and election contests; campaigns; determining Congressional districts; and provide penalties for violation of the election rules and procedures set forth in the statutes. State laws do not take priority over the Federal Election Campaign Act.

Election System

In the United States there are two types of elections—general and primary. General elections are held every two years in even-numbered years on the first Tuesday after the first Monday in November. The purpose of a general election is to make the final selection for an office. Elections that are held for the purpose of voting on members of the House of Representative are held every two years and are called mid-term elections. All members of the House of Representatives and one-third of the U.S. Senators are voted on in mid-term elections.

Primary elections are held before the general elections to select candidates to represent political parties in the general election. Primary elections are held for national, state, and local elections. The states, with the consent of the national party committees, decide the dates of the primary elections. States may also hold general and/or primary elections in odd-numbered years, but voting for members of Congress and the president take place only in even-numbered years.

Voters cast ballots for a presidential candidate in national general elections. The candidates have been chosen earlier in state primary elections (or by caucuses in some states), and are finally selected by each political party at its convention. Then, the candidate runs as the party's nominee in the general elections, and the country votes.

The Democrats have Super Delegates who represent the party and may cast votes as they wish. The Super Delegates are in addition to the number of committed delegates from each state. A nominating convention for the political party not holding the office of president is held before the political convention for the party who currently holds the presidential office. Each of the main parties will have a candidate, and often there will be third-party candidates on state ballots. There may also be candidates who can be "written-in." In order to vote for a "write-in" candidate, the candidate must have met the requirements of the state in which he/she wants to be included on the ballot.

The popular vote does not actually decide who will be president, but instead, the Electoral College serves that purpose. The Electoral College is provided for in the Constitution and consists of individuals who cast their votes for the president and vice-president. Each state is represented in the Electoral College and each state has the same number of electoral votes as they have Congressional districts. The electors meet in their states and send their ballots to Congress to be opened at a joint session of Congress in January. The Twelfth Amendment to the Constitution provides that if no candidate receives a majority of votes for president, the decision is made by the House of Representatives. The Senate decides upon the vice-president if no candidate has a majority of the electoral votes.

A state permits only residents of that state to vote in state elections. All states have an age requirement for voting and some states do not permit convicted felons to vote. If there is a provision for special elections, a state may hold a special election. One reason for holding a special election is to fill a vacancy due to the death or resignation of an office holder. In addition to voting for candidates, states may include on the ballot referendums for new legislation and recall questions relating to the removal of an official from office.

In the United States, voters must be at least 18 years old. The Twenty-sixth Amendment to the Constitution, which was ratified in 1971 and signed into law by President Richard Nixon, lowered the voting age from 21 to 18. The impetus for the change in voting age resulted from the belief that if eighteen-year-olds could fight for their country in the Vietnam War, they should be able to vote for the president. Voters are required to register and have some form of identification to show proof of age when they go to the polling places to cast their ballots. Each state has its own requirements for voting in national and/or state and local elections. Voter turnout may be high or low, depending upon a variety of factors. Voter turnout is usually better in general elections and in presidential elections. The economy, weather, and the predictability of an outcome of the election will result in different percentages of voter turnout. Voters may qualify for absentee ballots if they meet certain requirements and are unable to vote on voting day. States determine the qualifications for absentee voting.

Interest Groups And Political Action Committees_____

Interest groups and Political Action Committees all work towards a common agenda for their members. They act as influence-intermediaries on behalf of the public's interest.

Interest Groups

"Interest Group" is defined by *Merriam-Webster* as a group of persons having a common identifying interest that often provides a basis for action. An interest group may also be called an advocacy group or a special interest group. Not all interest groups are involved in politics. The interest groups that have shared ideas and attitudes about government or political issues will attempt to influence and change public policy about those issues or government policy in general. Generally an interest group focuses on a single issue, such as gun control or the environment, and tries to persuade government to pass legislation that is favorable to the interest group's position.

Interest groups have been involved in the political process since the colonial era when groups formed to support independence from England. Interest groups were also present in the early days of our nation. The First Amendment to the Constitution protects freedom of speech, the right to peacefully assemble, and the right to petition the government for redress of grievances. These protections guaranteed in the First Amendment support the creation of interest groups.

During the process of ratifying the Constitution, in the *Federalist Papers* James Madison proposed that the formation of multiple interests was beneficial to the new nation, and he encouraged the development of interest groups.

Types of Interest Groups

The anti-slavery groups were interest groups during the early to mid-1800s. The development of labor unions and the promotion of women's suffrage are examples of situations that led to the development of interest groups in the mid- to late 1800s. Today, interest groups advocate a variety of issues ranging from environmental issues and consumer issues to trade issues and benefits for retired people. The goal of any interest group is to make an impact on government decisions and to have those decisions favor the specific interest that the group is supporting. Examples of interest groups include the American Association for Retired Persons, the American Civil Liberties Union, the National Association for the Advancement of Colored People, the National Rifle Association, Planned Parenthood Federation of America, the Sierra Club, the Southern Poverty Law Center, and the U.S. Chamber of Commerce.

Interest groups can generally be divided into categories that relate to the economy, policy, public interest, and labor. Labor groups may promote issues such as collective bargaining with places of employment and stress their policies to legislators to obtain favored legislation on workers rights, for example. Public interest groups, as another example, may advocate more government oversight and budget reform.

Campaign reform is another focus of interest groups. In the 2016 campaign for the presidency, some candidates criticized other candidates for receiving huge amounts of money from Super Political Action Committees (PACs) and argued these donations affected the loyalty of the candidates receiving those funds. The details of Super PACs will be discussed later. Social policy and public interest groups may focus on one issue, such as abortion, animal rights, or gun control, while some groups such as the American Civil Liberties Union, focus on core beliefs.

Business, trade, and economic groups are the most common types of interest groups and represent nearly half of all interest groups in Washington, D.C. Professional groups, such as the American Medical Association and the American Bar Association are examples of economic or trade interest groups. Other examples include the oil and tobacco industries.

How Interest Groups Function

Interest groups function in two ways: direct interaction with the government legislators and indirect actions. Direct techniques can include lobbying, offering campaign assistance, and rating government officials for the public. During a campaign, the interest groups may share a candidate's voting record to bolster the candidate's campaign or to discredit the candidate. Interest groups also build alliances to increase support for their attempts to influence governmental actions. Indirectly, an interest group may influence government through third parties. Examples of indirect techniques include protest demonstrations, using constituents as lobbyists and policy promoters, and supporting candidates with financial campaign money through Super PACs. Interest groups may also join together to support an issue. This results in shared expenses and a stronger voice.

How Interest Groups Affect the Political Process and Public Policy

Interest groups affect the political process through their campaign contributions. An infusion of money into a candidate's campaign to boost the efforts of the candidate may keep a campaign on track that might otherwise need to be suspended for lack of funds. Interest groups also hope to work with legislators and public officials in influencing legislation and public policy. Campaign funding has been found to be one of the better ways to encourage elected officials to vote for legislation that favors specific policies of an interest group.

Lobbying

Lobbying is an effective method for affecting legislation and public policy. It is an attempt to directly affect government decisions by interacting, usually talking, with those who make the decisions — the members of Congress. Interest groups can also employ lobbyists, as third parties, to talk with members of Congress to attempt to sway votes. The pharmaceutical and insurances industries are two of the largest lobbying groups.

Lobbyists can be professional staff members of consulting firms or designated lobbyists employed by interest groups who attempt to direct the outcome of government legislation or policy. They may consult on the drafts of legislation, encourage voting for bills that represent the interests of their group or groups, or they may encourage a negative vote on legislation because the bill's contents may oppose the specific interest group's philosophy. Lobbyists may contact legislators directly to discuss the lobbyist's research and information about a specific subject and they may talk with reporters about their positions on upcoming legislation. Lobbyists may also testify before legislative committees in hearings. Effective lobbyists are well-spoken, have good "people" skills, and are knowledgeable about the industry they represent. Many have worked as interns or staffers for members of Congress before embarking on a career as a lobbyist.

Lobbying takes place at all levels of government. Much of the federal lobbying occurs in the halls of Congress. Each state has its own rules for lobbying even though all states have a similar definition of lobbying. The states also have their own rules about "gifts" and requirements for registration and disclosure.

In 1995, Congress passed the Lobbying Disclosure Act that requires paid lobbyists at the federal government level to register in the House of Representatives and the Senate. Lobbying firms, self-employed lobbyists, and groups employing lobbyists must also register and file reports about their lobbying activities. Members of Congress may not accept gifts from lobbyists or organizations employing lobbyists. The term "gift" means anything that has monetary value and includes such items as loans, entertainment, and hospitality.

In 2008, the Secretary of the U.S. Senate and Clerk of the U.S. House of Representatives issued a written statement of guidance, called the Lobbying Disclosure Act Guidance. The Guidance discussed disclosure and contribution rules under the Lobbying Disclosure Act and its amendments. The Guidance does not have the force of law but provides information and "guidance" for those who have questions relating to how the Clerk and Secretary will carry out their duties under the law.

Political Action Committee

A Political Action Committee (PAC) is a private group or committee that is formed to raise funds for a political candidate's campaign. The committee is a special-interest group that represents business or labor or some other interest. PACs are advocacy groups that have the goal of electing their candidates to the presidency, the U.S. Senate, or the U.S. House of Representatives. PACs may also use funds to promote a political agenda. They must register with the Federal Election Commission and are limited as to the amounts they may receive from individuals or other PACs. They are also limited in the amounts of cash they may give to an individual candidate, a party's national committee, or another PAC.

PACs were introduced into the political scene in the United States in the 1940s by the Congress of Industrial Organization (CIO). Before that time, labor unions and corporations were prohibited from making direct financial contributions to influence policy. As a result the CIO created the PAC as a separate political fund called the Political Action Committee. Another PAC was formed when the AFL and CIO merged in the 1950s. During the same period, a medical political PAC and a business PAC was formed. The number of PACS was at its highest in 1988 when there were more than 4,200 PACs.

"Super" PACs came into existence in 2010 as the result of two court cases. In *Citizens United v. Federal Election Commission* the Supreme Court decided that government could not prohibit independent spending by corporations and unions for political purposes. The dispute began when the group Citizens United objected to advertisements that were advocating against the re-election of George W. Bush and argued those ads were illegal. The Federal Elections Commission disagreed, so Citizens United formed a production company and made a documentary unsympathetic to presidential candidate Bill Clinton. The Federal Election Commission prohibited Citizens United from running ads that promoted the film. The issue was litigated and eventually reached the Supreme Court. The 2010 ruling eliminated all caps placed on the amount of money a PAC could receive from a person and declared corporations and unions could make unlimited donations.

Later, in the case of *Speechnow.org v. Federal Election Commission*, a decision by the federal court of appeals held that no limits could be placed on contributions to groups that only made independent expenditures. However, the Super PACs are required to disclose donors and are not permitted to coordinate with the candidates or the agendas they advocate. Today there are approximately 600 Super PACs.

The Mass Media

Mass media refers to various kinds of media—print, television, radio, and the Internet—that reach a large population and have an immense influence on the population. Mass media can be used for political communications, reporting the news, and attempting to impact the population's thinking about the candidates.

Functions of the Media

Probably the most important function of media is to report the news. This is equally true with respect to coverage of government, political parties, and elections. When the media reports the news, it provides voters and the population information, which they can use to make informative decisions. Today, the media practices objective journalism, but because many members of the media make their own interpretation of the news, the news report may become more of what the journalist believes than what is depicted by the facts. This type of reporting is called interpretive reporting. Because journalists often have the opportunity to select stories they want to report, their decisions let the population know which material the media considers most important.

The media is also a communication link between the people and the government. People learn what the government is (or is not) doing, and the government learns what the public is thinking. However, when the media attempts to make government officials accountable for an event, vote, or action, the reporter may be injecting his/her opinions as to why a government official should be accountable. This type of reporting can present a biased viewpoint and shape public opinion.

Impact of Media on Politics

The media often acts as gatekeepers by controlling which messages are presented to the public through decisions about which stories to tell and which stories not to tell. President Ronald Reagan used the media to the advantage of the presidency. By successfully reaching out to the people through the media, President Reagan became known as "the great communicator." The media in the United States is permitted freedom of speech and press, guaranteed in the First Amendment to the Constitution. However, the relationship between government and the media is also based on rules, such as reporters and broadcasters not being able to censor information or dictate the content of stories. Libel and slander laws are broad enough to allow for reporting that may be critical of public figures.

The media shapes politics in various ways. In addition to serving as a gatekeeper, the media can shape or alter the behavior of governmental officials and candidates. President Reagan was skillful at utilizing the press to his administration's advantage because he as a skilled movie and television actor his training permitted him to be an effective communicator. President Franklin Roosevelt used the radio to present "fireside chats" to encourage Americans during the Great Depression and the New Deal. President Obama used photo opportunities to show Americans the progress that had been made in the relations with Cuba when he visited Cuba in 2016 to establish diplomatic relations with the island nation.

During the 2016 campaign for the presidency, the media played a huge role in politics by having some of its members serve as moderators for the debates among the contenders for the office of president.

The media also believes it should have a right to keep sources of stories confidential. During the Watergate scandal, reporters did not want to disclose the name of "Deepthroat", the person who provided information on the scandal. The Watergate scandal, which resulted in the resignation of President Richard Nixon, made headlines in newspapers and was given widespread coverage by the media. In most cases, courts have been the decision-maker as to whether sources of news stories may remain confidential.

Impact of Media on Public Opinion

The impact of mass media on the public can be significant because the media can focus the attention on specific issues, individual personalities, and on polls. Polls are created by the media or other public interest groups to reflect changing attitudes and reactions to events, statements of candidates, and the popularity of the candidates. The Internet, as a source of news, can reach around the globe to all ages and levels of wealth. Individuals who own several media outlets can lessen the diversity of media communication. Although editorial endorsements may make an impact on presidential candidates, media endorsements for local and state officials may have an impact on the public and the outcome of elections.

Impact of Media on Voter Participation

Media can impact elections by shaping voter thinking. The media serves as a link between the people and government and reports news that can raise issues that are of importance in an election or shape and strengthen, or lessen existing issues.

People who are actively involved in, or interested in politics will probably not be swayed by media reports. However, the undecided voter or the voter whose opinion is not strongly formed can be swayed by what he or she hears from the media. Undecided voters can, and often do, decide elections and the impact of the media on them during close elections can be significant.

Campaign Strategies

Candidates use a variety of strategies and utilize the media in ways that were not available several years ago. Use of the Internet is now one of the most important tools that candidates use in their campaigns. Social media was an important tool that candidates used in the 2016 presidential campaign. The media reported "tweets" and other comments posted by candidates on sites such as Facebook and Twitter for the population as a whole. The media can present candidates' comments in a neutral, positive, or negative light, and possibly "spin" the news item in a way to influence voters.

Traditional methods of campaigning, such as distributing flyers and running ads in newspapers, have given way to more campaigning on radio and television. Some candidates make guest appearances on late night television. These appearances are less formal and more conversational than appearances at events such as the presidential debates. Although these appearances may not be considered in the terms of formal campaigning, they send messages to the voters on a more personal level.

The media can, and often does, affect the way the population perceives a candidate or an elected official. Television has a greater impact on voters than newspaper articles written about the same subjects. In television coverage, the questions that are asked, the manner of reporting a story, and the interpretation of news events can have a great effect on the undecided and independent voters. Television and Internet coverage of campaigns tend to give the voters a more personal glimpse of the candidate even though the image they gain may be from interpretive reporting.

The Growing Role of the Internet Media in Elections

The media of past elections has ranged from newspapers to radio to television. Now, the new media includes the Internet. Candidates still pay for advertising in print media, but social media on the Internet provides an expanding arena for candidates. Campaigning for donations through the Internet, using candidacy sites and social media sites such as Facebook and Twitter, was a successful method used in the 2016 campaign and will become increasingly important in future years. The "grass roots" of politics has become "tweeting" and texting, in addition to the in-person town hall meetings held by candidates.

Cell phones and "streaming" have become other sources of campaigning in the digital age. Cable television and blogging reach millions of voters and potential voters. People can select the methods of political communication they favor—and they can share their political ideas instantly by using modern technological devises and social media. In fact, President Obama announced his candidacy for the president by web video and, later, his vice presidential choice by text message.

Politicians and government officials use digital technology to find out how people are reacting to their policies. "Likes", "comments", and "thumbs up" on social media sites convey instantaneous opinions to politicians.

Relationship Between Elected Officials, the Media, and Candidates

There is a symbiotic but frequently conflicting relationship among the media, the candidates, and elected officials. One reason for this conflict is that the media is more focused on individuals running for office than on the political parties they represent. Candidates want media attention to draw them and their campaigns to the general public and, in particular, to the voters. As a result, claims of media bias may arise, whether from the stories that are reported or the positions the media take on the candidate's philosophy.

In the 2016 presidential debates Donald Trump and certain newscasters developed an antagonistic relationship. Trump refused to participate in one debate because of what he believed was an unfair attitude of a moderator during the debates.

The issues of media abuse, the role of media in national elections, the motives of media, and whether or not the media serves as a check to balance the factors in government and in the election process continue to be debated.

The issues involving insider stories and leaked news stories pose problems for the media, candidates, and government officials. The reasons why the media prints "leaked" stories, is seldom revealed. Sometimes those stories come from the government because the stories are favorable to the group leaking the stories. Sometimes the "leaked" stories result from an unidentified source and may have the purpose of exposing corruption or encouraging further research on the issue. As a result, the parties sometimes develop a distrust of the other parties and adversarial attitudes develop. This distrust can lead to verbal attacks on journalists, arguments about the purpose of journalism, and whether limitations should be placed on First Amendment rights. The goals of the media are usually focus on their rights to the freedoms guaranteed under the First Amendment, while the candidates and officials may argue that the media has overstepped its boundaries in defining freedom of the press.

Summary

Political parties that were formed more than 200 years ago have evolved to represent modern-day issues. However, the reasons for which political parties were formed exist for some of the same reasons today. Third parties have influenced the issues that are raised and resolved in government. Elections are an integral and important part of the political process. Interest groups and special interest groups, such as political actions committees, contribute to the election and government in a variety of ways. Lobbying can effectively encourage or discourage governmental action, and the mass media can significantly affect the political process. All of these groups link the political scene of America. They may have positive or negative interactions, and there may be reforms that are needed within the groups. Despite their strengths and weaknesses, they all affect the government and political processes in different ways and to varying degrees.

Chapter 4: Institutions of National Government

The framework for the government was created when the Constitution was written. The Constitution created three branches of government, described the powers of those branches, and provided for methods of amendment. The bureaucracy is included in a discussion of the Institutions of National Government because of the role it plays in American government.

This section of the study guide will discuss the organization of each of the branches of government and their powers and functions. You will also learn about the shared powers and relationships between the branches of government. You will also learn about the bureaucracy, its organization, and its functions. Finally, you will review the relationships between interest groups, the media, and state and local government and the national government.

What You will be Tested on

Questions on the test will focus on the lawmaking and institutional powers and processes of Congress, the president, the federal bureaucracy, and the judiciary. You will need to understand how each of these entities functions, is structured, and elects or appoints its members or representatives. A strong understanding of the nature of checks and balances under federalism is imperative, since it represents the counterbalance to all the powers granted by the Constitution to the branches of government. Also, it is important to remember that, while the branches of government have formal powers, they have also accumulated informal powers over the years. Finally, the court has power in interpreting and making new policies, but cannot enforce the rulings directly.

Congress

The legislative powers of the United States are vested in Congress, which consists of a Senate and House of Representatives. Each house is the judge of the election and qualifications of its own members. A simple majority of the members of each chamber (a quorum) must be present in order for the chamber to conduct business. Each house must also keep a journal of its proceedings including a record of the votes of the members, if one-fifth of those present at a vote want them recorded.

House Of Representatives

Members of the House of Representatives are chosen every two years, for two-year terms. A person who has reached the age of 25, has been a citizen of the United States for two years, and is an inhabitant of the state from which they are elected may serve as a member of the House of Representatives.

Representatives are chosen from each state, and the number of Representatives from each state is based on population. The number of Representatives from each state is determined by the census, which is conducted every ten years. For about the first 100 years, all members of free population and three-fifth of the slaves were counted to determine the number of Representatives each state was entitled to receive. Indians who were not taxed were not counted in the population. From the time of the ratification of the Constitution, each state has had a minimum of one Representative.

The Fourteenth Amendment eliminated the fractional count for slaves, and in the early 1940s, the "Indians, not taxed" language was no longer considered. In 1929, the number of Representatives was set at 435, and since then, the size of the House has remained the same.

The Reapportionment Act of 1929 created a Congressional district of approximately 674,000 people. When the census figures show a state's population has changed, the number of Representatives for the state also changes. For example, after the Civil War, the census of 1870 gave Indiana 13 Representatives. The number remained the same until the 1930 census, when the population of the state began decreasing. Today, Indiana has nine U.S. Representatives. When there is a vacancy in the House from a specific state, the executive officer of that state orders an election to replace the former Representative.

The Speaker of the House of Representatives is its presiding officer. Although the Constitution does not state the qualifications that a person must meet to be elected Speaker, all Speakers have been members of the House. The Speaker is a leader of the majority party in the House and is second in the line of succession for the presidency.

Senate

Article I, Section 3 of the Constitution provides that the Senate of the United States shall be composed of two Senators from each state. Each senator serves a six-year term. A senator must be at least 30 years old, have been a U.S. citizen for nine years, and be an inhabitant of the state from which he was elected.

In the beginning, the Senators were selected by legislatures of their states, and the membership was divided into thirds, with one group serving two years, one group serving four years, and one group serving six years. The senators were chosen by state legislatures until the Seventeenth Amendment was ratified in 1913.

The Vice President of the United States presides over the Senate but a president pro tem is chosen to preside in the absence of the Vice President. Unlike the Speaker of the House, the Vice President has no vote except at the time the Senate is equally divided. A president pro tem is chosen to preside when the Vice President is unavailable or is serving as President of the United States.

Committees

Committees have an important function in Congress because all bills begin and end in committees. Thousands of bills begin in committees but only about ten percent pass Congress and are signed into law. Members of the House and Senate are assigned to committees after each election. The member may make his or her wishes known as to which committee they wish to serve on, but the appointment will ultimately depend upon the needs of the committees. Since the House is the larger body, most Representatives only serve on one or two committees. Senators, however, are often assigned to several committees and subcommittees. There are four types of committees: standing committees, select committees, joint committees, and conference committees.

Standing Committees

Standing committees are probably the most important type of committee because they are continuing and because the members of the standing committees consider all major proposed legislation. Many standing committees have been in place for years. The House of Representatives and the Senate both have standing committees. In the process of passing legislation, once a bill is given to the presiding officer of the House or Senate, it is assigned to a committee. The committee discusses the proposed law, holds hearings, calls experts, and then may refer it to a subcommittee, which investigates the proposal in more depth. If the bill passes out of committee, it is sent to the other chamber to go through the same process.

These committees also perform the function of oversight, which means to review and monitor the work of the executive branch and its agencies. The standing committee may hold hearings as part of the process of investigating the actions of the agencies or executive branch. For example, during the Clinton presidency, the Senate Banking Committee investigated matters in the Whitewater scandal.

At the time of publication of this guide, the Senate has 16 standing committees and the House has 19. Some examples of standing committees include: agriculture, appropriations, armed services, banking, budget, commerce, education, foreign relations, rules, and finance. In addition to reviewing proposed legislation, standing committees may conduct investigations.

The House Ways and Means committee is one of the most important standing committees. It is the oldest committee in the House and is responsible for writing tax legislation. Its power is derived from the Article I provision in the Constitution that declares all revenue bills shall originate in the House of Representatives. The committee also is involved in revenue-related tariff issues, reciprocal trade agreements, and revenue aspects of Social Security and Medicare.

Select Committees

Select committees are formed for particular purposes. They may study an issue or investigate government actions. For example, a select committee was appointed to investigate the assassination of President John F. Kennedy. At the conclusion of its investigation, select committees are disbanded.

There are also times that a select committee may become a standing committee. The Committee on Intelligence is an example of a Senate select committee that has served as a de facto standing committee. Its purpose is to oversee the agencies and bureaus in the federal intelligence area. This select committee was established in the 1970s and its membership is temporary. Majority and minority members from the Appropriations, Armed Services, Foreign Relations, and Judiciary committees serve on the Intelligence committee. The committee reviews the intelligence budget and prepares legislation in addition to conducting investigations and inspections of intelligence programs. The committee has exercised oversight in the areas of communication, surveillance, and torture.

Joint Committees

Joint committees have members of both chambers of Congress. Sometimes joint committees handle routine matters and other times, they focus on major issues. One of the oldest, the Joint Committee on Printing was created in the 1840s and oversees the U.S. Government Publishing Office's operations. The Government Publishing Office is in charge of government printing for the federal agencies, legislative documents, and minimizing the cost of printing for the government. Another joint committee of Congress oversees the operations of the Library of Congress.

Conference Committees

A conference committee's function is to reconcile different versions of bills that are passed by the House and the Senate. The committee is composed of members of both chambers who were members of the committee that considered the bill in their chamber's committee. If the conference committee agrees on a compromise bill, then it is sent to both houses for approval.

Historical Background Of The Organization Of Congress

The Articles of Confederation had provided for a legislative branch of government, but because the states were given so much power, the newly created federal legislature was extremely weak. Also, each state had a single vote, which gave the less populated states the same vote as larger states with more population. Since states could legislate in ways that benefited them without regard to the country as a whole, the new nation's economic system could not grow, resulting in trade problems both domestically and abroad.

The Constitutional Convention of 1787 originally met to amend the Articles of Confederation. However, it soon became obvious that amending the document would not resolve the issues. Delegates at the convention represented differing interests, which were divided primarily as north vs. south, slave vs. free, and large vs. small states. As such, the final document was a result of compromise.

The organization of Congress was the result of one compromise. The Virginia Plan, or the large-state plan, favored a bicameral legislature (two-house legislature) with representation in each chamber based on population. The small states objected to this plan because more voting power would be given to the states with the largest populations. New Jersey, a small state, favored a unicameral (one-house) legislature like the single house legislature under the Articles of Confederation.

The Connecticut Compromise, called the Great Compromise, called for a two-house legislature, with a House of Representatives based on population and a Senate based on the number of states. The Senate, therefore, would give the small states equal representation. To satisfy the larger states, it was decided that all revenue-raising bills would be required to begin in the House of Representatives. Another part of the compromise was that the House members would be elected directly by the people and the senators would be elected by their respective state legislatures. The terms of the members of Congress were also the result of compromise. It was decided that Senators were to serve six-year terms, that would result in more stability and that House members would be elected for two-year terms, making them more responsive to the voters. Further compromise was made regarding how the population should be counted in determining the number of representatives a state has in the House of Representatives. The issue was primarily over how to count the slaves, if at all. The compromise resulted in counting three-fifths of the slaves in a state's total population to determine how many representatives the state would have in the House.

Powers And Functions

The function of Congress is to make the law. Once the process is complete and the bill has passed both the House and Senate, before it can become a law, it is presented to the President for approval. If the bill is approved and the President signs the bill, it becomes law. If the president vetoes the bill, it is returned to the chamber in which it originated and Congress, at that point has to decide whether the bill should become law even though the President has vetoed it. To override a presidential veto, the bill must be passed by a two-thirds majority vote. The second chamber must also pass the reconsidered bill by a two-thirds majority for Congress to override the presidential veto and the bill becomes law.

The Constitution provides that the House of Representatives has the sole power of impeachment. The term "impeachment" means to "charge with a wrong doing." The Senate has the sole power to try impeachments. If the President is being tried, then the Chief Justice of the Supreme Court presides over the trial. In order to convict a person, two-thirds of the members (of the Senate) that are present must concur. The Senate also has the power to determine the penalty if it enters a judgment against a person who has been impeached. The judgment may not be greater than removing the person from office and disqualifying the person to hold any office in the future. Even if the Senate enters a judgment, the person may still be subject to indictment, trial, and punishment according to the law.

Article I, Section 7 of the Constitution provides that all bills for raising revenue shall originate in the House of Representatives but that the Senate may propose or concur with amendments.

Enumerated Powers

Article I Section 8 of the Constitution itemizes a list of duties, referred to as enumerated duties that Congress shall perform. Among the enumerated powers are the power to lay and collect taxes, duties (fees), and excise taxes and to pay debts and provide for the common defense and general welfare of the country. However, Congress must make all duties and excises uniform throughout the United States. For example, if a duty is levied on molasses coming into the country, the same duty must be levied at all of the ports. For example, New York could not charge one rate and Charleston another. The idea of uniformity was to eliminate the power of the states to control, as they had under the Articles of Confederation.

Additional enumerated powers of Congress are to borrow money on the credit of the United States, to regulate Commerce with foreign nations, among the states, and with Indian tribes. The Constitution also provides that Congress shall establish a uniform rule of Naturalization, which means that the requirements for citizenship for foreigners living in Michigan are the same as requirements for citizenship in Florida or Wyoming or Kansas.

When a person files for bankruptcy protection, they are following the rules set by Congress because establishing uniform laws on bankruptcy is another of the enumerated powers of Congress. Congress also has the power to coin money, fix the standard of weights and measures, punish counterfeiters, establish post offices, and promote science and the arts by granting copyrights, patents, and trademarks.

Another power granted to Congress in the Constitution is to "constitute tribunals inferior to the Supreme Court." The word "inferior" means "lesser" and U.S. District Courts (which are the trial courts in the federal system) and the Circuit Courts of Appeal are examples of inferior tribunals.

Other enumerated powers of Congress identified in Article I Section 8 of the Constitution include: declaring war, raising and supporting armies, providing and maintaining an army, and to provide for the calling out of the militia to execute the laws of the United States.

Implied Powers

Congress has the power "to make all law which shall be necessary and proper for carrying into execution" all of the enumerated powers and other powers that are provided for in the Constitution and in any department or officer of the federal government. This clause is often referred to as the "necessary and proper" clause or the "elastic clause", and has been interpreted to mean that Congress can meet the changing needs of society by using this clause in voting in favor of bills for which specific authority is not given in the Constitution.

The clause is controversial because it can be interpreted differently as to what is necessary. Examples of implied powers can include the institution of the draft. Although the Constitution provides that Congress shall raise and support armies, there is no mention of how that shall be accomplished. Therefore, when Congress voted to institute the draft before the U.S. entered World War II, Congress based the institution of the draft on an implied power that flowed from its power to provide for and maintain an army.

The question of whether or not Congress had the power to create a national bank is an issue that was discussed in light of the enumerated powers and the "necessary and proper" clause. When it was decided that Congress did have the power to create a national bank, the issue then became whether a state had the right to tax the bank and resulted in the landmark case of *McCulloch v. Maryland*.

Prohibited Powers

In addition to setting the powers of Congress, Article I of the Constitution identifies which powers Congress does not have. One example is that Congress may not suspend the writ of habeas corpus unless there is a rebellion or invasion where the safety of the public requires it. "Habeas corpus" means "have the body." And a "writ of habeas corpus" is a writing that requires an arrested person to be brought before a court to show why they should not be released. The purpose of a writ of habeas corpus is for a court to determine whether the detention is valid. In 1863, during the Civil War, Congress passed an act that suspended habeas corpus.

Congress may not pass a bill of attainder or an ex post facto law. A bill of attainder is a bill passed by Congress that finds a person (or persons) guilty of a crime and punishing them, with or without a trial. An ex post facto law punishes a person for something that was not illegal when the person committed the act. This type of law is a retroactive law that changes the legal status of a person because what is illegal today was not illegal earlier when the person acted.

Congress may also not tax articles exported from a state or show favoritism to ports in one state over ports in other states. Congress is also prohibited from granting titles of nobility. This prohibition would have been important to steer the new country in the direction of being independent from Great Britain and would prevent members of Congress from restoring that type of rule.

State Prohibitions

The Constitution was written to correct the problems with the Articles of Confederation, which provided a loose arrangement or association between the federal and state governments. The Articles of Confederation gave states more power than the legislative branch of the new federal government. The drafters of the Constitution included the concept of federalism, which provides for shared powers of state and federal government. As a result, the framers identified powers that states did not have under the new organization of government. Some of the itemized prohibitions included the states not being able to enter into treaties, coin money, pass bills of attainder or ex post facto laws, or grant titles of nobility. States were also prohibited from imposing import or export duties without the consent of Congress unless those funds were absolutely necessary for executing inspection laws. Also, states were prohibited, without consent of Congress, from keeping troops or war ships in time of peace or engage in war unless they were actually invaded or in "such imminent" danger that they should not delay.

Formal and Informal Duties of Congress

The duties of Congress that are identified in Article I of the Constitution and known as the enumerated powers are the formal powers of Congress. The "necessary and proper" clause provides the basis for most of the informal powers of Congress. Congress also has the informal power, or power not specifically granted, of investigating the executive branch of government and the agencies of the executive branch. A third informal power is the power to hold hearings.

Checks and Balances

The system of government established by the Framers provides for separation of powers but it also provides for checks by each branch on the other two branches in order to maintain balance between the three branches.

Congress checks on the executive branch in several ways.

- It is the body that declares war even though the President is the commander-in-chief. The Senate must also ratify treaties negotiated by the Executive branch.

- The President will ask for money for programs but it is Congress that appropriates the funds.
- One of the most obvious checks on the executive branch is the power of Congress to override a presidential veto. Congress must override the veto by a two-thirds vote, which is greater than the simple majority of votes required to pass the bill originally.
- Congress also can check the action of presidential appointments through the Senate that must approve and confirm the appointment.
- An example of the struggle between the two branches was apparent when President Obama named an individual to replace retiring Justice Scalia in 2016. The Republican-controlled Congress decided not to hold confirmation hearings to replace the Supreme Court Justice until the 2016 presidential elections were held, claiming the next president should be the president to nominate a Justice.
- One of the checks Congress has on the executive branch is to impeach and remove a president from office. This power has been used very infrequently. No president has been removed, but Presidents Andrew Johnson and Bill Clinton have both been impeached by Congress.
- Congressional oversight is another check Congress has on the executive branch. When Congress exercises this power, it reviews and monitors actions of the executive branch and its agencies, policies, and programs. Much of the oversight is conducted by legislative committees and often includes the use of Congressional hearings. As an example: the hearings that were held to obtain more information about the attacks and the role of the State Department in the 2012 deaths of U.S. officials in the American compound in Benghazi, Libya, when terrorists attacked the compound.

Congress also has checks on the judicial branch of government. The Constitution authorizes Congress to establish inferior tribunals. The final determination as to whether or not there is a need to create additional federal courts is within the discretion of Congress. Congress approves or rejects nominees for federal court judgeships and can impeach and remove federal judges from serving. Another very important check that Congress has on the judicial branch, is the power to amend laws in response to a decision of the courts.

The Presidency

Article II of the Constitution creates the Executive branch of government. The primary function of the Executive branch is to faithfully execute the laws. Article II creates the position of President to be head of the Executive branch and establishes the term of office at four years. Section I also states that the Vice President's term will be for four years. In order to become President, a person must be 35 years old, a resident within the United States for fourteen years, and be a natural born citizen.

The "natural born citizen" issue arose during the election of 2008 when Barack Obama was nominated for the presidency. Some people believed that Obama had been born in Kenya rather than in Hawaii as he claimed.

Historical Background

The Articles of Confederation did not provide for an executive officer to carry out, or enforce, the laws of the legislature. The Framers of the Constitution agreed that this was one of the weaknesses of the Articles that needed to be corrected in the new form of government they were proposing; however, despite the fact they agreed on the need for an executive, they did not know, in the beginning, how the president would be elected or the term of office for the president. The delegates debated over the length of the term because some feared the possibility of returning to a monarchy or the possibility of a single individual serving for so long that he took over the rule of the country. The reign of King George III had not been favorable to the colonists in the eyes of many of the delegates; therefore, they hesitated to vote in favor of a powerful executive branch of government. There were different proposals as to the length of the term, which finally was decided to be four years.

Today's executive branch is very different than the first executive branches. The Constitutional requirements remain the same but the personalities of the presidents and their interpretations of the use of the implied powers have created more influential presidencies. Throughout most of the country's history, until the 1930's, the legislative branch was dominant.

Beginning with the presidency of Franklin D. Roosevelt during the Great Depression, the balance began to shift, and the executive branch began to become more dominant. Roosevelt's "hands on" decision-making policies to institute new program to improve the country's economy is one example. He also became very involved in making foreign policy decisions as the country approached, entered, and fought in World War II. He met with the Prime Minister of England, Winston Churchill, and agreed to the Atlantic Charter. He met with Churchill and Joseph Stalin, the Soviet leader, to discuss the conduct of the war and how the defeated countries would be governed after the war. From the presidency of Franklin Roosevelt to modern day presidencies, the role of the executive has evolved and become stronger.

Term Limits for the President

Although there were discussions as to whether there should be term limits, none were included in the Constitution. Presidents served one or two terms until the election of Franklin D. Roosevelt. President Roosevelt was elected during the

Great Depression and began the New Deal in an attempt to bring the country out of the Depression. Although unprecedented, he was elected to a third term and was president when the U.S. entered World War II. He was then elected to a fourth term during the war but died before he completed his term of office.

A concern over the possibility of numerous presidential terms became apparent and an amendment to the Constitution was proposed. The issue of the number of terms a president could serve was resolved by the ratification of the Twenty-second Amendment to the Constitution in 1951. The amendment provides that no person shall be elected to the office more than twice but if a person has held the office for more than two years during another's term, then the person may only be elected to one term. This provision means that if, for example, if a president died and a vice-president would take over the presidency and serve more than two years of the former president's term, the person could only be elected to one more term. However, if the vice-president served less than two years of the former president's term, then he or she could be elected to a second term.

Election Of The President

The delegates to the Constitutional Convention voted more than 60 times before they decided how the president would be elected. Some of the delegates favored direct election but others believed the common man would not have the ability to make that kind of a decision. Some believed the common man would not have the intellect to judge the correct characteristics needed for a president and others believed the vastness of the nation would exclude those in rural areas from being able to vote, or make a knowledgeable decision. Some delegates believed that the state legislatures should elect the president but others believed this type of election would not result in a person with independent judgment.

The delegates finally decided that the president should be elected by electors in each state. The electors, who were to be chosen by the state legislatures, would vote for two people. However, the elector could not vote for two people from the same state.

Because of this limiting caveat, we have never had a President and Vice President run from the same state. The closest was in the 2000 election where both George W. Bush and Dick Cheney had called Texas home in the run-up to the nomination. But, Cheney sidestepped the issue by registering to vote in Wyoming, the state he once represented in the House. It's good he did. Bush/Cheney wound up with 271 electoral votes. Take away Texas' 32 electoral votes from the Bush/Cheney tally and they would not have gotten the required 270 votes.

The person with the most votes would become president and the person with the second highest number of votes would become vice president. If no person had a majority of the votes of the electors, the job of deciding who would become president would fall upon the House of Representatives and would be decided among the top five candidates. The vote in the house would be taken by state and each state would have one vote.

The first time the House of Representatives had to decide who would become president was in 1800. Thomas Jefferson and Aaron Burr were both Democrat-Republican candidates who had the same number of votes in the Electoral College. Because of the tie, the decision was made by the House of Representatives. The House of Representatives, at that time, was dominated by the Federalists and most of the Federalists preferred Aaron Burr. After many ballots, Alexander Hamilton, a Federalist who believed Jefferson would be the better choice of the two, secured enough votes to elect Jefferson on the thirty-sixth ballot.

In 1804, the Twelfth Amendment cured the problem that had presented itself in 1800. This amendment provided there would be separate ballots for president and vice-president. Despite the provisions of the Twelfth Amendments, the House of Representatives was again the decision-maker in the 1824 election.

In the election of 1824, there were ten candidates. One of the contenders was Secretary of State John Quincy Adams, who was from Massachusetts and was the son of the second president, John Adams. Adams was supported by the business interests of the Northeast. Henry Clay, a Kentucky slaveholder, was Speaker of the House of Representatives. Clay supported the needs of the West—roads and canals. Andrew Jackson, also a Westerner, was from Tennessee. His claim-to-fame was his victory over the British at New Orleans during the War of 1812. He was a Senator from his state of Tennessee but his political views were mainly unknown. The fourth serious contender was William Crawford, a Georgia slaveholder and President James Monroe's Secretary of the Treasury. Crawford had suffered a stroke in 1823 but remained one of the frontrunners. The campaign became heated, the candidates were called various uncomplimentary names, and when the vote was taken in the Electoral College, no candidate has won a majority. In the popular vote, however, Andrew Jackson had won the most, gaining 42 percent. Jackson had also won 99 electoral votes but was 32 votes short of obtaining a majority. Based upon the wording of the Twelfth Amendment, the House of Representatives considered the top three candidates—Jackson, Adams, and Crawford.

Henry Clay, who was still Speaker of the House because the president did not begin office until March, attempted to gain votes for Adams even though he disliked Adams because he believed that he and Jackson would be rivals in the future. It was also rumored that if he won, Adams had agreed to make Clay Secretary of State. Adams did win, gaining the 13 states he needed. Jackson won seven of the states. The Jackson supporters believed a "corrupt bargain" had been made that had kept their candidate, who had won the largest share of the popular vote, out of the White House. Jackson, also as a result of losing the vote in the House of Representatives, called for eliminating the Electoral College and selecting the president by direct election.

The issue of whether the Electoral College should be eliminated remains to be answered. In the election of 2000, Al Gore's popular vote count was approximately 500,000 more than George W. Bush's votes. However, Gore's narrow loss in Florida gave Florida's Electoral College votes to Bush, and Bush became president by a margin of five Electoral College votes.

Succession

Article II provides that the Vice President will become president in the event the president is removed from office, dies in office, resigns, or is unable to discharge the duties of the presidency. The 1787 Constitution provided that Congress would establish the order of succession. The Twenty-fifth Amendment provides that if the President dies in, resigns from, or is removed from the office, the Vice President shall become President. Section 2 of the amendment provides that if there is a vacancy in the office of Vice President, the President shall nominate a person to fill that office. A nominee, who is approved by a majority vote of both houses, then becomes the Vice President.

Another provision of the Twenty-fifth Amendment allows the President to notify, in writing, the *president pro tem* of the Senate and the Speaker of House, and indicate that he is unable to discharge the duties of the office and that the Vice President will serve as acting President until the President notifies Congress otherwise. The wording of this provision refers to "he." The Vice President may also, along with other government officials, notify the presiding officers of both houses of Congress that the President is unable to fulfill the obligations of the office. In that event, the Vice President will assume the duties of the presidency.

Up until the time the Twenty-fifth Amendment was ratified, seven vice presidents had died in office and one had resigned, meaning that in those instances there would not have been a Vice President to assume the presidency if needed. But more importantly, the amendment was an effort to deal with the issue of the disability of a President. Three times in the history of our country, a Vice President assumed the duties of the President. President Garfield had been assassinated and lay in a coma for more than two months before he died. President Wilson had suffered a stroke and was an invalid for more than a year, and after President Lyndon Johnson became President upon the death of John F. Kennedy, the country did not have a Vice President.

In 1973, Vice President, Spiro Agnew, resigned from office. President Nixon nominated, and the Congress appointed Gerald Ford of Michigan the new Vice President. The following year, in 1974, President Nixon resigned and Vice President Ford became President. The Twenty-fifth Amendment came into play again when President Ford nominated New Yorker Nelson Rockefeller to be his vice president. Both chambers of Congress confirmed the appointment and Mr. Rockefeller became Vice President.

Formal Powers and Functions

Article II of the Constitution identifies the duties of the President, which include serving as Commander-in-Chief of the Armed Forces and of the National Guard in the various states.

The Constitution also gives the President the authority to grant pardons and reprieves for federal offenses but does not allow the President to grant either if the case involves a person who has been impeached. A famous one is the pardon President Ford granted Richard Nixon for Nixon's involvement in the Watergate scandal. Ford's intention was to heal the nation but many think that the granting of the pardon greatly affected the outcome of Ford's loss in the subsequent presidential election.

The president also has the power to make treaties, with the advice and consent of the Senate; make appointments, subject to confirmation; and is required to periodically report to Congress on the state of the Union.

Informal Powers

The specific powers listed for the executive branch of government in the Constitution are considered the formal powers of the President. In addition to specific powers, the President exercises informal powers.

Presidents have exercised their authority to make executive orders. The earliest use of this informal power is thought to have been used by President Jefferson when he purchased the Louisiana Territory in 1803 without the approval of Congress; However, the use of this power is controversial in many situations, such as when it can be argued the executive orders fall within the range of legislative responsibilities.

In 1954, the U.S. Supreme Court decision in *Brown v. Board of Education* held that separate schools were inherently unequal schools and ordered the desegregation of public schools in the United States. When it was necessary to enforce the high court's decision, President Eisenhower, using the executive order, sent the National Guard to Little Rock, Arkansas, to integrate Central High School.

In 1965, President Lyndon Johnson issued an executive order for companies holding government contracts to implement new programs for hiring minorities.

During President Clinton's administration, noncontroversial executive orders were given the name, Presidential Decision Directives.

The use of executive privilege is also an example of an implied power. If a president is asked to disclose information which the president believes is privileged and could compromise the activities of the Executive branch, then the president will invoke "executive privilege" to avoid disclosing the information. The idea behind invoking the privilege is to protect the national security of the country.

At the end of World War II, the Soviet Union, who had been an ally of the U.S. during the war, gained power and became the Cold War enemy of the United States. The fear of Communism spread throughout the United States and a Republican Senator from Wisconsin, Joseph McCarthy, began a search for Communists working in the government. McCarthy claimed to have a list of more than 200 State Department employees who were Communists. McCarthy lowered the number to under a 100 when he was forced to give details of the information he claimed he held. McCarthy began to widen his search for Communists and set his goal on finding Communists who were serving in the army.

President Dwight Eisenhower, who had been the Supreme Commander of the Allied Forces during World War II, was angered by McCarthy's actions and refused to give the documents relating to meetings between Eisenhower's personnel and the Army officials. In refusing to turn over the notes of the meetings, Eisenhower invoked executive privilege and stated that national security might be breached if the notes were turned over. Eisenhower also invoked executive privilege to avoid testifying about those matters.

Executive privilege is also used by Presidents to protect members of their administration. When the privilege is invoked to avoid a subpoena, presidents may face resistance, which was the case in 1974 when President Nixon invoked executive privilege. The events that led up to the claim of executive privilege involved a break-in at the Democratic National Committee's offices in the Watergate building in Washington, D.C. The purpose of the break-in was to obtain information, by setting up eavesdropping devices in the Committee's phones, that would benefit Richard Nixon in his re-election bid. The first break-in was successful, but the burglars were caught on a second attempt. The Nixon administration attempted to cover up the activities and their priority was to protect the President from the investigation of the break-in and burglary and to keep the investigation from pursuing whether or not Nixon was aware of or involved in the activities. Some information about the break-in had leaked to the press and the prosecutor wanted President Nixon to release some White House tapes that may have contained discussions related to the break-in. Nixon offered to release a statement about the contents but not the tapes themselves. The issue of whether the President was required to turn over the tapes was heard by the U.S. Supreme Court and the court decided the tapes were to be turned over to the prosecutor. President Nixon released the tapes and the tapes implied his guilt. The House Judiciary Committee recommended that articles of impeachment be prepared against the President, and as a result, he announced he would resign.

President Clinton invoked executive privilege several times, and lost the privilege by a court ruling, as had President Nixon. Clinton had invoked executive privilege in the Monica Lewinsky scandal but the judge in the federal court case ruled that Clinton's aides could be called to testify in the case. During the George W. Bush administration, the President invoked executive privilege to prohibit the disclosure of information about a former Attorney General. This scandal involved the misuse of organized-crime informants by the Federal Bureau of Investigation, and Vice President Cheney's meetings with energy officials. President Bush also invoked executive privilege to resist congressional subpoenas that would require testimony of staff persons.

The first time President Obama asserted executive privilege, he wanted to withhold Department of Justice documents relating to "Operation Fast and Furious," a program where, for about fifteen months, the Bureau of Alcohol, Tobacco, Firearms and Explosives allowed illegal gun sales—thought to be to Mexican drug cartels—in an attempt to track purchasers and sellers.

A third informal power allows the president to commit troops in peacetime, under certain conditions, without Congressional approval. President Lyndon Johnson committed troops to the Vietnam War even though there was never a formal declaration of war by Congress. In 1973, Congress passed the War Powers Act to limit the president's deployment of troops into a foreign, hostile, peacetime situation for more than 60 days without Congressional approval, providing a check on the executive branch of government.

Checks And Balances

The president has several checks on the legislative branch. The veto power is an important check on the legislative branch because it stops a bill from becoming a law, unless Congress has the final say by overriding the veto. Under certain circumstances, the president can utilize a pocket veto. A pocket veto occurs when the president does not sign a bill after Congress has adjourned and is, therefore, unable to override a veto. Pocket vetoes are not used frequently. James Madison was the first president to use the pocket veto and President Franklin D. Roosevelt used this type of veto the most, using it 263 times. In more recent times, President Reagan vetoed a total of 78 bills, 39 nine of which were vetoed with a pocket veto. President Clinton used the pocket veto one time, and Presidents George W. Bush and Barrack Obama (as of May 2016) did not use a pocket veto to keep a bill from becoming a law.

A second check that the executive branch has on the legislative branch is the power of the president to propose legislation. President Obama's 2015 proposed legislation to curb gun violence is an example. In the proposal the administration made multiple requests that included additional background checks that sellers are required to make and the requirement that the FBI modernize its background check system

A president can also call a special session of Congress. There have only been 27 times when presidents have Congress into session, and each time it has been to deal with a crisis. President Lincoln called a special session in 1861, and Woodrow Wilson called one in 1917. President Franklin called three special sessions. The first was to pass a banking bill in 1933 and his last was to repeal the bans on arms sales to the countries involved in the war in Europe. In 1948, President Truman, who is the last president to call a special session, asked Congress, which he had called a "do nothing Congress," to pass laws that improved civil rights, extended the Social Security system, and to create a national health system.

Negotiating treaties is also a check on the legislative branch. Although the Senate must ratify the treaty by a two-thirds majority, the terms of many treaties come from the negotiations entered into by the executive branch.

The executive branch also has checks on the judicial branch. Two examples are: appointing federal judges and granting pardons and reprieves for federal offenders.

The Bureaucracy

A bureaucracy is a form of administration within a business or government that organizes the business of government mainly through bureaus and departments that are staffed by non-elected officials. The term "bureaucracy" comes from a French word that means "rule by desks or offices." You may have heard people refer to bureaucracies as having so much red tape to go through or being not-well organized or a place where there is a lot of "paper pushing" or statements such as, "What else would you expect when you are dealing with a bureaucracy?" Usually, comments such as these are expressions of frustrations about the inefficient, wasteful, tedious, and time-consuming processes involved in dealing with bureaucracies to accomplish a task or result. Comments such as these impart beliefs that bureaucratic administration is slow and impersonal. And while a bureaucracy can be said to be inefficient, this type of organization provides a hierarchy within an organization where a multitude of people can work together every day in a compatible way because each person's role is defined.

Powers And Functions

The job of a person working in a bureaucracy (a bureaucrat) is to implement policy. The policy may be for the government or a specific business. In government for example, some bureaucrats take laws and create practical working solutions for the laws. Some government bureaucrats write rules and regulations and others work with citizens to implement the rules. There are many types of government agencies, and the function of each type of agency is different. Some agencies promote the public good, others protect the nation, and others help maintain a strong economy.

Each designated agency or group within a bureaucracy has a hierarchy. At the top of the hierarchy is one individual who oversees the bureau or agency. There is a chain of command and the person at the top of the chain has the most power.

Bureaucratic agencies are also specialized, dealing with one issue or one aspect. For example, in government there may be an agency dealing with environmental affairs, another dealing with some aspect of education. People who work within a specialized governmental agency have specialized backgrounds that are relevant to their specific aspect of government.

There is a division of labor within each agency and within each task. Each person has a specific job. Different people work on different parts of a task so that each of the smaller parts or tasks comes together to make a final result that takes into account all aspects of a situation. Job productivity is the basis for determining job performance.

The bureaucratic organization also functions under formalized rules. These rules are referred to as "standard operating procedure" and each employee, or part of the chain of command, must adhere to the rules. By following a standard operating procedure, tasks are completed more efficiently and the results in similar situations will be predictable.

In today's governmental agencies (bureaucracy), jobs are awarded as the result of merit. This was not always the case. During Andrew Jackson's administration, for example, many government jobs were given to friends and political supporters. This system is called patronage. Qualifications for the job were not necessarily considered. The system for appointing friends and supporters to government became known as the "spoils system" and was relevant to the phrase, "To the victor goes the spoils," meaning that it was all right to reward those who helped someone attain victory. Some of the friends and supporters met with Andrew Jackson to make policy decisions. This group of Jackson's friends became known as the "Kitchen Cabinet." Eventually, Congress passed the Pendleton Civil Service Reform Act to award government jobs on merit.

The Development Of The Federal Government Bureaucracy

The departments of State, Treasury, and War were the departments that made up the original bureaucracy of the federal government. Today, there are more than three million people working in the executive branch alone.

Patronage is the system of putting people into political positions as a way of thanking them for support and friendship and has been part of the federal system from the early days of our country. Although, political parties did not exist when George Washington became President, many of the government employees had Federalist beliefs. Thomas Jefferson was a Democratic-Republican and dismissed the Federalist party employees and filled the positions with those who supported his political views.

As the country expanded westward, developed better methods of transportation, and grew in population, new demands were placed on government to manage the expanding nation. The government created new jobs and new departments during the Civil War and as the nation's urban areas developed during the American Industrial Revolution more government agencies were created.

The system of patronage continued throughout the Civil War and into the early 1880s and President Garfield's administration. In 1881 a disappointed office seeker, denied a government job by President Garfield, assassinated the president. Congress then passed the Pendleton Act, creating the Civil Service Commission in an attempt to lessen the practice of patronage. The Pendleton Civil Service Reform Act created the merit system and required applicants for government jobs to take and pass an exam that would show they were qualified for the position. In the early years of the merit system, not even one-fourth of the federal employees were hired as the result of the civil service examination. Today that number is greater than 85 percent.

During the ages of Progressivism and Imperialism, the economy expanded and "bigness" became a word for many businesses. The trusts, such as Standard Oil, the rail industry, the steel industry and other companies became ever larger. Citizens began demanding that the government protect them from the abuses of big business, and laws such as the Sherman Anti-Trust Act were passed. Also in that time period, the first government agencies were established to monitor abuses and regulate industry.

In 1887, the Interstate Commerce Act created the first regulatory agency, the Interstate Commerce Commission, to reduce abuses in the rail industry. The commission members were nominated by the president and confirmed by the Senate. The commission was created because railroad companies were creating monopolies and discriminating in the areas of rates, markets, and other shipping practices. The five-member commission monitored the actions of the railroads to ensure they charged "just and reasonable" rates, did not provide special rates to special shippers, did not give rebates to preferential shippers, and did not discriminate between long-haulers and short-haulers. The Act required railroads to submit annual reports to the Commission so the Commission could monitor acts that might be discriminatory. As the first regulatory agency in the United States government, the Interstate Commerce Commission became the model for regulatory agencies that were established later.

Franklin Roosevelt's administration created a large number of agencies to help the country through the Great Depression. Because many of the agencies could be identified by the first letters in each of the words in their names, the agencies became known as the "alphabet" agencies. The Civilian Conservation Corps (CCC) is one example. This agency employed young men who worked to plant trees and reforest areas. Other examples were the Works Progress

Administration (WPA), the Public Works Administration (PWA), the Puerto Rico Reconstruction Administration (PRRA), and the Tennessee Valley Authority (TVA). Additional agencies were created when the United Stated entered World War II, and the need for civilian employees became greater. During President Lyndon Johnson's administration in the 1960s, the new civil rights legislation and other Great Society legislation increased the federal government bureaucracy. After "911" and President George W. Bush's efforts to fight terrorism, the federal bureaucracy was further expanded and new departments, such as the Department of Homeland Security were created.

Agencies each have an area of specialization but their duties may overlap, making it more difficult to administer them. States and local governments also have agencies, and many of them are counterparts to the federal agencies.

Congress creates, organizes, and has the power to end federal agencies. Most agencies are executive agencies but many are legislative agencies. There are five main types of bureaucracy in the federal government: Cabinet departments, independent agencies, regulatory agencies, commissions, and government corporations.

The Cabinet Departments

Article II, Section 2 provides the president may "require the opinion, in writing, of the principal officer in each of the executive departments, upon any subject relating to the duties of their respective offices." President George Washington's Cabinet consisted of four departments: State, Treasury, War, and Attorney General. Cabinet members are selected by the president and serve at the president's pleasure. Most serve the entire time the president serves, but when a president leaves office, the Cabinet members resign.

Throughout the years, the number of Cabinet departments increased to 15, some have been removed or renamed, and the Vice President has been added as a member of the Cabinet. For example, the Post Office Department had its beginnings in the 1790s and as the country grew in size, the post office's importance increased. When Andrew Jackson became president in 1828, the post office department was the largest employer in the executive branch of government and he invited the Postmaster General to become a Cabinet member. The Post Office Department, however, did not become an actual Cabinet position until 1872. In 1970, during President Nixon's administration, Congress passed the Postal Reorganization Act, which transferred the government ownership of the department to a quasi-private ownership, which meant that the post office would be run like a business and rely on public revenue from postage sales rather than on taxpayer monies.

President Washington's Department of War has now become the Department of Defense and includes all agencies involving national security. The Department of Labor was created in the early 1900s to handle the issues involving big business. The department changed names and became the Department of Commerce and Labor, adding duties of workplace issues, such as safety, hours and wages, and re-employment. Today, they are separate Cabinet departments. As an interesting note, the first woman Cabinet member was Frances Perkins, Secretary of Labor. Ms. Perkins served as Secretary of Labor during Franklin D. Roosevelt's administration and was instrumental in obtaining legislation to form the Social Security program and the first minimum wage laws. The Department of Homeland Security now includes the Federal Emergency Management Agency (FEMA), which had originally been a Cabinet position. The Office of Strategic Services was formed during World War II and eventually became the Central Intelligence Agency. In 2004, Congress passed legislation to create the office of the Director of National Intelligence, which oversees the Central Intelligence Agency. At that time the CIA was eliminated as a Cabinet position, but the president continues to appoint a head of the CIA. Today, the Cabinet departments include:

- Department of State
- Department of Treasury
- Department of Defense
- Department of Justice
- Department of the Interior
- Department of Agriculture
- Department of Commerce
- Department of Labor
- Department of Transportation
- Department of Housing and Urban Development
- Department of Health and Human Services
- Department of Energy
- Department of Education
- Department of Veterans Affairs
- Department of Homeland Security

All of the Cabinet departments have broad responsibilities and their organizations are complex. Each department has a special area of expertise, and although there are differences in each Cabinet department, their organization is similar. Each Secretary has a deputy or undersecretary, as well as multiple assistant Secretaries who direct specific programs within each department. Each department is further divided into bureaus and sections.

Government Entities

Corporations

Government businesses that are created by Congress and charge fees for their services are identified as government corporations standing alone, and not considered as part of any department. Two such examples are Amtrak and the United States Postal Service. Congress passed the Rail Passenger Service Act in 1970, which established the National Railroad Passenger Corporation. The new corporation took over intercity passenger rail service that private railroads had previously operated. Amtrak began operations in May 1971 and serviced 43 states.

Fourth Branch of Government

U.S. governmental agencies are often referred to as the fourth branch of government. Most of the government agencies are part of the executive branch but some are part of the legislative branch. The agencies usually exercise each of the constitutional powers, legislative, executive, and judicial. Agencies legislate through their rulemaking authority. In their executive power, they investigate and enforce the rules, and in their judicial power they apply, interpret, and enforce the rules.

Independent Legislative Agencies

Most of the agencies are executive branch agencies, but they are independent agencies because they are not a subordinated part of a Cabinet department. There are also a small number of agencies that fall under the authority of Congress. They are the Library of Congress and the Congressional Budget Office. The single independent agency within the judicial branch of government is the U.S. Sentencing Commission

Functions of Agencies

Rulemaking, investigating, and adjudicating are the three main functions of administrative agencies. Federal agency rulemaking is governed by the Administrative Procedure Act. When Congress passes legislation, the legislation will be general but will direct an agency to take action to issue rules. For example, if the law involves the safety of children's furniture, the federal agency will be responsible for devising standards for manufacturers to make furniture safer to reduce the number of accidents or deaths. The agency posts a notice in the Federal Register to announce that it will be proposing a new rule on the subject and ask for public comment. The agency will set a time during which the public can express its views and then considers such factors as: whether there are new technologies to make furniture safer; what have been the concerns or reasons for the new law; whether the Congressional committees studying the legislation has developed any guidelines; whether there have been petitions or input from lobbying groups or the public in general; whether lawsuits have been filed; and whether the President has issued any directives on the topic.

Agency members use their expertise to find answers to the various questions that have been posed by investigating and finding answers to the questions that will lead to new rules for the manufacture of children's furniture. For example, if the agency finds that several infant deaths have resulted from babies who have had their heads stuck between side rails in a crib, then the agency may want to hear testimony from individuals in families who have been affected by crib deaths of this type before making a decision about a new manufacturing rule. The committee may also want to investigate the names of the manufacturers whose products have allegedly caused the deaths. The agency may investigate the design specifications of items manufactured to consider possible defects and improvements in design. If, after investigation the agency decides that the deaths appear to have been caused by the distance between crib slats being too great, they will formulate a rule and create new standards that need to be established to narrow the distance between crib slats.

When an agency decides the language of the new rule, it publishes the new rule in the Federal Register. It is the agency's responsibility to enforce the rule, and if there is a violation, the enforcement role of the agency comes into play. If there is a violation of the new rule, it can be settled by negotiation, the way in which most violations are settled. If a manufacturer fails to comply with the new rule, for example, and a negotiated settlement cannot be reached, then the agency can file a formal complaint against the violator and the case will be decided by an administrative law judge.

Federal regulatory agencies have responsibility over rules, regulations, and legislation for a specific area of the government. The Environmental Protection Agency is an example of a federal regulatory agency. Another is the Bureau of Alcohol, Tobacco and Firearms (ATF), which is part of the Department of Justice and protects society against criminal organizations, violent criminals, illegal use of firearms and the illegal use and storage of explosives. The Federal Trade Commission focuses on anticompetitive, unfair, and deceptive trade practices. The Commission was established in the early 1900s to deal with the problems of big business, such as predatory pricing. The FTC handles issues involved with the No Call List, deceptive advertising, and similar issues. The more than 2,000 agencies and departments that make up the American government bureaucracy serve as government watchdogs to protect the consumer, the general public, and the economy.

The Courts

Article III of the Constitution establishes the judicial branch of government. Section 1 provides that the judicial power of the United States shall be "vested in one supreme court and in such inferior courts as the Congress may from time to time ordain and establish." These courts are often referred to as "Article II Courts" because they are provided for in Article III of the U.S. Constitution.

The Supreme Court is the highest court in the land and has original and appellate jurisdiction.

Throughout the history of our country, Congress has established other federal courts. As previously mentioned, the term "inferior" means "lesser." These "lesser" federal courts include the District Courts and the U.S. Circuit Courts of Appeal. If you were to draw a triangle to describe the federal court system, the Supreme Court would be at the top. The base of the triangle would contain the U.S. District Courts, and the narrowing middle section of the triangle would consist of the U.S. Circuit Courts of Appeal.

The District Courts are the trial courts of the federal court system. At present there are 94 U.S. District Courts. Each state has at least one District Court. There is also a U.S. District Court in Washington, D.C. If a state has two District Courts, the state is divided into geographic districts, e.g., the U.S. District Court for the Northern District of Indiana and the U.S. District Court for the Southern District of Indiana or they are divided by east and west. The U.S. District Court may be divided into geographic districts and identified by division, which may be named after a city in the state. The District Courts are presided over by a judge, and the cases that are filed in these courts include felonies and misdemeanors. There is a unit in the U.S. District Court that is the Bankruptcy Court. Bankruptcy laws are U.S. laws that have been passed by Congress, and for this reason, the courts that decide bankruptcy cases are federal courts. Juries are used in the U.S. District Courts. There are also U.S. District Courts in four of the U.S. territories—Puerto Rico, Guam, the Virgin Islands, and the Northern Mariana Islands.

In the federal court system, there are 13 appellate courts below the Supreme Court, called the Circuit Courts of Appeals. The U.S. District Court system is divided into 11 geographic areas and cases that are appealed from a federal trial court will be heard in the Circuit Court of Appeal for those states. For example, the territorial jurisdiction of the Tenth Circuit Court of Appeals includes the states of Colorado, Kansas, New Mexico, Oklahoma, Utah, Wyoming, and the parts of Yellowstone Park that extend into Idaho and Montana. The other two Circuit Courts of Appeal are for Washington, D.C. and the Federal Circuit. The Federal Circuit Court of Appeals hears cases being appealed from the Court of Veteran Affairs, the U.S. Court of Federal Claims, the Court of International Trade, and cases from U.S. administrative agencies.

Congress has created two other special courts, the Court of International Trade that hears cases involving international trade and customs laws and the U.S. Court of Federal Claims that hears cases involving money damage claims against the U.S. government.

Judges

Article III, Section 1 of the Constitution also provides that the judges of the Supreme Court and inferior courts will hold their offices "during good behavior." Federal judges are appointed by the President and confirmed, or approved, by the Senate. While "good behavior" usually means "for life," a few federal U.S. District Court judges have been impeached and convicted. The first federal judge was convicted in 1804, and the most recent was in 2010. One Supreme Court Associate Justice, Samuel Chase, was impeached by the U.S. House of Representative in 1804 for arbitrary and oppressive conduct of trial but was acquitted by the U.S. Senate.

Judicial Power

The Supreme Court can hear cases involving law and equity that arise under the Constitution, U.S. laws, or treaties. Cases at law involve money, and cases in equity involve remedies other than money. The high court can also hear cases that affect ambassadors and other diplomats, cases involving maritime law, and cases in which the United States is a party. The Supreme Court also hears cases where there is a controversy between two states and cases where the parties are from different states.

Jurisdiction

Jurisdiction is the power of a court to hear a case. The U.S. Supreme Court has original jurisdiction over cases affecting ambassadors and diplomats and cases in which states are the parties. The term "original jurisdiction" means that it is the first court to hear a case. For example, in the case of *United States v. Utah*, 283 US. 64 (1931), the United States sued the state of Utah to determine ownership of the lands that formed the riverbeds in some rivers in the State of Utah. The Supreme Court had original jurisdiction to hear the case because it involved a dispute between a state and the U.S. government. In this case, the State of Utah claimed that the lands under the streams belonged to the state because they were located under streams that were navigable waters. The Supreme Court held that the title to the riverbeds passed to the state of Utah when it was admitted to the Union, if the rivers were navigable. If the rivers were unable to be navigated at the time the territory became a state then the land making up the river beds would have belonged to the United States.

The Supreme Court also has original jurisdiction in cases involving disputes between two states. An example is the 2009 case between North Carolina and

South Carolina over the apportionment of the Catawba River, a river that begins in the mountains of North Carolina, flows through North Carolina, and enters South Carolina at Lake Wylie. The dispute arose because the river had severe fluctuations in water level and is affected by droughts. Both states use the river for water supplies and hydroelectric power. South Carolina believed that a North Carolina law harmed South Carolina because the law required a permit to transfer more than the specified amounts of water from the river and, as a result, North Carolina transferred more than its fair share of the water.

Appellate Jurisdiction

Article III, Section 2 of the Constitution provides that in all cases other than original jurisdiction cases, the Supreme Court shall have appellate jurisdiction. Appellate jurisdiction means that the case has been decided by a lower court, and one of the parties is asking the Supreme Court to hear the case. Many cases that are appealed to the Supreme Court involve a federal question. A federal question is an issue that involves the Constitution, a law of Congress, or a treaty.

In 1954 the Supreme Court decided on the case of *Brown v. Board of Education of Topeka*. The facts of the case involve a young black girl who was unable to attend her neighborhood school because the city had separate schools for blacks. Her father filed suit in the federal district court to challenge the school board's policy and alleged that the racial segregation violated the Constitution's Equal Protection Clause because the schools were not equal. The federal district court followed the decision of the U.S. Supreme Court in an earlier case, *Plessy v. Ferguson*, and dismissed the case.

Plessy, 163 U.S. 537, had been decided in 1896 and involved a Louisiana law that required separate railroad cards for blacks and whites. Plessy, who was one-eighth black and had very fair skin color, purchased a ticket and attempted to sit in the car for white people. He was arrested for violating the Louisiana law. He filed a lawsuit in the Louisiana state court, alleging Thirteenth and Fourteenth Amendment violations and lost. The U.S. Supreme Court accepted his case, but he also lost there. His argument on appeal was that state laws requiring people of different races to use segregated facilities violated the Constitution because segregated facilities were not equal facilities. The U.S. Supreme Court upheld the Louisiana courts and decided that separate facilities were equal facilities.

Approximately fifty years later in Brown, Thurgood Marshall, who became the first black to serve on the U.S. Supreme Court, argued for the Browns that the "separate but equal" doctrine handed down in Plessy was unconstitutional because the ruling violated the Equal Protection clause of the Fourteenth Amendment. This time, the U.S. Supreme Court agreed and held that in education, separate facilities were inherently unequal facilities.

Both the Plessy case and the Brown case are examples of cases that were heard by the U.S. Supreme Court through the appellate jurisdiction authority granted the court in Article III of the Constitution. In Plessy, the case began in a state court and was appealed after the highest court of the state found against a person's constitutional issue. In Brown, the case began in the federal courts and was appealed after the case was dismissed by the court. Both cases involved a federal question because they involved constitutional issues.

Another type of case that Article III gives the Supreme Court authority to hear cases, involves citizens from different states. An example of this type of case is where the parties are from different states and the amount of the controversy exceeds a certain level. The dollar amount has increased over the years and today the minimum amount in a controversy between citizens of different states is $75,000. An example of a diversity action case is an airplane crash where a plaintiff is seeking damages. Corporations are legal entities that are considered "persons" and, therefore, diversity actions often involve a company and an individual (or individuals).

Article III also requires that all crimes, except cases of impeachment shall be by jury. This right was expanded in the Sixth Amendment to the Constitution, which states,

> In all criminal prosecutions, the accused shall enjoy the right to a speedy and public trial, by an impartial jury of the state and district wherein the crime shall have been committed…and to be informed of the nature and cause of the accusation; to be confronted with the witnesses against him; to have compulsory process for obtaining witnesses in his favor, and to have the assistance of counsel for his defense.

The final section of Article III of the Constitution defines treason and provides that treason against the United States shall consist only of levying war against the U.S. or adhering to the enemies of the U.S. by giving the enemies aid and comfort. The section further provides that a person may only be convicted of treason by confessing in open court or by the testimony of two witnesses.

Checks And Balances

The judicial branch can review the actions of the executive to decide whether executive actions are unconstitutional. It also can check Congressional action by declaring laws passed by Congress as unconstitutional. The concept of judicial review can be traced to the early 1800s and the case of *Marbury v. Madison* when the Supreme Court first declared an act of Congress unconstitutional.

The facts of *Marbury v. Madison* involve the appointment of "midnight judges." In 1800, Thomas Jefferson, a Democratic-Republican, became President. He was replacing John Adams, a Federalist. Between the time of the Electoral

College vote and the March inauguration, Adams began making appointments of justices of the peace for the District of Columbia. The commissions for the appointments had been approved by the Senate, signed by President Adams, and affixed with the seal of the United States. However, the commissions were not delivered to those named to fill the positions of justice of the peace. After Jefferson was inaugurated, he ordered his Secretary of State, James Madison not to deliver the commissions.

William Marbury was one of the appointees whose commission had not been delivered. He asked the Supreme Court for an order requiring Madison to deliver the commissions (a writ of mandamus, which is an order from a court to an inferior government official ordering the government official to properly fulfill their official duties or correct an abuse of discretion.)

The Supreme Court had three issues to resolve: first, whether Marbury was entitled to the writ (the order he requested); second, whether the laws of the United States permitted courts to grant the order; and third, if the laws permitted the grant of the order, whether the Supreme Court could grant it. John Marshall, a Federalist, was Chief Justice of the Court and wrote the opinion. The Court found that Marbury had been properly appointed, but that the Judiciary Act of 1789 used to support Marbury's claim did not give the Supreme Court original jurisdiction over cases like Marbury's. The law gave the Supreme Court original jurisdiction in cases involving ambassadors, other public ministers and consuls and where the state was a party.

Marbury's case did not fall within any of those categories because he was an appointee for a District of Columbia court. The high court held that the Court was obligated to uphold the Constitution because it was the "law of the land." Marbury was not awarded his commission, and the Supreme Court established the doctrine of judicial review, the right to review acts of Congress.

In 1944, the U.S. Supreme Court heard the case of *Korematsu v. U.S.*, 323 U.S. 214, which involved an Executive Order. The Order was issued in response to Congressional legislation and required people of Japanese ancestry to leave restricted military areas and placed in internment camps during World War II. It also directed the exclusion of the Japanese Americans from a particular West Coast military area. Other orders required them to report to assembly centers and provided for their detention in relocation centers. Mr. Korematsu was an American citizen of Japanese descent who remained in a California "military area" contrary to exclusion orders. He was convicted in a federal district court of violating the order. The U.S. Circuit Court of Appeals affirmed the conviction. Mr. Korematsu filed a writ of certiorari (a "writing" asking the Supreme Court to hear the case) and the Supreme Court heard the case to decide the constitutional issue he raised. The issue was whether or not the restriction that curtailed the civil rights of a single racial group was constitutional. The Supreme Court decided that such restrictions may be justified when there is pressing public necessity. The Court held that because the country was at war with Japan it was necessary to protect against espionage and against sabotage to the country's national defense and that the actions were not beyond the war power of Congress or the power of the Executive. The Court did not address the issue of whether the order requiring reporting for relocation was constitutional because Mr. Korematsu had only been convicted of not leaving the military area. In this case, the judicial review of an executive action resulting in affirmance and was deemed to be constitutional.

More than forty years later, Congress awarded restitution to the survivors of the relocation camps.

Another example of judicial review on executive actions involves the case of *Nixon v. U.S.* in 1974. In this case the high court addressed the issue of executive privilege. President Nixon claimed executive privilege in refusing to turn over to the Watergate prosecutor tapes of conversations he and others had in the Oval Office in connection to the Watergate break-in and criminal charges being brought against members of his administration. The Supreme Court stated there was a valid need to protect communications within government but that because the President had only argued a "generalized need" to protect the documents, the argument was not strong enough to take precedence over the larger public interest in obtaining the truth in the context of a criminal investigation.

Arrangements Of Institutions

The Constitution provides that each branch of the federal government will have separate powers, but the branches also have shared powers, many of which become checks on the other branches to maintain a balance among the branches.

Separate Powers

The concept of "separation of powers" means that each branch of government has separate, independent functions, and that the powers need to be separated to maintain a balance within the government. Historically, the concept can be traced to the Enlightenment and promotes the idea that if government responsibilities are separate and distinct, no one part of government will have a concentration of power and that each part of government can provide checks upon the other parts of government. Realistically, no one branch of American government can work absolutely independently from the others because their powers and responsibilities overlap.

Shared Powers

The executive branch and legislative branch both have responsibilities in the appointment process. The President nominates appointments, and the Senate must confirm or approve the appointments. The treaty-making responsibilities provide another example. The President and State Department personnel negotiate treaties with foreign nations, but they cannot be approved without the consent of the Senate. The Treaty of Versailles that ended World War I is one such example. President Woodrow Wilson and his advisors traveled to Paris, France, to meet with dignitaries from other nations to write the terms of the treaty. President Wilson had the vision he called the Fourteen Points. Those ideas were to become the basis for maintaining peace in the future, and those points included creating an organization called the League of Nations to discuss global matters and avoid future wars. The European powers at the conference wanted retribution from Germany and were not interested in most of the Fourteen Points. The provisions for the League of Nations, however, were included in the treaty.

President Wilson had worked hard to negotiate a treaty that would make the world safer, but when the treaty was sent to the Senate to be approved some Senators objected to terms relating to the League of Nations and some Republican Senators also objected to the fact that a prominent Republican had not been invited to be part of the treaty delegation. As a result, the treaty failed approval by the Senate by not garnering the two-thirds majority vote that was required for ratification.

The executive branch and legislative branch also share responsibility with legislation. Congress passes the laws, but the president can veto the laws.

Relationships Within Government And With Groups _____

The relationships between the branches of government and the interactions between government and groups within society are instrumental in making important policy decisions. Public policy is the result of a course of action taken by the government that deals with problems and issues that reflect the priorities and attitudes of the public. Public policy is goal oriented because its purpose is to resolve problems.

One example of public policy is minimum wages. The federal government has enacted a minimum wage law, which some 2016 presidential candidates, for example, believe is not high enough. Public policy is more than a rule or regulation. Public policy is the result of recognizing a problem, formulating a way to resolve the problem, and adopting a way (a policy) to resolve the problem. The dollar amount contained within the minimum wage law is a statement that the problem being addressed is the maintenance of living standards above a poverty level, but is not the policy. The policy is to help American workers maintain a higher standard of living. The 2016 presidential candidates who believe the minimum wage needs to be increased recognize there should be a policy helping people to earn a living wage but disagree as to the amount that the law should require as the minimum wage.

Public policy can also relate to issues ranging from protecting the environment to limiting campaign finance abuse. Much public policy is implemented by administrative agencies.

Public Opinion

The Founding Fathers realized the importance of maintaining a link between the government and the citizenry. They provided this link in the legislative branch when they created a House of Representatives that had terms of office for two years. The members of the House represent the views of their constituents. They are responsible for the wellbeing of those in their Congressional districts. By having one chamber of a legislature that was more directly connected with the people, the framers of the Constitution recognized the importance of the link between the government and the citizens.

In today's society, public opinion is extremely important because it drives political action. Public opinion also indicates to the politicians what the public wants and is concerned about in a politician. Public opinion also reflects why specific policies come into being.

Public opinion consists of a variety of views that can range from liberal to conservative. In the area of politics, for example, the range can be from far right (ultra conservative) to moderate to far left (ultra-liberal). Public opinion can change as people consider various options to resolve an issue, whether the issue is deciding which candidate to vote for, how best to resolve the homeless problem, or which option is best for the placement of a landfill.

Measuring public opinion is important for public officials. If the subject of public opinion is a presidential race, for example, one way to measure public opinion is the survey. Public opinion surveys indicate how people view the effectiveness of their leaders. The results may show whether they think the government is doing well, accomplishing goals outlined in their platforms, and whether government should be trusted. The evaluations are indicators of how people will vote in an upcoming election. Since the 1960s, the public's opinion of government has declined and the surveys show people have a lower level of trust in government. Recent public opinion surveys have focused on issues such as terrorism, global warming, gay rights, immigration, healthcare, economic conditions, and abortions and other social issues.

Public opinion is an indicator of what people expect in government. In the early 2000s, public support for the war in Iraq lessened. As a result, more Democrats were voted into office and the Democrats gained control of both houses of Congress and the presidency. In the 1960s the civil rights movement gained momentum because of public opinion. The Supreme Court overturned the "separate but equal" doctrine and found that, in education, separate facilities were not equal facilities. The emphasis on eliminating discrimination shifted to public accommodations, employment, and other aspects of society. Public opinion about civil rights for women also resulted in government action. The National Organization of Women (NOW) wanted to eliminate discrimination against women in the workforce. They focused on equal pay for equal work and entry for women into some of the more male-dominated professions. The group supported the Equal Rights Amendment to the U.S. Constitution. The proposed amendment did not become part of the Constitution but public opinion concerning women's rights resulted in many changes for greater equality.

Today, public opinion focuses on social issues such as eliminating gender discrimination and discrimination against the disabled, the elderly, and other minorities.

Political Parties

Political parties offer people choices about how the government should be run. Their goals are to elect people to positions in government so the elected officials can turn their beliefs and philosophies into public policy. In the 2016 campaign the Democrats and Republicans had different ideas on how to repair America's economy; how to deal with the illegal immigrant issue; whether to raise or lower taxes, and if so, to what extent; and whether the states or the federal government should decide on increasing the minimum wage.

Each political party wants to attract the public to vote for its candidates. In order to do so, their candidates run campaigns to get the voters' support. When they explain their party's platform to the candidates, they are serving a function by informing the public. Campaigns last for long periods of time and cost millions of dollars. However, campaigns also inform the public about the positions the candidates take on various issues.

The Role of Political Parties

In addition to having the purpose of electing political candidates to office, a political party serves as a check on the other political parties. In Congress, the minority party assumes the role of criticizing the majority party and its proposed legislation. Partisanship can increase to the point where Congress is unable to accomplish its legislative objectives. When politicians ask for bipartisan legislation they are asking for members of Congress to "work across the aisle" and "cross the party line" to work with members of the majority party to enact legislation that is beneficial for the country rather than to defeat the majority party's legislation for the sake of party alignment.

The Two-Party System

President Washington, in his farewell address, warned Americans about "factions." The "factions" developed into political parties, and the political-party system we have today is the two-party system. The first two American political parties were the Federalists and the Democratic Republicans. The Whigs became a second major political party during the early 1800s and opposed the Democrats. William Henry Harrison was the Whig nominee who won the presidency and served approximately two months because he died from contracting a cold at the inauguration.

The Republican Party became the second major party in the 1860 election and ran Abraham Lincoln as its candidate. During the 1860s the donkey was used as a symbol of the Democrat Party and the elephant was used as a symbol of the Republican Party. The symbols remain as party symbols today.

Third parties have played a role in American politics, also. One of the strongest third parties was the Progressive Party that was known as the Bull Moose Party. The party candidate for President was former President Theodore Roosevelt who had supported his Vice President William Howard Taft until he believed Taft was too conservative. The Bull Moose Party was formed to advocate progressive ideas and reform and its members were more progressive than the members of the Republican Party.

Campaigns and Elections

The American system of elections is a "winner-take-all" system. The person with the highest number of votes is elected to fill a government position. Campaigns take place before elections and in recent years, the campaigns have lasted longer, cost more money, and involved more issues. And, because of the enormous amounts of money being spent on the campaigns, there have been cries for campaign finance reform.

Before the general election is held, each party must narrow its choices of possible candidates to one. The process of elimination can be done through caucuses or primary elections. Both are party functions. Primary elections replaced the nomination of a candidate by influential party members. There are three types of primary elections—direct, closed, and open. In direct primaries all party members may vote to choose a candidate for the general elections. Closed primaries are held in most states and the voters in a closed primary must be a registered party member to vote for a nominee. Open primaries are held in a few states. Open primaries do not require a person to be affiliated with a party to vote for a nominee.

Caucuses are held in fewer states. The Iowa caucuses are the first where votes are cast for presidential candidates. A caucus is different from a primary because in a caucus people meet in groups and attempt to persuade others to vote for their candidate. As voters move from group to group or from one side of a caucus center to another, the outcome for the candidates becomes more obvious. Votes are taken when debate is cut off and the winner is announced.

Often the primary elections result in a candidate receiving the required number of votes to be chosen at the party's convention the summer before the general election. If not, then the convention becomes an "open convention" where other individuals may be nominated.

General elections are held on the first Tuesday after the first Monday in even numbered years. The voters vote for the President and Vice President every other election cycle because those terms are for four years. Often, state and local elections are held at the same time. Voter who select all candidates from one party are said to vote a "straight ticket." Those who choose candidates from each party are said to vote a "split ticket." Today many voters prefer to identify themselves as "independents" because they do not favor either political party. In states where a voter must align with a political party to vote in a primary election, independent voters may not be able to vote, and for some, providing further confirmation of the reasons for maintaining an independent status.

Campaigns and Finance Reform

The Federal Election Commission (FEC) was formed to administer and enforce the Federal Elections Campaign Act that governs the financing of federal elections. Because a presidential campaign can cost millions of dollars, there is much opportunity for abuse. Special interest groups can have considerable influence on candidates and the outcome of elections. As a result, political action committees (PACs) have been formed to address abuses and pursue campaign finance reform. The PACs pool campaign contributions from members of the committee and donate those funds to campaign for or against a candidate or legislation. Advocates of campaign finance reform want to put the electorate in a stronger position during elections by taking power away from the special interest groups. Implementing reforms that will make primary elections and campaigns more transparent will help strengthen the link between citizens and the government.

Interest Groups

People who want to influence government organize with others who share their interest. When they attempt to pressure the government to adopt policy that benefits their group, they are called interest groups. Interest groups usually represent only one issue or a set of attitudes and concerns that are closely related. The interest groups are another way that citizens can link to their government.

There are several types of interest groups. Public interest groups promote their interests for the public in general. The group may be interested in environmental issues or animal rights issues. Or, they may be interested in voter awareness and better government. The League of Women Voters is an example of a public interest group. Business and trade associations are interest groups that are formed by people with business-related interests. These groups represent large and small businesses and an example is the Chamber of Commerce. The National Association of Manufacturers is another example of a business or trade association interest group.

Professional interest groups have members of occupations that require training and / or specialization. Examples include teachers' organizations such as the National Education Association; the American Medical Association, an interest group of doctors; and the professional group for lawyers, the American Bar Association.

Some interest groups promote or oppose causes. Examples include the National Rifle Association, Planned Parenthood, the American Civil Liberties Union, and the National Wildlife Federation. Agricultural groups comprise another type of interest group. Organizations such as the National Grange and the American Farm Bureau Association focus on protecting the interests of the American farmers and monitoring and promoting the government's agricultural policies. These interest groups are often broad based and include a variety of farming groups that represent different interests ranging from livestock and sheep to grain and fruit production.

Labor union interest groups have members who either work in the same industry or share the same type of job. They focus on government action that will benefit their members and job-related matters. An example of a labor union interest group is the American Federation of Labor and Congress of Industrial Organizations (AFL-CIO). Religious interest groups are active at the state and federal levels of government. Some are conservative, pro-family organizations interested in legislation that may affect their beliefs and others support prayer in school and attempt to influence public policy in matters involving religion. Examples of religious interest groups are the National Council of Churches, the Christian Coalition, and the American Jewish Congress.

Interest groups that want to promote the welfare of certain groups are also important links between the citizens and the government. The American Legion is an example. Also, the American Association of Retired People (AARP) and the National Association for the Advancement of Colored People (NAACP) are also interested in promoting welfare for specific groups of people.

How Interest Groups Work

Interest groups have lobbyists in Washington, D.C. and in state capitals to encourage legislators and policymakers to adopt policies that are beneficial to their groups. Lobbying can include testifying at legislative hearings or contacting legislators and government officials with research and technical information to support their points of view. Lobbyists can also present proposed legislation or help draft legislation. They can also grant interviews to members of the media to express their views on specific subjects.

Interest groups are involved in the political process to help elect candidates who are favorable to their position. They also work to defeat candidates who oppose their views. Interest groups sometimes form an organization called a Political Action Committees (PAC). A PAC pools campaign contributions from its members and donates those funds to campaign for or against a candidate, policy or legislation. For example, the pharmaceutical industry is an interest group and a political action committee may be associated with it. The PACs list the donations of members and the contributions they make in favoring or opposing candidates. The reason people donate to PACS is because Congress has passed legislation to limit the amounts individuals may make as contributions to political campaigns. When people want to support a candidate who favors a certain issue, they can make a contribution to the PAC that represents the group or issue and the PAC will then make direct contributions to candidates who support those views. As a result, the interest groups help citizens have more and better links to their government.

Media

The media serves as an important link between the people and government. Think about the types of media you use in a single day—the Internet, television, newspapers, and perhaps the radio—and think about how your ideas about government and candidates have been influenced by the media.

In an election year, the media broadcasting companies will hold debates between the candidates. In 2016, there were more than ten such debates. The Republican debates began with 17 candidates and as the debates progressed, the number of candidates decreased. Did the debates have an impact on the voters? The debates were held before primary elections in various states and it is likely the decrease in number of candidates was the result of voters forming opinions of the candidates from a variety of sources, including the debates.

Presidents have benefited from media exposure leading to a gain in popularity. President Ronald Reagan used his ability as a former movie star turned politician to become known as "The Great Communicator." Other presidents have used the media to their advantage in promoting their policies and goals for the nation. Franklin D. Roosevelt presented "fireside chats" to the public to help the country work its way out of the Great Depression. Media telecasts of the State of the Union addresses provide the public with an awareness of government and telecasts of Congressional hearings provide the opportunity to understand issues and the positions elected officials are taking on those issues.

The Internet is playing an increasing role in the link between government, the political scene, and the people of America. The Internet provides a candidate the opportunity to reach millions of voters. Candidates can send messages and information on platforms such as Facebook and Twitter to convey political philosophy, encourage voting, and argue against their opponents' ideas. The interactive aspect is important because citizens can use social media to respond to the messages they receive. Candidates have websites, campaign donations can be made through the website, and information about the candidate's stance on issues can be read on websites.

In addition to the Internet being an excellent source of media content, the Internet has been used to test voting practices. More than ten countries now have online voting, and Arizona experimented with online voting in the 2000 primary elections. The expanded use of Internet voting will likely cause new guidelines and rules to be implemented as to the extent, type, and scheduling of media coverage of the candidates and the elections. Internet voting even has the possibility of redirecting the citizens to a more "direct democracy" where each citizen can be directly involved in the political process.

The media has a significant impact on the voters and on campaigns. Today, more than ever, the campaigns focus on the candidate rather than the party. Negative media coverage can turn a positive, forward-thinking campaign into a losing campaign for candidates. Candidates want "good press" and want favorable attention from the press to attract voters. The media is an important link between the citizens and government because the media can influence voters' opinions. The media attempts to present information objectively but there are times when the individual reporter's biases are apparent. These subjective reports can change voters' views and sway uncommitted voters. The media can also affect the behavior of candidates. Print media can affect the public's image of a candidate by the pictures it prints. If the media focuses on an issue that might be considered a scandal, the public can draw a negative conclusion about the candidate. However, another conclusion might be drawn if a candidate is photographed while working on a social service project. The power of the press and the opportunity for photo shoots can be used by the media to shape public opinion.

The media plays an important role in linking the citizens to their government. It can be a positive role, or a negative role, but in either situation the media acts as watchdogs over elected candidates and those running for office. The media believes its function is consistent with the concept of freedom of the press to report news as it sees fit and to prevent politicians and government officials from harming their constituents or abusing their power.

State Government

The framers of the Constitution adopted a federal system of government. Federalism divides the power of government between a central federal government and district or regional governments, such as states. Both levels of government in the United States have a great deal of sovereignty. Some federal laws preempt, or take priority over, state laws. Certain types of railroad legislation present examples. The Constitution identifies expressed powers belonging to each branch of the central government and it lists the powers that the states do not have. However, the Tenth Amendment to the Constitution provides that "the powers not delegated to the United States by the Constitution, nor prohibited by it to the states, are reserved to the states, respectively, or to the people."

Article IV

Article IV of the U.S. Constitution provides that "full faith and credit shall be given in each state to the public acts, records, and judicial proceedings of every state." It also provides that "the citizens of each state shall be entitled to the privileges and immunities of citizens in the several states." These provisions mean that if, for example, a person is married in one state, all other states must recognize the marriage. In the 2010 to 2016 time period an issue arose over states' recognition of marriages of the same sex and the Supreme Court of the United States ultimately decided the issue. Another example is a judgment for money obtained in one state. If a person is sued for not paying a bill and the creditor files suit and obtains a judgment against the debtor in Hawaii, the judgment must be recognized in all of the other 49 states.

The U.S. Constitution also addresses the issue of extradition, which is the process of returning a person to the state in which they are charged with a crime if they have fled to another state.

Organization of State Government

Each state is organized in a manner that is similar to the U.S. government. Each state has three branches of government and each branch has the same type of powers as its counterpart in the federal government. All states have executive, legislative, and judicial branches of government. One state has a unicameral (one house) legislature but its function is the same as legislatures with two chambers. Judicial branches of state government have trial courts and appellate courts, with one appellate court being the highest. Most states, for example, call the highest state court a supreme court, but not every highest state court is called a supreme court.

States also have administrative agencies and most of them are similar to its counterpart in the federal government. And the parallel agencies perform similar services. States may have additional types of administrative agencies. For example, the states that allow gambling will likely have established a gaming commission to regulate the gaming activities. If states have parallel administrative agencies and the rules and regulations of a state agency conflict with those of the federal agency, the federal agency rules will control.

The extent to which states can provide services to their populations depend on available cash, just the same as it does with the federal government. Many state budgets receive funding from lottery revenues. Lotteries and lottery funding are controversial because of the belief that many poor people use money on the lottery needed for other purposes. Taxes and fees from licenses are also used to fund state and local budgets. Some state constitutions have provisions that prohibit the state from going into debt; other states do not have such provisions. In some instances state and local expenditures become an election issue and are voted on for approval. In some localities, increases in taxes are voted upon by the people.

Many powers of the states are concurrent with those of the federal government. An example of a concurrent power is the power to regulate transportation and highways within a state. The federal government has the power to regulate aspects of the interstate highway system but states have the power to build and maintain roads and set speed limits. The federal and state governments provide funding to build roads.

Local Governments

Local governments usually consist of two tiers or levels, the county government and the municipal government. The organization of local governments is also similar to the organization of the U.S. government. Local governments have bodies to make, enforce, and interpret laws. Some local governments have an executive department that is headed by one person; other communities have a commission that forms their executive departments. Local governments make laws, which are usually called ordinances and have courts or boards to interpret laws. Some agencies within a local government have similar responsibilities as state and federal agencies. For example, a city may have a commission for historic preservation, which may be parallel to a state organization.

The interest that citizens show in local government is often less than the interest show in national government. However, the foundation and issues of government are as important at the local level as they are at the national level. One reason is that local politicians sometimes use their local government experience as a stepping stone for political advancement.

Local elections tend to draw fewer voters than national elections. Citizens tend not to be concerned with local issues because most local issues are not controversial and only when a controversial issue arises do citizens become involved. At that point, the issue will, or could, affect their lives. An example is a locality seeking to extend its boundaries and provide additional services to the residents in an area the city government wants to annex. If the people do not want to pay additional taxes as a result of the annexation or if they have recently put in new wells and do not want to be hooked up to city water, then they will respond and take more of an interest in local politics.

Summary

American government is based on the concept of federalism, which includes a central government and governments within districts or regions. Government at the national, state, and local levels all have an executive, legislative, and judicial branch. Each level of government is similarly organized and operated. The U.S. Constitution provides the framework for the central government and states have constitutions that provide their framework. The institutions of government are linked closely to the citizens, public opinion, interest groups, and the media and together, determine the type of society in which Americans live.

Chapter 5: Public Policy

What is public policy? Is it under the control of the public? What is the role of the government in public policy? These are some of questions that you will need to know how to answer at the end of this section.

Public policy is essentially policy developed and executed by the government to support public services, infrastructure, or public programs. The study of public policy, its theories and concepts are the content of political science. Public policy is a goal-oriented course of action that the government follows in dealing with a problem or issue in the country. Public policies are based on law, but many people other than legislators affect them.

Public policy is the result of interactions between actors, institutions, processes, and self-interest groups. Congress, the President, the Cabinet, advisers, agency bureaucrats, federal and state courts, political parties, interest groups, the media—all these groups interact to make political decisions in the United States.

The policy process involves the formulation of policy agendas, the legislation creating the policy, the implementation of the policy by the bureaucratic branch, and the judicial branch weighing in with legal interpretations when required. Individuals, groups, and even government agencies that do not comply with policies can be penalized.

What You Will Be Tested On

In the AP exam you will be tested on your understanding of the creation of public policy, the various institutions that play a role in generating and executing public policy, the citizen's role in public policy, and how the different players (or actors) co-opt their self-interests in coming to a policy decision.

You will have to understand the linkages between the different institutions, how policy is formed in the American system, how some agendas (or issues) come to the forefront of the political debate while others don't get through. The role of institutions in the enactment of policy is also important—and this includes Congress and the President. Once policy is passed, the implementation of the policy is in the hands of the various government agencies. Any legal issue that arises from the legislation or execution of the legislation falls under the purview of the federal court system.

Finally, you will need to understand the various policy networks and how they support the policy process.

Policymaking in a Federal System

Policymaking in the federal system refers to the issue of who makes policy decisions and how it is passed into law. Four key groups in the American political system make policy: the executive branch, the legislative branch, the courts, and the bureaucracy.

Federal public policy refers to any "official" decision made by the Congress and the President about public expenditures, regulations, or any other issue affecting the United States and its citizens. The President can issue an Executive Order mandating something that then becomes law and must be implemented by the federal agencies. Congress passes legislative bills and when the President signs them, they become law. In both cases, those laws constitute public policy. Government agencies also make policy, by passing U.S. Code or mandates that companies or people must follow. Finally the courts, through its judgments on cases that interpret policy, make adjustments to policy, thereby validating or invalidating it.

The power to formulate and implement policy is often divided between several entities. As you know from previous sections, the President of the United States cannot declare war; only the U.S. Congress can declare war. This is part of the checks and balances system. After the bombing of Pearl Harbor in December 1941, President Franklin Roosevelt addressed a joint session of Congress to ask the body to declare war against Japan. This was a policy decision, made by the President, supported by public opinion, and declared by Congress. The policy was executed by the War (the Defense) Department.

Cooperation between the executive and legislative branches is necessary for any policy agenda. While the executive branch forms and executes a policy, the legislative branch makes the policy a law (i.e. official) and provides funding for the execution of the policy.

Some common areas where public policy is passed are social welfare programs, social policies, economy, environment, the budget, and national security. In each of these cases, the government has passed laws that better the conditions of the citizens or the economy or the security environment of the United States. These are also hot-button policy topics in the U.S, with interest groups, lobbyists, public opinion, media, and the various government organizations involved in developing the final policy solution.

Finally, the relationship between the states and federal government on policy is somewhat divided—in most cases, issues that are national in scope and impact and become federal problems, while regional and local issues become state or city/county policy issues. There are cases, where two or three levels of government share the responsibility for administering the policy—for example, the federal government might set standards of care or coverage in education, health, or highway safety, but states have to execute and evaluate the policy. Also, the federal government provides some funding for programs, which is then supplemented by state coffers. For example, education programs receive both federal and state funds, transportation (especially highways) also receive both funding from the federal Department of Transportation and from the state governments. Innovation is another example of where the federal government might support the creation of a technology incubator which the state subsequently owns and operates.

The Formation of Policy Agendas

An agenda is a set of problems that the government wants to solve. This list is generally quite long and therefore must be prioritized, with some problems getting earlier and more attention than others. Agenda setting may be a response to pressure from interest groups, political parties, the media, and other branches of government. Agendas usually are reshaped when a new president takes office or when the majority party in Congress changes after an election. A crisis such as war, depression, natural disasters, or a tragic accident can also re-prioritize issues.

Around the turn of the 20th century, muckrakers and concerned citizens brought to light the unethical practices rampant in the food and medicine industries and pressed the government to take action. The result was legislation such as the Pure Food and Drug Act of 1906, and lead eventually to the creation of regulatory agencies like the Food and Drug Administration.

Many things disturb or distress people, such as unsafe workplaces, natural disasters like tornadoes and earthquakes, crime, pollution, or the cost of medical care. However, not all types of distress automatically become problems. People have to recognize that government can and should do something about them. For example, most citizens probably do not expect government to prevent hurricanes. However, they may expect quick relief actions by the government to help hurricane victims.

When a problem is identified, often, conflicting plans from various political interests take shape. Various players — the President and White House aides, agency officials, specially appointed task forces, interest groups, private research organizations, and legislators — may take part in formulating new policy.

Generally policy agendas "bubble up" from the bottom—meaning that something is not functioning correctly at the citizen or individual level. If the issue impacts or affects a large number of people, then it comes to the government's attention and might lead to the formation of a taskforce to study it. Eventually, the issue works its way towards becoming a policy issue.

However, sometimes, there is the "top-down" approach to policy formulation. This is when a group or organization drives the agenda with a specific policy solution in mind. Some policy researchers believe that there is a right time for a top-down versus bottom-up approach to policy formulation. The top-down perspective is more appropriate in the early planning stages, but a bottom-up view is more appropriate in the later evaluation stage. There are different and specific instances when each approach is best utilized. When the policy goal seeks incremental change, can use stable technology, has a stable environment, low-conflict within the goal, and a tightly coupled institutional setting then top-down is the appropriate implementation strategy. Conversely, uncertain technology, goal conflicts, and an unstable or loosely coupled environment should use the bottom-up approach.

Policy incrementalism is another phenomenon in the policy world. Incrementalism refers to the slow tweaking or changing of policy to meet new needs or unforeseen impacts of the original policy. In this case, often multiple interests intervene, and sometimes policymakers use the incremental approach to slow down the policy's full set of deliverables. Policies relating to healthcare, education, and the environment often fall under this approach.

The Role of Institutions in the Enactment of Policy

All public policies are implemented by bureaucracies. These are the various government agencies at the federal or state and local levels that receive appropriations from Congress and supporting guidance on policy execution. However, despite this guidance, the agencies become the experts on the subject matter of the policy. They hire experts and retain staff with knowledge regarding the policy and they hold meetings with affected constituents. They monitor progress, evaluate policy impact, and then report back to Congress or their state or local leaders.

The environment of some government agencies is more political, volatile and tumultuous than others. For example, an agency like the Bureau of Engraving and Printing and the U.S. Geological Survey, might have less visibility than the Social Security Administration or the Department of Defense.

Policy makers often try to determine what a policy is actually accomplishing or whether or not it is being carried out efficiently. Often the evaluation process takes place over time with contributions from many of the interacting players. Most evaluations call for some degree of change and correction, and inevitably, at least some of the players will disagree. The whole process then begins again and the problem is readdressed.

The Role of the Bureaucracy and the Courts in Policy Implementation and Interpretation

As you now know, policy is a complex intertwined effort among all branches of government. Government agencies (bureaucracies) and the courts play a key role in implementing, interpreting, or enforcing the policy—and through this they sometimes refine the policy. Often a policy issued work for a decade or so, but the technology changes and the policy comes up for reinterpretation.

Policy is often built in a series of small steps passed over time by different players, and eventually, a complex negotiated policy emerges. As described earlier, a policy is passed by Congress and signed by the President to become law. Or the President issues an Executive Order, or a government agency issues a mandate or a U.S. Code of Federal Regulations. Government agencies, in combination with the President's approval, have been key in issuing much of the existing safety legislation in the United States. They have also issued policy mandates for the economy and for the defense of the country.

Most public policies are carried out by administrative agencies in the executive branch, although sometimes the courts get involved in implementing decisions they make. Agencies use many techniques to see that policy is carried out. Sometimes they punish people and organizations that do not comply with policy. For example, a state can take a driver's license away from a bad driver; or the government may offer incentives, like tax breaks for contributing to the presidential election campaign. They even appeal to people's better instincts, such as using the slogan, "Only you can prevent forest fires."

Below a quick set of examples of government agency policies.

- Economy – International trade regulations, for example the North American Free Trade Agreement (NAFTA), allow for the growth of the U.S. economy and international expansions of businesses.
- Environment – the Clean Air Act, the Clean Water Act, the National Environmental Protection Act, the Endangered Species Act, etc. are examples of key federal policy legislation passed to protect people from living in over-polluted environments, and the environment from over-consumption.
- National Security – The war on Japan and Germany (World War II), the Vietnam War, the War on Terrorism are examples of U.S policy in national security.

Policies and enactment of policy by government agencies might be greatly affected by the judiciary's use of its power of judicial review and statutory interpretation. Agencies may have their statutory authority expanded or reduced by courts or their policy implementation overruled by the courts.

Several landmark policy decisions have been passed by the courts over the last several decades. You know many of these already, but here is a brief list of policy decisions for each of the areas mentioned above.

- Social welfare programs – Obamacare passed in 2010, Social Security, Medicare and Medicaid are examples of policies that provide assistance.
- Social policies – Civil rights legislation, right to vote for women and minorities, the right to choose abortion, and gay marriage policies passed by states are examples that represent social change for everyone in the United States.

Congress plays an important role annually in policy decisions through the passage of the budget or appropriations for the federal agencies.

- Budget – any and all appropriations and authorization bills passed by the Congress, and or State legislatures or city governments. These indirectly represent policy decisions because they provide funding for government programs.

Linkages Between Policy Processes

Given the number of players in the process of American governance, a policy process can look like "sausage making." Each player or actor is self-interested in the outcome, and this leads to some interesting linkages and deal-making, especially in large policy initiatives. Federalism, with its levels of government and checks and balances, means that the various players have different powers and levels with which they control the outcome of the policy process. Below, we'll look at some key linkages and inter-relationships as it relates to public policy-making.

The Iron Triangle

In the United States world of public policy, you might hear the word "iron triangle." This refers to the three points of an imaginary triangle—where points are represented by the bureaucracy, Congress, point interest groups. These three entities have linkages with each other in terms of power, resources, and self-interest.

1. Congress and interest groups – Interest groups provide campaign funds and access to congressional members in return for legislation and funding benefiting their lobbying interests.
2. Interest groups and bureaucracies – Government agencies execute the policy and interest groups want favorable policies for their constituents, while agencies want congressional support via lobbying by the interest groups (since the agencies themselves cannot lobby Congress).
3. Congress and Bureaucracies – Congress provides appropriations or funding to the agencies to execute the policy. Once accomplished, they only have minimal oversight over the policy. Agencies want

continued support of the program and budgets, so they work with Congressional Members and Committees on policy choices and execution decisions.

The rational model of policymaking states that all players involved will fairly and knowledgeably evaluate all the options, and select the optimal option to benefit the group. However, this means that everyone is aware of their biases and do not let those biases enter or influence their decision. This is rarely the case, of course. Herbert Simon (a Nobel Prize winner in economics) stated that bounded rationality is when individuals are limited in their decision-making, by the available information, the difficulty or complexity of the decision, their ability to understand the problem, and the amount of available time. So, they act as "satisfiers", seeking a satisfactory solution rather than an optimal one.

There are subtle and direct linkages between the institutions that make up government and influence government. Federalism creates checks and balances and this ensures that policymaking allows all the players to have an opinion. Let's look at a few of these interactions.

- Political parties – The two major political parties lobby on behalf of national policy decisions. For example the Democratic Party tends to support issues relating to the environment, increasing taxes on big business, providing funds for welfare and assistance programs, etc. The Republican Party on the other hand tends to support big business and their policy recommendations try to alleviate the tax and regulation burden on businesses.

- Interest groups – These groups tend to form around large issues or sometimes niche issues. They help craft legislation, they provide experts on the issue and they directly lobby Congress and the Executive branch for support on their agenda.

- Public opinion – As you've already explored in the chapter on mass media, you understand how public opinion impacts government decision making. The public's level of understanding and support of a policy agenda can make passage of a new policy easier or more difficult. Examples include school shootings and the passage of more restrictive gun laws after the Sandy Hook school shooting.

- Elections – Candidates running for office have to make their stances or opinions public on a variety of issues like immigration, health reform, national security, budget deficits, trade, etc. They essentially create a policy platform of the issues they "promise" to work on if they are elected.

Summary

Policy decision making is a continuous process with numerous people participating. At any given time, the government is at various stages of policy-making in a never-ending quest to provide solutions to countless societal problems.

In summary, let's revisit the steps for the policy process from identification and formulation, to implementation and evaluation of the policy. Through each of these steps, various actors and organizations intervene and have an impact on the policy.

- Agenda setting or problem identification – An issue comes to the public's attention. Usually brought to attention through the mass media. Interest groups and political parties grow awareness for the issue.
- Policy formation – The legislature and bureaucracies begin discussing the issue. Many politicians support the policy to gain votes and support and brainstorm strategies to deal with the problem.
- Policy Adoption – A policy is formally chosen as the solution. Usually, this is in the form of legislation.
- Policy Implementation – Government agencies create procedures, guidance, and grants to support the policy.
- Policy Evaluation – Policy analysts decide whether the policy is effective. The analysts are both government members and outside experts. At this stage, the policy can be revised for optimal success.

Chapter 6:
Civil Rights and Civil Liberties

From the beginning of the nation, the basic rights of mankind have been held sacred in the United States. The majority of individual states adopted a declaration or a bill of rights at the time they drafted their first state constitutions in the 1770s. These state bills of rights protected the basic rights of the people, such as free speech, freedom of the press, and free exercise of religion, or in other words the "civil liberties" of the people.

The fact that the Constitution did not contain a bill of rights to safeguard the people was the chief argument of the debates from 1787-1788. Supporters of the Constitution promised that a bill of rights would be inserted if the Constitution was ratified. During the first session of Congress in 1789, this promise was fulfilled. James Madison introduced a number of rights and protections that were briefly debated, and most of which were adopted. These became known as the federal "Bill of Rights" which applied only to the federal government, and were quite similar to the rights listed in the various state bills of rights.

After the Civil War, the protection of rights was again a chief concern of many. In particular, many in the north wanted to protect the rights of newly freed black slaves. The Fourteenth Amendment was enacted during this time, guaranteeing equal protection of the law to all citizens. Thereafter, the Supreme Court began to selectively "incorporate" parts of the federal bill of rights so they would apply directly to the states.

Although African Americans were granted rights by constitutional amendments and statutes after the Civil War, in reality, it took 100 years before their "civil rights" were truly respected. For decades a variety of discriminatory acts were practiced by local and state governments, especially in the south. There were separate schools for blacks and whites, and laws were set in place to separate the two races in public places and on public transportation. It was only in the 1950s and 1960s that these laws were seriously challenged, and ultimately overcome.

What You Will Be Tested On

When people refer to the Constitution today, a close examination of what they are saying will usually reveal that they are really talking about the rights protections in the amendments to the Constitution, and particularly how those protections apply to all of the people in all of the states. In other words, when the "Constitution" is debated today, or attacked, or is said to be under attack, what is usually being talked about are rights, and not the structure-oriented wording in the Constitution itself.

You will be tested on your understanding of a civil liberty and a civil right. You will have to be knowledgeable on the key decisions of the U.S. Supreme Court as they relate to civil liberties and civil rights. Nuances of the right to freedom of speech, rights of the accused, and of women and minorities are also important to know. The Fourteenth Amendment and its role in extending interpretations of rights and liberties are also important.

The Development of Civil Liberties and Civil Rights by Judicial Interpretation

Civil liberties are generally understood to be those rights, which safeguard all men from intrusions of government. These include the basic rights of freedom of religion, freedom of the press and speech, and a variety of protections of the criminally accused. In particular, persons accused of a crime have a number of rights and protections, including the right to an attorney to represent them, the presumption that they are innocent until proven guilty in a court of law, the right to confront witnesses and the right to not be forced to testify against themselves if they do not want to. They also have the fundamental right of 'habeas corpus,' or in other words if they are in jail, they have the right to quickly bring their incarceration to the attention of a judge, so that they will not be held without a charge.

Closely connected with the concept of civil liberties are civil rights. These are commonly understood to be the legal protections against discrimination based on race, gender, religion, national origin, age, disability, or other factors. All Americans are guaranteed the "equal protection of the law" by the Fourteenth Amendment. Curiously however, the equal protection clause in the Fourteenth Amendment is worded to only apply against the states, and not the federal government. Discrimination by the federal government is not technically prohibited by the Fourteenth Amendment, but is prohibited by a variety of federal statutes and laws.

Civil War and Slavery

It is known that one of the reasons for the Civil War was the debate over the future of slavery.

The agrarian South utilized slaves to tend its large plantations. On the eve of the Civil War, some four million Africans and their descendants toiled as slave laborers in the South. Slavery was interwoven into the Southern economy even though only a relatively small portion of the population actually owned slaves. Slaves could be rented or traded or sold to pay debts. Ownership of more than a handful of slaves bestowed respect and contributed to social position; and slaves, as the property of individuals and businesses, represented the largest portion of the region's personal and corporate wealth, as cotton and land prices declined and the price of slaves soared.

Meanwhile, one by one, the states of the North gradually abolished slavery. A steady flow of immigrants, especially from Ireland and Germany during the potato famine of the 1840s and 1850s, ensured the North a ready pool of laborers, many of whom could be hired at low wages, diminishing the need to cling to the institution of slavery.

However, for a century after the Civil War that freed them, slaves remained free but not equal. They were not truly free. While they could no longer be put in chains or sold like cattle, they were nonetheless treated unfairly, especially in the south. So great was the oppression against them and the institutionalized structure of "keeping them in their place", that their status was little improved from when they had been slaves.

The discriminatory attitude toward former slaves was often supported by government. Southern states in particular enacted a number of laws providing for segregation and discrimination based on race. It is not surprising that such laws were ultimately challenged in the courts.

The Supreme Court and Desegregation

Unfortunately, in the decades immediately after the Civil War, the Supreme Court did not protect the former slaves, as it should have done. The primary case in which discriminatory laws were challenged was *Plessy v. Ferguson*. In 1892 Homer Plessy deliberately sat in the "white only" railroad car of the East Louisiana Railroad. He intentionally indicated that he was a black, knowing that under laws enacted by the Louisiana legislature he was not entitled to be there. The purpose of his act was to challenge the constitutionality of the discriminatory laws in the courts. The case progressed through the court system until it reached the United States Supreme Court in 1896. This highest court proclaimed by a 7-2 majority that the "separate but equal" laws in Louisiana were acceptable, and did not violate the Thirteenth and Fourteenth Amendments to the Constitution.

Armed with this decision, southern states lost no time in establishing "separate but equal" schools, restrooms and other public places, and to allow for segregation to exist in public transportation theaters. The theory was that the separate facilities were equal in quality, but the reality was that usually the black facilities were far worse.

Sixty years later, the extensive segregation laws in the south were challenged again, and were gradually eliminated. The process largely began with a number of court challenges, which were raised in respect to school segregation in Kansas, Delaware, Virginia and South Carolina. Many of these separate cases were consolidated together into a single case by the name of *'Brown v. Board of Education of Topeka.'* This case was decided by a unanimous ruling of the Supreme Court in 1954, in which the 'separate but equal' doctrine of *Plessy v. Ferguson* was shot down as an unconstitutional denial of equal protection guaranteed by the Fourteenth Amendment. The black schools were found to be inferior to those for whites, and the very concept of segregating blacks from whites in public schools was found to be damaging to both races, and particularly to blacks.

Armed with this victory, many leaders of the new civil rights movement undertook a series of efforts to change other laws and practices, which discriminated against blacks. One of the chief of these efforts occurred in Alabama. In December of 1955, Rosa Parks, a highly respected black female, refused to yield her bus seat to a white passenger, contrary to laws of the City of Montgomery. Laws allowing for segregation in public transportation were challenged. Long before courts ruled on the issue, members of the black community joined together in a boycott of the public bus system in Montgomery, as a peaceful demonstration of protest against their treatment. Martin Luther King, Jr. was one of the leaders of the Montgomery bus boycott, and ultimately became one of the leading figures of the civil rights movement in the 1960s. Ultimately the Supreme Court in the case of *Browder v. Gayle* (a separate case from the one involving Rosa Parks) determined that segregation in public transportation was an unconstitutional violation of the equal protection guarantee in the Fourteenth Amendment.

Legislation Granting Civil Rights

The Civil Rights Act of 1964 was a landmark work of legislation which outlawed discrimination based on race, national origin, gender or religion. This was followed by the Voting Rights Act of 1965, which re-enthroned the basic right of blacks to vote, and the Fair Housing Act of 1968 which prohibited discrimination in the selling or renting of houses based on race.

Because blacks and women had suffered so many abuses for so long, many believed they should be given special consideration to advance their standing in society to a level considered equitable had there been no discrimination. Policies that have this equalizing goal are known as "affirmative action." Such policies are usually implemented by colleges and universities in an attempt to obtain percentages of enrollment by race that are roughly equal to race percentages in the population at large. As recently as 2003 the Supreme Court has upheld affirmative action as a legitimate goal in the case of *Grutter v. Bollinger*. However, affirmative action is controversial in the view of many. Some white males have even brought lawsuits on the basis of "reverse discrimination," alleging that the affirmative action goals of colleges and universities have caused them harm. Such cases have not always met with success.

Other Civil Rights Protections

It was not only African Americans that gained protections and rights, which had been denied for so long. Women also gained significant new rights and protections, as did those with disability and older persons. The Equal Pay Act of 1963 required that equal pay be made to both men and women for the same job. The Act to Prohibit Age Discrimination in Employment, was passed by Congress in 1967, prohibiting employment discrimination against persons over 40. The Americans with Disabilities Act was passed in 1990, prohibiting discrimination against those who are disabled.

Following closely on the heels of the civil rights movement there have been a number of court cases which have recognized a "right of privacy" in sexual matters. This right of privacy was derived from the Fourteenth Amendment. These cases have tended to be more controversial. One of the first of these cases occurred in 1965, in *Griswold v. Connecticut*. In this case the court recognized a right of privacy and ruled that state laws preventing married couples from using contraceptives were unconstitutional.

Perhaps the most controversial of the right of privacy cases was *Roe v. Wade*, decided in 1973. In this case, the court overturned laws in most states which outlawed abortion. The court in this case adopted a "trimester" system under which states were completely forbidden from regulating abortion during the first trimester of pregnancy. States were allowed to enact regulations to protect a woman's health in the second trimester, and could prohibit abortion during the third trimester as long as the mother's health was not at risk. The third trimester is when the fetus was considered to be "viable" (able to live on its own outside the womb, with life support). Later in 1992, the Supreme Court in *Planned Parenthood v. Casey* revised this structure, acknowledging that advancing medical technology allowed for viability and survival of an infant earlier than the third trimester, and therefore allowed states to enact laws protecting the unborn from the point of viability onward during the second trimester. To this day, abortion continues to be one of the most hotly contested issues in the United States, with many believing that the *Roe v. Wade* decision made the right to life of the unborn secondary to the mother's elective choice.

Most recently, the right of privacy derived from the due process and equal protection clauses of the Fourteenth Amendment has been cited in support of "gay marriage" in the 2015 case of *Obergefell v. Hodges*. In the years immediately preceding this decision, many states had enacted amendments to their state constitutions defining marriage as being between a man and a woman. The Supreme Court toppled these state constitutional amendments in its ruling, which recognized same sex marriages as legal in all states.

Knowledge of Substantive Rights and Liberties _____

The rights and liberties enjoyed by Americans are codified in the Constitution through the Bill of Rights, are interpreted through key Supreme Court cases, and are found in legislation passed by the federal government. As stated at the start of this chapter, most of the modern-day revisions to our rights and liberties have been in interpreting the Bill of Rights as it applies to the situation at hand. The following paragraphs, describe the "modern" liberties and rights we have assimilated as Americans in addition to our Bill of Rights.

Challenges to Interpretation

Some of the most fundamental rights and liberties of the people are found in the First Amendment to the Constitution. Included in this amendment are the right to free exercise of religion, to freedom of speech and the press, and the right of the people to peaceably assemble. As often happens with the passage of time, new or unusual events challenge the interpretation of the right, often attempting to broaden the meaning. Three instances are discussed below: flag burning, prayer in schools and workplace discrimination.

The U.S. flag is sometimes burnt as a symbol of protest, often against the policies of the American government. The flag can also be used in other symbolic ways, such as wearing it in an offensive manner or displaying it upside-down. While burning a flag is actually an action, other non-verbal actions have been used over the years to make similar statements. Through Supreme Court interpretations, these actions are protected as symbolic speech under the First Amendment.

The interpretation of free speech was a result of incensed citizens when demonstrators burned the flag as part of their protest against government actions or decisions. In the 1989 case of *Texas v. Johnson*, the Supreme Court ruled that flag burning is a protected act of free speech. The Supreme Court decided the First Amendment to the Constitution says it's unconstitutional for a government (whether federal, state or town) to prohibit the desecration of a flag, because it is seen as "symbolic speech."

This decision overturned laws in 48 out of 50 states, and resulted in Congress enacting the Flag Protection Act, that year, which outlawed flag burning. In the 1990 case of *United States v. Eichman* the Supreme Court reaffirmed its prior decision and ruled that the Flag Protection Act was unconstitutional. Attempts have been made to enact a constitutional amendment outlawing flag burning, but so far none have been successful.

Prayer in public schools has been another contested issue addressed by the courts. The First Amendment prohibits the establishment of a state religion and has been interpreted to guarantee the free exercise of religion pursuant to individual beliefs. In the 1962 case of *Engel v. Vitale* the Supreme Court ruled that a Christian oriented prayer drafted by school officials could not be recited in school and was an unconstitutional violation of the First Amendment. The prohibition of prayer in public schools has been reaffirmed in subsequent cases such as *Wallace v. Jaffree* in 1985, where a law permitting one minute of prayer in school was declared unconstitutional and *Lee v. Weisman* in 1992, where a clergy-led prayer at a middle school graduation ceremony was not allowed.

As covered earlier in this chapter, the Fourteenth Amendment and the Civil Rights Act of 1964 prevent discrimination based on race, gender, religion or national origin. These federal laws prohibiting discriminatory treatment have been applied in the workplace to protect against harassing or inappropriate behavior. Hence, if an employee is treated differently than other employees due to their gender, race or religion they have a cause for action against their employer. They are then entitled to bring a discrimination claim before the Equal Employment Opportunity Commission (EEOC) under Title VII of the Civil Rights Act. This is true whether their employment has been terminated or they have been subjected to a "hostile work environment."

Right to Due Process Under the Law

Among the most significant rights protections possessed by Americans are those pertaining to the criminally accused. Many people do not realize just how significant these protections are. Numerous countries across the world to this day do not maintain such protections for their people. Roughly half of all rights cases in the United States today relate directly to rights of the criminally accused, with the other half being all other rights cases, combined.

Several of the amendments that make up the Bill of Rights relate to the criminally accused. The Fourth Amendment protects against the unlawful search and seizure of personal items without a search warrant. Without this protection, people's homes or cars could be invaded at will by government officials looked for incriminating evidence which then could be used to accuse them.

The Fifth Amendment prohibits a person from being "twice put in jeopardy" for the same offense. This so-called "double jeopardy" clause mandates that all accusations against a person related to a particular crime must be decided in one single case, and cannot ever be raised again in a later case. The Fifth Amendment also grants protections against self-incrimination, meaning a person cannot be forced to testify against themselves. This "right against self incrimination" is sometimes called "pleading the fifth." The standard or burden to be proven in criminal cases is that conviction can only occur if the jury is convinced "beyond a reasonable doubt" that the accused person committed the crime. The mere fact that a person refuses to testify will not automatically lead to their conviction. In other words, silence is not sufficient evidence for conviction—there must be some actual, solid proof of the crime.

The Sixth Amendment has the most to say about rights of the criminally accused, and is entirely devoted to protecting these rights. It mandates that every person accused of a crime has the right to a speedy trial before an impartial jury of their peers. The accused must be fully informed of the crimes they are accused of and have the right to confront witnesses called against them. The accused also has the right to an attorney to help with their defense and the right to call witnesses to testify on their behalf.

Many of these rights are encapsulated in the "Miranda warning" which is derived from the 1966 Supreme Court case of *Miranda v. Arizona*. Mr. Miranda in that case was acquitted because he had not been adequately informed of his rights before being interrogated by the police. Since that time, police officers have been more aware of their duty to inform accused persons of their "Miranda rights" at the time of arrest. This includes the right to remain silent (to not testify against oneself according to the Fifth Amendment). If the accused person chooses not to be silent (to cooperate with the authorities) then anything said may later be used against them. The accused is also informed that they have the right to an attorney (according to the Sixth Amendment), and that they have the right for an attorney to be present during questioning. They are also told that if they do not have an attorney, one will be appointed for them.

Finally, the Eighth Amendment deals with punishment of the criminally accused. Authorities cannot require excessive bail of a person indicted or inflict "cruel and unusual punishment." Of course, one of the cruelest of punishments is to be left sitting in jail with no means to bring one's case to the judge. The criminally accused not only can call on rights derived from the Eighth Amendment to protect them from such a situation, but they can also rely on the Sixth Amendment's guarantee of a speedy trial and the promise in Article 1, Section 9 of the Constitution that "the privilege of the writ of habeas corpus shall not be suspended." This right to a writ of habeas corpus allows prisoners to file a request for judicial review of their case.

Other Important Rights

A few other rights from the Bill of Rights are also important and need to be understood. Among these are the right to bear arms from the Third Amendment, the right to compensation if private property from the Fifth Amendment, and the right to a jury trial. In civil cases this jury trial right is found in the Seventh Amendment and in criminal cases is found in Article III, Section 2 of the Constitution.

In recent years, the right to bear arms has been a hotly debated issue in the United States with passionate supporters on both sides of the issue. Notwithstanding this, the Supreme Court in the 2008 case of *District of Columbia v. Heller* affirmed the right of individuals to own and maintain guns in their home and struck down as unconstitutional certain parts of the federal Firearms Controls Regulations Act of 1975. The right to keep private guns was later "incorporated" through the Fourteenth Amendment as applicable to the states in the 2010 Supreme Court case of *McDonald v. Chicago.*

The right to compensation in the cases of government taking property for public use has a long history. When government needs property for public purposes, it has the power to "take" that property from private individuals, if necessary. Indeed, the private property owner cannot prevent such a "taking," but is entitled to a court hearing if he or she feels the government is not taking the property for a "public purpose," or is not paying adequate compensation for the land. Usually "takings" cases by the courts relate to taking of tangible, touchable land, but have sometimes also applied to circumstances where a government action has taken something intangible and caused economic harm to someone. For example, the Supreme Court stated in the landmark takings case of *Penn Central v. New York* that the "air rights" to build a 20 story building above Grand Central station could not be "taken", because the station was protected under New York City law which preserved the station as a historic landmark, and prohibited any building over the top of it.

The Seventh Amendment is unique in its specific mention of the "common law." The "common law" is the traditions and decisions handed down by the courts of England and the U.S. over a period of many years, in situations where the legislature has not passed a specific law that addresses an issue. Courts turn to the common law to help make their decisions only when they have no other applicable law.

The amendment has been used relating to the right of a jury trial in civil (non criminal) cases. A civil case is one in which there is no accusation of a crime, but two parties are disputing a "wrong" that they believe has been committed. This could be anything from a slip-and-fall at a grocery store that causes injury, because of a store's negligence, to a property or contract dispute in which two parties are fighting over who owns a certain piece of land. While a jury trial is guaranteed in criminal cases by Article III, Section 2 of the Constitution, it was considered important to guarantee a trial by jury in non-criminal disputes as well, as granted in the Seventh Amendment.

The Impact of the Fourteenth Amendment on the Constitutional Development of Rights and Liberties _____

It is state in Section 1 of the Fourteenth Amendment that "no state shall... deny to any person within its jurisdiction the equal protection of the laws." The Fourteenth Amendment, passed in 1868 as one of the post Civil War Amendments, is unique among all the amendments to that point, since it was the first to use the specific language "no state shall ..." All of the prior amendments had applied to acts of Congress or the federal government, and none had used this language to apply directly to the states.

It should be noted however that Article I, Section 10 of the Constitution does contain the language "no state shall ..." A number of prohibitions are then listed in this section, including a prohibition of any state passing an "ex post facto" law (a law which makes a past act a criminal offense) or any law "impairing" a contractual obligation. Hence, the idea that a provision in the federal Constitution could apply directly to the states was not new; rather, the prior understanding was that only the items listed in Article I, Section 10 applied directly on the states, and everything else (including all of the Bill of Rights) applied only to the federal government. Indeed, the Supreme Court in the 1833 case of *Barron v. Baltimore* specifically said that the federal Bill of Rights applied only to the federal government.

This all changed with the advent of the "incorporation doctrine." Starting with the 1897 case of Chicago, Burlington and *Quincy Railroad v. City of Chicago*, the Supreme Court began "incorporating" some of the rights protections in the federal Bill of Rights (the first ten amendments) directly onto the states. The amendment "incorporated" in the 1897 Chicago case was the Fifth Amendment and its "just compensation clause," when private railroad property was taken by the City of Chicago as part of the widening of one of its streets.

Since that time a number of the rights derived from the federal Bill of Rights have been "incorporated" as applying directly to the states. While not all rights have been "incorporated," it is generally assumed that all of them could be and most of the important ones have been. For example, in 1925 in the case of *Gitlow v. New York*, the Supreme Court said that the guarantee of free speech in the First Amendment cannot be violated by the states, thereby "incorporating" this amendment. The process of "incorporation" has continued on occasions over the years as more and more of the Bill of Rights guarantees have become applicable to the states. As discussed earlier, most recently the Third Amendment's guarantee of the right to bear arms was "incorporated" as being directly applicable to the states in the 2010 Supreme Court case of *McDonald v. Chicago*.

It should be noted that in most states, the state Constitution and state Bill of Rights contain very similar rights protection to those in the federal Bill of Rights. While this suggests that "incorporating" the Bill of Rights protections does not seem to be necessary, the "incorporation doctrine" has the effect of unifying the interpretation of rights protections across the country as a whole. This is particularly true since the various bills of rights in the states do not all use the same language and would not necessarily all be interpreted the same way. By applying the federal Bill of Rights provisions directly to the states, a single, federal interpretation of rights holds sway, which leads to greater consistency and ease of interpretation in rights disputes.

The impact of the Fourteenth Amendment on the development of rights and liberties due to the "incorporation doctrine" cannot be overstated. Perhaps the clearest example of this is also the most controversial today - the right of privacy, as mentioned above. It is noteworthy that the Bill of Rights does not use the words "right of privacy," and indeed there is no use of these words anywhere in the first ten amendments. While the Ninth Amendment was crafted by the founders to cover those rights which are not specifically listed in the Bill of Rights, the U.S. Supreme Court in the cases where it has gradually come to recognize the "right of privacy" has done so based primarily on the equal protection and due process clauses of the Fourteenth Amendment. While the court has sometimes referenced the Ninth Amendment, it has usually concluded that it is unclear what unlisted rights the Ninth Amendment was meant to include. However, the due process and equal protection clauses of the Fourteenth Amendment, which are directly applicable to the states, include the general concept of a right of privacy for all.

Not everyone has agreed with this characterization of course. To this day, the most controversial rights cases decided by the Supreme Court are the sexually oriented "right of privacy" cases that deal with such topics as gay marriage or abortion. Many people maintain that the Supreme Court has invaded the province of the legislative branch in crafting moral and social policy for the country at large. They decry "Judicial Activism," in which the Supreme Court has exercised powers beyond what it should. Others support the positions assumed by the Supreme Court as the branch of government that acts to protect the rights of the people. This is a debate not likely to be concluded anytime soon.

Summary

Americans love their rights. Throughout the world, the United States and its citizens have the reputation of being a "rights-loving" people, who are seemingly obsessed with rights and the protection of their rights. Many leaders of other nations look on this obsession with disdain. However, people throughout the world and across the decades have been attracted to come to America, where they know they will be protected in their rights.

The civil liberties of the people are mostly encapsulated in the Bill of Rights of the federal Constitution. While each state has its own Bill of Rights, which usually tends to mirror the federal version, it is almost always the federal Bill of Rights that gains attention today. This is largely due to the "incorporation doctrine" of the last 100 years, whereby the Supreme Court has gradually incorporated most of the federal Bill of Rights to apply directly to the states under the Fourteenth Amendment.

Civil rights are a subset of civil liberties. The idea behind the protection of civil rights is that there are certain groups who have been denied their rights and the equal protection of the laws in the United States. These groups have had to fight for recognition of their basic civil rights. The groups usually identified as having suffered from unjust discrimination are blacks and women, but other groups are also beneficiaries of the civil rights movement which equalized the treatment of all persons in the country, such as disabled persons, older persons, Hispanics and Native Americans.

Since rights continue to be so fundamentally cherished today, it is essential to understand what these rights are, and where they are described. It is also important to know how the Supreme Court has interpreted these rights in many landmark rights cases over the years. The rights protections in the amendments to the U.S. Constitution continue to be a bastion of protection in a world where, all too often, rights are still ignored.

SECTION V:
Practice Test One

Time – 45 minutes
60 Questions

Directions: Each of the questions or incomplete statements below is followed by five suggested answers or explanations. Select the one that is BEST in each case.

1. Which of the following two essential powers were not given to the federal government by the Articles of Confederation and were largely the reason why a new constitutional convention was called?

    (A) The power to declare war and the power to regulate commerce

    (B) The power to fix weights and measures and the power to tax

    (C) The power to make foreign treaties and the power to declare war

    (D) The power to regulate commerce and the power to tax

    (E) The power to borrow money and the power to tax

2. The due process clause is found in which of the following amendments?

    (A) The Fifth and the Fourteenth

    (B) The Sixth and the Fourteenth

    (C) The Second and the Tenth

    (D) The First and the Fifteenth

    (E) The Fourth and the Fifteenth

3. Which of the following is not true of the Fourteenth Amendment?

    (A) It defines whether a person born in the United States is a citizen.

    (B) It says the U.S. government will not pay any claim for loss of a slave.

    (C) It mentions the denial of due process in respect to life, liberty or property.

    (D) It says the federal government cannot deny equal protection of the law.

    (E) It mentions the privileges and immunities of citizens.

4. **Which of the following rights was not specifically protected in either the body of the Constitution or an amendment to the Constitution?**

    (A) The right against double jeopardy, which means an individual cannot be tried twice for the same crime

    (B) The right to a speedy trial

    (C) The right to confront witnesses against the accused

    (D) The right to the presumption that a person is innocent until proven guilty

    (E) The right of women to vote

5. **The Constitution provides for impeachment as follows:**

    (A) The House of Representatives shall initiate the process, and the Supreme Court will hold the actual impeachment trial; conviction requires a two-thirds vote.

    (B) The Senate shall initiate the process, and the House of Representatives will hold the actual impeachment trial; conviction requires a two-thirds vote.

    (C) The Supreme Court shall initiate the process, and both houses of Congress will hold the actual impeachment trial; conviction requires a two-thirds vote of each house.

    (D) The House of Representatives shall initiate the process, and the Senate will hold the actual impeachment trial; conviction requires a two-thirds vote.

    (E) The details of impeachment are not defined in the Constitution, but are set by laws passed by Congress.

6. **The best description of public opinion is that it is**

    (A) The distribution of the public expression of the will of the people.

    (B) The distribution of the population's beliefs about politics and policy issues.

    (C) The distribution of the media's reflection of public attitudes.

    (D) The distribution of the public expression of voter attitudes.

    (E) The distribution of random samples of attitudes.

7. **Which of the following is the most common form of political participation in the United States?**

    (A) Expressing one's ideas in a public opinion poll

    (B) Participating in a mass demonstration

    (C) Voting in a presidential election

    (D) Contacting a public official regarding a public issue

    (E) Joining an interest group for the purpose of influencing legislation

8. **Which of the following is a major weakness of public opinion polls?**

    (A) Polls only measure the opinions of political elites.

    (B) Polls cannot measure the intensity of feelings about issues.

    (C) Polls are so fraught with error that their results are nearly meaningless.

    (D) The opinions of the poor and politically active individuals are overrepresented.

    (E) All of the above.

9. **Liberals are likely to support all of the following EXCEPT**

    (A) Freedom of choice in abortions.

    (B) Government regulation.

    (C) Increased taxes on the rich.

    (D) Social welfare programs.

    (E) Prayer in schools.

10. **The "gender gap" refers to the idea that women**

    (A) Are denied equal protection of the law in economic matters in the United States.

    (B) Cannot work in all combat roles in the military.

    (C) Are more likely to vote for Democrats than are men.

    (D) Are proportionally under-represented among members of Congress.

    (E) Live on average longer than men, affecting their Social Security costs.

11. **Which of the following would older Americans be more likely to support than younger Americans?**

(A) Protection of Social Security

(B) Decreased military spending

(C) Gays serving in the military

(D) Increased spending on education

(E) Increased spending on environmental protection

12. **Political socialization is the process by which**

(A) The use of private property is regulated by the government.

(B) Governments communicate with each other.

(C) Public attitudes towards government are measured and reported.

(D) Political values are passed to the next generation.

(E) Children are trained for successful occupations.

13. **Which of the following is not a core value of United States political culture?**

(A) Legal equality

(B) Political equality

(C) Economic equality

(D) Freedom of religion

(E) Freedom of speech

14. **Which of the following defines and describes the ideals and positions of a political party?**

(A) The national committee

(B) The state level committees

(C) The local party level of committees

(D) The party platform

(E) The presidential candidates

15. **Which of the following statements characterizes George Washington's thoughts about political parties?**

    (A) The national government should be strong and active.

    (B) The government should be focused on states' rights.

    (C) Political parties were a threat to national unity.

    (D) Government should remain small.

    (E) Government should be limited.

16. **Which of the following helped shape the ideologies of the Republicans and Democrats and the development of those two political parties?**

    (A) The War of 1812

    (B) The Great Depression

    (C) The American Revolution

    (D) World War I

    (E) World War II

17. **Which type of media was the dominant form of media in the 1800s and early 1900s?**

    (A) Radio

    (B) Print

    (C) Billboards

    (D) Television

    (E) Social media

18. **What group from the media worked to expose injustices and political corruption during the Progressive Era?**

   (A) Propagandists

   (B) Yellow journalists

   (C) Writers of the Federalist Papers

   (D) Muckrakers

   (E) Presidential candidates

19. **How was mass media used during the 1960 campaign and election?**

   (A) To televise the Republican convention that nominated Dwight Eisenhower

   (B) To televise the Democratic convention that nominated Adlai Stevenson

   (C) To broadcast up-to-date information about the Vietnam War

   (D) To present news coverage on the attempted assassination of Ronald Reagan

   (E) To present the debates between John Kennedy and Richard Nixon

20. **During the 2016 presidential debates, moderators asked people to send them questions to ask the candidates during the debates. What type of media is an example of this process?**

   (A) Social media

   (B) Print media

   (C) Mass media

   (D) Broadcast media

   (E) Political media

21. **What majority is needed to override a presidential veto?**

   (A) Simple

   (B) Two-thirds

   (C) Three-fifths

   (D) Three-fourths

   (E) Four-fifths

22. What is the meaning of the term "impeach"?

(A) To bring charges against

(B) To remove from office

(C) To re-elect an official

(D) To override a presidential veto

(E) To arrest an official

23. Why was the Election of 1800 significant?

(A) John Adams became president.

(B) Thomas Jefferson became president after an orderly transition.

(C) John Quincy Adams became the first president to be a member of one family.

(D) James Monroe announced the Monroe Doctrine.

(E) James Madison was the first president who had signed the Constitution.

24. How many presidents have been impeached?

(A) None

(B) One

(C) Two

(D) Three

(E) Four

25. Which president served more than two terms?

(A) Theodore Roosevelt

(B) Franklin Roosevelt

(C) Harry Truman

(D) Jimmy Carter

(E) William Clinton

26. **Which U.S. Supreme Court case established the doctrine of judicial review?**

    (A) *McCulloch v. Maryland*

    (B) *Brown v. Board of Education*

    (C) The Dred Scott decision

    (D) *Plessy v. Ferguson*

    (E) *Marbury v. Madison*

27. **Which president tried to "pack" the Supreme Court?**

    (A) Theodore Roosevelt

    (B) Harry Truman

    (C) Franklin Roosevelt

    (D) Thomas Jefferson

    (E) William Clinton

28. **Which is the only court referred to in the Constitution?**

    (A) State trial court

    (B) U.S. Supreme Court

    (C) State Supreme Court

    (D) Federal District Court

    (E) U.S. Circuit Court of Appeal

29. **What does the term "inferior" court mean?**

    (A) A court that can only hear cases involving small claims

    (B) A court that can only hear cases involving family law and probate matters

    (C) A bankruptcy court

    (D) A court that is lower than the U.S. Supreme Court

    (E) A court that hears patents and copyrights

30. What does the term "constitutional court" mean?

(A) A court that can only hear cases involving the Constitution

(B) A court that has been set up for a special purpose

(C) A court whose judges have fixed terms of office

(D) A court that has a specific number of judges

(E) A court that exercises powers found in Article III of the Constitution

31. How do judges become constitutional court judges?

(A) They are nominated by the President and approved by the Senate.

(B) They are nominated by members of the House of Representative from their "home districts" and approved by the President.

(C) They are nominated by the Senate and approved by the President.

(D) They are nominated by the Senate and approved by the House of Representatives.

(E) They are nominated by the President and approved by the existing judges of the court to which they are nominated.

32. What is a writ of certiorari?

(A) A written decision by a court

(B) A written order

(C) A written request for a court to hear a case

(D) A written certification explaining a court decision

(E) A writing that presents the pleadings of one of the parties in a case

33. If a case is remanded, what is the meaning of "remand?"

(A) Reversed

(B) Affirmed

(C) Judges agree for different reasons

(D) To send back

(E) To dispose of

34. **What does "stare decisis" mean?**

 (A) Follow earlier cases

 (B) Decide to reverse

 (C) Decide to affirm

 (D) Let the decision stand

 (E) Concurring decision

35. **Which was the first independent regulatory commission?**

 (A) Interstate Commerce Commission

 (B) Federal Trade Commission

 (C) Consumer Products Division

 (D) Federal Aviation Agency

 (E) Department of Revenue

36. **During what time period was the largest growth of the bureaucracy?**

 (A) 880–1890

 (B) 890–1930

 (C) 930–1945

 (D) 945–1960

 (E) 960–1990

37. **What is the highest appellate court in the United States?**

 (A) National Court of Appeals

 (B) Circuit Court

 (C) District Court

 (D) Supreme Court

 (E) Court of Claims

38. Which is a shared power of the federal and state governments?

(A) The power to declare war

(B) The power to build roads

(C) The power to coin money

(D) The power to regulate interstate trade

(E) The power to educate

39. What was an outcome of the Great Compromise in the framing of the Constitution?

(A) It provided for two year terms for the House of Representatives but made the Senate six year terms.

(B) Also known as the three-fifths compromise, this determined how to count slaves in determining the population of the states.

(C) It delegated all powers to the states not explicitly granted to the federal government in the Constitution.

(D) It outlined the country's plans for expansion.

(E) It guaranteed states equal representation in the Senate, but based representation on proportional population in the House of Representatives.

40. Which of the following was referred to as "a league of friendship?"

(A) The Constitution

(B) The Virginia Plan

(C) The New Jersey Plan

(D) The Connecticut Plan

(E) The Articles of Confederation

41. **Which president is noted for using the "spoils system"?**

   (A) Andrew Johnson

   (B) Andrew Jackson

   (C) Zachary Taylor

   (D) George Washington

   (E) Theodore Roosevelt

42. **Which is the trial court at the federal level?**

   (A) Circuit Court

   (B) District Court

   (C) Supreme Court

   (D) Court of Claims

   (E) Bankruptcy Court

43. **Which Amendment provides for a "two-term" president?**

   (A) Twenty-second

   (B) Twenty-third

   (C) Twenty-fourth

   (D) Twenty-fifth

   (E) Twenty-sixth

44. **The United States legislature is bicameral, which means _____.**

   (A) It consists of several houses

   (B) It consists of two houses

   (C) The legislature meets twice a year

   (D) The legislature meets every other year

   (E) It has an upper house and a lower house

45. Before the Seventeenth Amendment, how were U.S. Senators chosen?

(A) By the House of Representatives

(B) By the people

(C) By the state legislatures

(D) By the courts

(E) By the President

46. A Supreme Court that shows a willingness to change public policy and alter judicial precedent is engaging in

(A) Due process

(B) Judicial restraint

(C) Judicial activism

(D) Judicial review

(E) Ex post facto lawmaking

47. Which of the following institutions established in the Constitution make public policy?

(A) The Senate, the president, and political parties.

(B) The Congress, the president, and the courts.

(C) The Congress, the courts, and the military.

(D) The Congress, the president, and the military.

(E) The Congress, the president, and the bureaucracy.

48. Which of the following best defines a set of institutions linking government, politics, and public policy?

(A) An educational system

(B) A political system

(C) A social system

(D) An economic system

(E) A socioeconomic system

49. **Which of the following best illustrates a use of the "elastic clause"?**

   (A)   The Supreme Court allows a lower court ruling to stand by refusing to hear
         an appeal.

   (B)   A congressional committee prevents the full chamber from voting on legislation
         by delaying its report.

   (C)   Congress passes legislation establishing a national speed limit.

   (D)   A member of the House of Representatives introduces a bill to increase federal
         income tax rates.

   (E)   A governor issues an executive order requiring all state employees to submit to
         drug testing.

50. **The programs of the New Deal are examples of**

   (A)   The safety net

   (B)   The state sponsored era

   (C)   The federal era

   (D)   Grant blocks to states

   (E)   The New Federalism

51. **The main purpose of the National Environmental Policy Act was to**

   (A)   Require government agencies to issue environmental impact statements if their
         policies would have a negative impact on the environment

   (B)   Require the Environmental Protection Agency to monitor clean air standards

   (C)   Establish clean water standards

   (D)   Establish a superfund to clean up environmental abuses

   (E)   Require the Department of the Interior to establish criteria for ocean dumping

52. **All of the following choices represent features of the Clean Air Act of 1990 EXCEPT that**

    (A) It established standards to protect the ozone layer.

    (B) It set overall carbon dioxide standards.

    (C) It established standards to attack the acid rain problem.

    (D) It directed factories to reduce emissions.

    (E) It directed auto manufacturers to sell electric cars.

53. **The role of a conference committee in Congress is to**

    (A) Hold hearings on proposed legislation.

    (B) Oversee the actions of the executive branch of the government.

    (C) Decide which bills should be considered by the full Senate.

    (D) Conduct hearings that make information available to the public.

    (E) Reconcile differences in bills passed by the House and Senate.

54. **Supreme Court justices were given tenure subject to good behavior by the framers of the Constitution in order to ensure that**

    (A) Justices are free from direct political pressures.

    (B) Justices remain accountable to the public.

    (C) Justices are encouraged to make politically popular decisions.

    (D) Cooperation between the judicial and legislative branches is assured.

    (E) Presidents are encouraged to seek younger nominees for the Supreme Court.

55. **The committee system is more important in the House than in the Senate because**

   (A)   The seniority system plays no role in the House and therefore committees must play a larger role.

   (B)   The Constitution mandates the committee structure in the House.

   (C)   Committee members are appointed by the President.

   (D)   The House is so large that more work can be accomplished in committees than on the floor.

   (E)   The majority party in the House prefers to give priority to the work of the committees.

56. **Which of the following is NOT true of the privilege of habeas corpus?**

   (A)   It is a right, which can prevent unlawful arrest.

   (B)   It is a right that can be suspended in times of rebellion or threats to public safety.

   (C)   It is a right, which can only be exercised after criminal conviction.

   (D)   It is a right which can prevent ongoing unlawful imprisonment.

   (E)   It is intended to safeguard individual freedom against arbitrary and lawless state action.

57. **Which of the following relates most directly to the admissibility of wrongly obtained evidence in court?**

   (A)   The right against self-incrimination

   (B)   The right against double jeopardy

   (C)   Amicus curiae

   (D)   The exclusionary rule

   (E)   The Miranda warning

58. The right of a convicted felon to vote in the United States is

(A) Guaranteed by the Fourteenth Amendment.

(B) Denied by the Twenty-fourth Amendment.

(C) A matter of state law, which varies from state to state.

(D) Not addressed in either federal or state law.

(E) Only allowed for "lesser" felonies.

59. Which of the following relates to making an action criminal after it was committed?

(A) A bill of attainder

(B) Self incrimination

(C) Ex post facto law

(D) Double jeopardy

(E) Cruel and unusual punishment

60. The "Lemon Test" is

(A) A test followed by the Supreme Court when reviewing legislation concerning free speech.

(B) A test followed by the Supreme Court when reviewing legislation concerning religion.

(C) A test followed by the Supreme Court when reviewing legislation concerning the right to bear arms.

(D) A test followed by the Supreme Court when reviewing legislation concerning government "takings."

(E) A test followed by the Supreme Court when reviewing whether to take a case regarding automobiles.

Section II: Free Response Questions

Time – 1 hour and 40 minutes (100 minutes)

Directions: You have 100 minutes to answer all four of the following questions. Unless the directions indicate otherwise, respond to all parts of all four questions. It is suggested that you take a few minutes to plan and outline each answer. Spend approximately one-fourth of your time (25 minutes) on each question. In your response, use substantive examples where appropriate. Make certain to number each of your answers as the question is numbered below.

1. **Interest groups play political roles in the democratic process.**

   a. How are interest groups formed? How are they structured?

   b. Discuss the outcome/result of different types of representation of interests.

   c. Describe some types of interest groups.

2. Checks and balances serve an important purpose in government.

a. Why did the framers of the Constitution include checks and balances?

b. What are examples of checks each branch of government has on the other branch?

c. What balance(s) result from the checks?

3. Assume for a moment that you are from the state of _____, the year is 1789, and you have been given the task of creating a list of proposed rights to be sent to James Madison, who will be taking suggestions from all the states and compiling a single list of rights to be proposed to Congress. However, also assume that you have the benefit of knowing the history (especially of Supreme Court decisions) that has taken place in the United States between 1789 and the present day.

a. Please describe the rights you would include on your list. Which would you list first?

b. Please indicate any added descriptive terminology or definitions you would give to your listed rights based on the history of the U.S. since 1789. Specifically, are there words you would use to clarify your intended meaning, words you would avoid using, or that you would define differently if you did use them? Where possible, give reasons for your changes in wording.

4. **The U.S. Congress and the President together have the power to enact federal law. Federal bureaucratic agencies have the responsibility to execute federal law. However, in the carrying out of these laws, federal agencies have policy-making discretion.**

a. Explain two reasons why Congress gives federal agencies policy-making discretion in executing federal laws.

b. Choose one of the bureaucratic agencies listed below. Identify the policy area over which it exercises policy-making discretion AND give one specific example of how it exercises that discretion.

> Environmental Protection Agency (EPA)
> Federal Communications Commission (FCC)
> Federal Reserve Board

c. Describe two ways in which Congress ensures that federal agencies follow legislative intent.

Section I: Multiple Choice Answer Sheet

1. Ⓐ Ⓑ Ⓒ Ⓓ Ⓔ
2. Ⓐ Ⓑ Ⓒ Ⓓ Ⓔ
3. Ⓐ Ⓑ Ⓒ Ⓓ Ⓔ
4. Ⓐ Ⓑ Ⓒ Ⓓ Ⓔ
5. Ⓐ Ⓑ Ⓒ Ⓓ Ⓔ
6. Ⓐ Ⓑ Ⓒ Ⓓ Ⓔ
7. Ⓐ Ⓑ Ⓒ Ⓓ Ⓔ
8. Ⓐ Ⓑ Ⓒ Ⓓ Ⓔ
9. Ⓐ Ⓑ Ⓒ Ⓓ Ⓔ
10. Ⓐ Ⓑ Ⓒ Ⓓ Ⓔ
11. Ⓐ Ⓑ Ⓒ Ⓓ Ⓔ
12. Ⓐ Ⓑ Ⓒ Ⓓ Ⓔ
13. Ⓐ Ⓑ Ⓒ Ⓓ Ⓔ
14. Ⓐ Ⓑ Ⓒ Ⓓ Ⓔ
15. Ⓐ Ⓑ Ⓒ Ⓓ Ⓔ
16. Ⓐ Ⓑ Ⓒ Ⓓ Ⓔ
17. Ⓐ Ⓑ Ⓒ Ⓓ Ⓔ
18. Ⓐ Ⓑ Ⓒ Ⓓ Ⓔ
19. Ⓐ Ⓑ Ⓒ Ⓓ Ⓔ
20. Ⓐ Ⓑ Ⓒ Ⓓ Ⓔ

21. Ⓐ Ⓑ Ⓒ Ⓓ Ⓔ
22. Ⓐ Ⓑ Ⓒ Ⓓ Ⓔ
23. Ⓐ Ⓑ Ⓒ Ⓓ Ⓔ
24. Ⓐ Ⓑ Ⓒ Ⓓ Ⓔ
25. Ⓐ Ⓑ Ⓒ Ⓓ Ⓔ
26. Ⓐ Ⓑ Ⓒ Ⓓ Ⓔ
27. Ⓐ Ⓑ Ⓒ Ⓓ Ⓔ
28. Ⓐ Ⓑ Ⓒ Ⓓ Ⓔ
29. Ⓐ Ⓑ Ⓒ Ⓓ Ⓔ
30. Ⓐ Ⓑ Ⓒ Ⓓ Ⓔ
31. Ⓐ Ⓑ Ⓒ Ⓓ Ⓔ
32. Ⓐ Ⓑ Ⓒ Ⓓ Ⓔ
33. Ⓐ Ⓑ Ⓒ Ⓓ Ⓔ
34. Ⓐ Ⓑ Ⓒ Ⓓ Ⓔ
35. Ⓐ Ⓑ Ⓒ Ⓓ Ⓔ
36. Ⓐ Ⓑ Ⓒ Ⓓ Ⓔ
37. Ⓐ Ⓑ Ⓒ Ⓓ Ⓔ
38. Ⓐ Ⓑ Ⓒ Ⓓ Ⓔ
39. Ⓐ Ⓑ Ⓒ Ⓓ Ⓔ
40. Ⓐ Ⓑ Ⓒ Ⓓ Ⓔ

41. Ⓐ Ⓑ Ⓒ Ⓓ Ⓔ
42. Ⓐ Ⓑ Ⓒ Ⓓ Ⓔ
43. Ⓐ Ⓑ Ⓒ Ⓓ Ⓔ
44. Ⓐ Ⓑ Ⓒ Ⓓ Ⓔ
45. Ⓐ Ⓑ Ⓒ Ⓓ Ⓔ
46. Ⓐ Ⓑ Ⓒ Ⓓ Ⓔ
47. Ⓐ Ⓑ Ⓒ Ⓓ Ⓔ
48. Ⓐ Ⓑ Ⓒ Ⓓ Ⓔ
49. Ⓐ Ⓑ Ⓒ Ⓓ Ⓔ
50. Ⓐ Ⓑ Ⓒ Ⓓ Ⓔ
51. Ⓐ Ⓑ Ⓒ Ⓓ Ⓔ
52. Ⓐ Ⓑ Ⓒ Ⓓ Ⓔ
53. Ⓐ Ⓑ Ⓒ Ⓓ Ⓔ
54. Ⓐ Ⓑ Ⓒ Ⓓ Ⓔ
55. Ⓐ Ⓑ Ⓒ Ⓓ Ⓔ
56. Ⓐ Ⓑ Ⓒ Ⓓ Ⓔ
57. Ⓐ Ⓑ Ⓒ Ⓓ Ⓔ
58. Ⓐ Ⓑ Ⓒ Ⓓ Ⓔ
59. Ⓐ Ⓑ Ⓒ Ⓓ Ⓔ
60. Ⓐ Ⓑ Ⓒ Ⓓ Ⓔ

Section I: Multiple Choice Answer Key

Question Number	Correct Answer	Question Number	Correct Answer	Question Number	Correct Answer
1.	D	21.	B	41.	B
2.	A	22.	A	42.	B
3.	D	23.	B	43.	A
4.	D	24.	C	44.	B
5.	D	25.	B	45.	C
6.	B	26.	E	46.	C
7.	C	27.	C	47.	B
8.	B	28.	B	48.	B
9.	E	29.	D	49.	C
10.	C	30.	E	50.	A
11.	A	31.	A	51.	A
12.	D	32.	C	52.	E
13.	C	33.	D	53.	E
14.	D	34.	D	54.	A
15.	C	35.	A	55.	D
16.	B	36.	C	56.	A
17.	B	37.	D	57.	D
18.	D	38.	B	58.	C
19.	E	39.	E	59.	C
20.	A	40.	E	60.	B

Section I: Multiple Choice Explanations _____

1. **Which of the following two essential powers were not given to the federal government by the Articles of Confederation and were largely the reason why a new constitutional convention was called?**

   (A) The power to declare war and the power to regulate commerce

   (B) The power to fix weights and measures and the power to tax

   (C) The power to make foreign treaties and the power to declare war

   (D) The power to regulate commerce and the power to tax

   (E) The power to borrow money and the power to tax

   Answer: D.
   The power to regulate commerce and the power to tax. Article IX of the Articles of Confederation denies Congress the power to regulate commerce contrary to the wishes of the states. Article VIII states that taxes are to be paid by the states according to a levy suggested by the Congress. On the other hand, Article IX grants Congress the power to declare war, borrow money and make treaties with the consent of the nine states, and to fix weights and measures throughout the country.

2. **The due process clause is found in which of the following amendments?**

   (A) The Fifth and the Fourteenth

   (B) The Sixth and the Fourteenth

   (C) The Second and the Tenth

   (D) The First and the Fifteenth

   (E) The Fourth and the Fifteenth

   Answer: A.
   The Fifth and the Fourteenth. Due process is mentioned only twice in the Constitution and only in amendments, the Fifth and Fourteenth Amendments.

3. **Which of the following is not true of the Fourteenth Amendment?**

(A) It defines whether a person born in the United States is a citizen.

(B) It says the U.S. government will not pay any claim for loss of a slave.

(C) It mentions the denial of due process in respect to life, liberty or property.

(D) It says the federal government cannot deny equal protection of the law.

(E) It mentions the privileges and immunities of citizens.

Answer: D.

It says the federal government cannot deny equal protection of the law. The wording of the amendment only says that States may not deny equal protection. It does not say this applies also to the federal government. All the other provisions are found in the amendment.

4. **Which of the following rights was not specifically protected in either the body of the Constitution or an amendment to the Constitution?**

(A) The right against double jeopardy, which means an individual cannot be tried twice for the same crime

(B) The right to a speedy trial

(C) The right to confront witnesses against the accused

(D) The right to the presumption that a person is innocent until proven guilty

(E) The right of women to vote

Answer: D.

The right to the presumption that a person is innocent until proven guilty. The right against double jeopardy is found in the Fifth Amendment. The right to a speedy trial and to confront witnesses is found in the Sixth Amendment. A woman's right to vote is found in the Nineteenth Amendment. The presumption of innocence is stated nowhere in the Constitution or its amendments. It has subsequently been found in the case of *Coffin v. United States*, 156 U.S. 432 (1895).

5. The Constitution provides for impeachment as follows:

(A) The House of Representatives shall initiate the process, and the Supreme Court will hold the actual impeachment trial; conviction requires a two-thirds vote.

(B) The Senate shall initiate the process, and the House of Representatives will hold the actual impeachment trial; conviction requires a two-thirds vote.

(C) The Supreme Court shall initiate the process, and both houses of Congress will hold the actual impeachment trial; conviction requires a two-thirds vote of each house.

(D) The House of Representatives shall initiate the process, and the Senate will hold the actual impeachment trial; conviction requires a two-thirds vote.

(E) The details of impeachment are not defined in the Constitution, but are set by laws passed by Congress.

Answer: D.
The House of Representatives shall initiate the process, and the Senate will hold the actual impeachment trial; conviction requires a two-thirds vote. The very last line of Article I section 2 states that the House of Representatives "shall have the sole power of impeachment." Article I section 3 states that "the Senate shall have the sole power to try all impeachments," after which the procedure they are to follow is given, including the requirement that conviction be by two-thirds vote.

6. The best description of public opinion is that it is

(A) The distribution of the public expression of the will of the people.

(B) The distribution of the population's beliefs about politics and policy issues.

(C) The distribution of the media's reflection of public attitudes.

(D) The distribution of the public expression of voter attitudes.

(E) The distribution of random samples of attitudes.

Answer: B.
The distribution of the population's beliefs about politics and policy issues. Public opinion as it relates to government and politics means that some means were exercised to determine the leanings or opinions of the citizens. It is not the will of the people, it is not about the media or voter attitudes, or about random samples. When public opinion is measured, it is important to ensure a representative and random sample, but public opinion is not about random samples, per se.

7. **Which of the following is the most common form of political participation in the United States?**

(A) Expressing one's ideas in a public opinion poll

(B) Participating in a mass demonstration

(C) Voting in a presidential election

(D) Contacting a public official regarding a public issue

(E) Joining an interest group for the purpose of influencing legislation

Answer: C.

Voting in a presidential election. Statistically, the most common form of political participation in the United States is voting in a presidential election. The estimated turn out as a percent of eligible voters in 2000 was 54.2%; in 2004 was 60.4%; 2008 was 62.3%; and 2012 was 57.5%.

8. **Which of the following is a major weakness of public opinion polls?**

(A) Polls only measure the opinions of political elites.

(B) Polls cannot measure the intensity of feelings about issues.

(C) Polls are so fraught with error that their results are nearly meaningless.

(D) The opinions of the poor and politically active individuals are overrepresented.

(E) All of the above.

Answer: B.

Polls cannot measure the intensity of feelings about issues. While polls can capture a person's sentiment of an issue, they cannot capture the intensity of that sentiment.

9. **Liberals are likely to support all of the following EXCEPT**

(A) Freedom of choice in abortions.

(B) Government regulation.

(C) Increased taxes on the rich.

(D) Social welfare programs.

(E) Prayer in schools.

Answer: E.

Prayer in schools. Liberals would support all of the other choices, except prayer in schools, especially public (or government) sponsored schools. Prayer in schools would find more support among conservatives.

10. **The "gender gap" refers to the idea that women**

(A) Are denied equal protection of the law in economic matters in the United States.

(B) Cannot work in all combat roles in the military.

(C) Are more likely to vote for Democrats than are men.

(D) Are proportionally under-represented among members of Congress.

(E) Live on average longer than men, affecting their Social Security costs.

Answer: C.

Are more likely to vote for Democrats than are men. Gender gap does not refer to the protection of law, the military, the Congress or life expectancy. It was coined in reference to the fact that since 1980 women tended to be more supportive of Democrats than have men, and this trend is especially strong among unmarried women.

11. **Which of the following would older Americans be more likely to support than younger Americans?**

(A) Protection of Social Security

(B) Decreased military spending

(C) Gays serving in the military

(D) Increased spending on education

(E) Increased spending on environmental protection

Answer: A.

Protection of Social Security. Older voters tend to be more supportive of social security benefits, while younger voters have tended to focus on social issues, education and the environment.

12. Political socialization is the process by which

(A) The use of private property is regulated by the government.

(B) Governments communicate with each other.

(C) Public attitudes towards government are measured and reported.

(D) Political values are passed to the next generation.

(E) Children are trained for successful occupations.

Answer: D.

Political values are passed to the next generation. The socialization that occurs between families, communities, and peers is the way by which political values and leanings are passed to successive generations.

13. Which of the following is not a core value of United States political culture?

(A) Legal equality

(B) Political equality

(C) Economic equality

(D) Freedom of religion

(E) Freedom of speech

Answer: C.

Economic equality. Economic equality is not guaranteed by any legal document such as the Constitution, federal or state laws. In a capitalist economy like the United States, the economic wellbeing of an individual is incumbent on oneself.

14. Which of the following defines and describes the ideals and positions of a political party?

(A) The national committee

(B) The state level committees

(C) The local party level of committees

(D) The party platform

(E) The presidential candidates

Answer: D.

The party platform. The national committee creates the document, called the party platform, which defines and describes the ideals and positions of the political party.

15. **Which of the following statements characterizes George Washington's thoughts about political parties?**

   (A)   The national government should be strong and active.

   (B)   The government should be focused on states' rights.

   (C)   Political parties were a threat to national unity.

   (D)   Government should remain small.

   (E)   Government should be limited.

Answer: C.

Political parties were a threat to national unity. George Washington believed political parties were a threat to national unity and popular government. The Federalists believed in a strong and active government. The Democratic-Republicans believed in smaller, limited government in favor of states' rights.

16. **Which of the following helped shape the ideologies of the Republicans and Democrats and the development of those two political parties?**

   (A)   The War of 1812

   (B)   The Great Depression

   (C)   The American Revolution

   (D)   World War I

   (E)   World War II

Answer: B.

The Great Depression. The issue of slavery helped the development of the two main political parties and the Depression and New Deal helped shape ideologies of the Republicans and Democrats.

17. **Which type of media was the dominant form of media in the 1800s and early 1900s?**

    (A) Radio

    (B) Print

    (C) Billboards

    (D) Television

    (E) Social media

Answer: B.

Print. Print media includes books, magazines, and newspapers. It also includes newsletters and anything that is published on paper. The reason that print media became the dominant form of media is that the newspapers used the telegraph to receive a supply of news and then used the printing presses to distribute news from all over the world. Print media dominated the media scene before the Internet and World Wide Web became an important factor in the lives of people throughout the world.

18. **What group from the media worked to expose injustices and political corruption during the Progressive Era?**

    (A) Propagandists

    (B) Yellow journalists

    (C) Writers of the Federalist Papers

    (D) Muckrakers

    (E) Presidential candidates

Answer: D.

Muckrakers. The Muckrakers were writers such as Ida Tarbell and Upton Sinclair who exposed the evils of society, the injustices, and political corruption during the period from the late 1800s to the early 1900s. These writers were known as 'muckrakers' because they dug up muck/dirt about business conditions and corruption. Ida Tarbell, for example attacked the business trusts, and Upton Sinclair wrote The Jungle, a book about the mistreatment of workers in the meatpacking industry.

19. How was mass media used during the 1960 campaign and election?

(A) To televise the Republican convention that nominated Dwight Eisenhower

(B) To televise the Democratic convention that nominated Adlai Stevenson

(C) To broadcast up-to-date information about the Vietnam War

(D) To present news coverage on the attempted assassination of Ronald Reagan

(E) To present the debates between John Kennedy and Richard Nixon

Answer: E.

To present the debates between John Kennedy and Richard Nixon. The correct choice is E. The conventions were first televised in the 1950s. Choices A and B did not occur in 1960. The Vietnam War was not a debate issue in 1960. Choice D also did not occur in 1960. So, the only choice is the Kennedy-Nixon debates, which were televised during their campaigns.

20. During the 2016 presidential debates, moderators asked people to send them questions to ask the candidates during the debates. What type of media is an example of this process?

(A) Social media

(B) Print media

(C) Mass media

(D) Broadcast media

(E) Political media

Answer: A.

Social media. Social media is an extension of Internet media. Social media is Internet-based social interaction between users.

21. What majority is needed to override a presidential veto?

(A) Simple

(B) Two-thirds

(C) Three-fifths

(D) Three-fourths

(E) Four-fifths

Answer: B.

Two-thirds. Although a simple majority is required for the passage of legislation, to override a presidential veto requires a two-thirds majority.

22. **What is the meaning of the term "impeach"?**

(A) To bring charges against

(B) To remove from office

(C) To re-elect an official

(D) To override a presidential veto

(E) To arrest an official

Answer: A.

To bring charges against. The House of Representatives may impeach, or bring charges against, an official. The Senate tries the official and decides whether or not to remove the official from office.

23. **Why was the Election of 1800 significant?**

(A) John Adams became president.

(B) Thomas Jefferson became president after an orderly transition.

(C) John Quincy Adams became the first president to be a member of one family.

(D) James Monroe announced the Monroe Doctrine.

(E) James Madison was the first president who had signed the Constitution.

Answer: B.

Thomas Jefferson became president after an orderly transition. There had been a tie vote for Jefferson and Aaron Burr in the Electoral College. The House of Representatives had to make the decision as to who would become president. The transition occurred in a smooth manner.

24. **How many presidents have been impeached?**

(A) None

(B) One

(C) Two

(D) Three

(E) Four

Answer: C.

Two. Presidents Andrew Johnson and Bill Clinton have both been impeached. Neither was convicted.

25. **Which President served more than two terms?**

(A) Theodore Roosevelt

(B) Franklin Roosevelt

(C) Harry Truman

(D) Jimmy Carter

(E) William Clinton

Answer: B.

Franklin Roosevelt. Franklin Roosevelt was elected to four terms as President. He served as President from 1933 to 1945. He died during the fourth term and his Vice-President Harry Truman became president.

26. **Which U.S. Supreme Court case established the doctrine of judicial review?**

(A) *McCulloch v. Maryland*

(B) *Brown v. Board of Education*

(C) *The Dred Scott decision*

(D) *Plessy v. Ferguson*

(E) *Marbury v. Madison*

Answer: E.

Marbury v. Madison. The case of *Marbury v. Madison* involved the appointment of the "midnight judges" and established the doctrine of judicial review.

Practice Test One

27. **Which president tried to "pack" the Supreme Court?**

    (A) Theodore Roosevelt

    (B) Harry Truman

    (C) Franklin Roosevelt

    (D) Thomas Jefferson

    (E) William Clinton

    Answer: C.

    Franklin Roosevelt. Franklin Roosevelt wanted to increase the number of justices on the Supreme Court to lessen the possibility of his New Deal legislation being declared unconstitutional.

28. **Which is the only court referred to in the Constitution?**

    (A) State trial court

    (B) U.S. Supreme Court

    (C) State Supreme Court

    (D) Federal District Court

    (E) U.S. Circuit Court of Appeal

    Answer: B.

    U.S. Supreme Court. The Constitution establishes the U.S. Supreme Court and permits other inferior courts to be established.

29. **What does the term "inferior" court mean?**

    (A) A court that can only hear cases involving small claims

    (B) A court that can only hear cases involving family law and probate matters

    (C) A bankruptcy court

    (D) A court that is lower than the U.S. Supreme Court

    (E) A court that hears patents and copyrights

    Answer: D.

    A court that is lower than the U.S. Supreme Court. Inferior courts are courts that are lower than the U.S. Supreme Court. Bankruptcy courts and courts that hear patent and copyright cases are special federal courts. Small claims, probate, and family law courts are state courts and are examples of inferior courts to the U.S. Supreme Courts but are established by states rather than Congress.

30. **What does the term "constitutional court" mean?**

(A) A court that can only hear cases involving the Constitution

(B) A court that has been set up for a special purpose

(C) A court whose judges have fixed terms of office

(D) A court that has a specific number of judges

(E) A court that exercises powers found in Article III of the Constitution

Answer: E.

A court that exercises powers found in Article III of the Constitution. The correct choice is E. The U.S. Supreme Court is an example of a constitutional court. A constitutional court is a court that exercises powers found in Article III of the Constitution.

31. **How do judges become constitutional court judges?**

(A) They are nominated by the President and approved by the Senate.

(B) They are nominated by members of the House of Representative from their "home districts" and approved by the President.

(C) They are nominated by the Senate and approved by the President.

(D) They are nominated by the Senate and approved by the House of Representatives.

(E) They are nominated by the President and approved by the existing judges of the court to which they are nominated.

Answer: A.

They are nominated by the President and approved by the Senate. The President nominates individuals to serve as judges on constitutional courts. The U.S. Senate approves the nominations.

32. What is a writ of certiorari?

(A) A written decision by a court

(B) A written order

(C) A written request for a court to hear a case

(D) A written certification explaining a court decision

(E) A writing that presents the pleadings of one of the parties in a case

Answer: C.

A written request for a court to hear a case. A writ of certiorari is a writing that requests a court to hear a case. A writ of certiorari is filed with the Supreme Court to request the high court accept a case and make a decision on the case.

33. If a case is remanded, what is the meaning of "remand?"

(A) Reversed

(B) Affirmed

(C) Judges agree for different reasons

(D) To send back

(E) To dispose of

Answer: D.

To send back. To "remand" is to send back to a lower court for some reason(s). The reason may be to change a sentence or to give the defendant a new trial.

34. What does "stare decisis" mean?

(A) Follow earlier cases

(B) Decide to reverse

(C) Decide to affirm

(D) Let the decision stand

(E) Concurring decision

Answer: D.

Let the decision stand. Following earlier cases is following precedent. Stare decisis means that a court is letting an earlier decision stand.

35. **Which was the first independent regulatory commission?**

    (A) Interstate Commerce Commission

    (B) Federal Trade Commission

    (C) Consumer Products Division

    (D) Federal Aviation Agency

    (E) Department of Revenue

    Answer: A.
    Interstate Commerce Commission. The Interstate Commerce Commission was created in 1887 to monitor abuses in the railroads.

36. **During what time period was the largest growth of the bureaucracy?**

    (A) 1880–1890

    (B) 1890–1930

    (C) 1930–1945

    (D) 1945–1960

    (E) 1960–1990

    Answer: C.
    1930-1945. The greatest period of growth in the federal bureaucracy occurred during the New Deal and the period before and during World War II.

37. **What is the highest appellate court in the United States?**

    (A) National Court of Appeals

    (B) Circuit Court

    (C) District Court

    (D) Supreme Court

    (E) Court of Claims

    Answer: D.
    The Supreme Court. The Supreme Court is a court of original and appellate jurisdiction. It is the highest court of appellate jurisdiction.

38. **Which is a shared power of the federal and state governments?**

(A) The power to declare war

(B) The power to build roads

(C) The power to coin money

(D) The power to regulate interstate trade

(E) The power to educate

Answer: B.

The power to build roads. The state governments and the federal government have the shared power of building roads.

39. **What was an outcome of the Great Compromise in the framing of the Constitution?**

(A) It provided for two year terms for the House of Representatives but made the Senate six year terms.

(B) Also known as the three-fifths compromise, this determined how to count slaves in determining the population of the states.

(C) It delegated all powers to the states not explicitly granted to the federal government in the Constitution.

(D) It outlined the country's plans for expansion.

(E) It guaranteed states equal representation in the Senate, but based representation on proportional population in the House of Representatives.

Answer: E.

It guaranteed states equal representation in the Senate, but based representation on proportional population in the House of Representatives. The New Jersey Plan advocated for equal representation in the New Congress. This would be of benefit for smaller states. The Virginia Plan proposed giving each state representation in Congress based on the proportion of the state's population to the American population. The compromise was to create a bicameral legislature with one body, the Senate, composed of equal representation from each state, and the House of Representatives, based on population.

40. Which of the following was referred to as "a league of friendship?"

(A) The Constitution

(B) The Virginia Plan

(C) The New Jersey Plan

(D) The Connecticut Plan

(E) The Articles of Confederation

Answer: E.

The Articles of Confederation. While the U.S. Articles of Confederation was a plan of government based upon the principles fought for in the American Revolutionary War, it contained crucial flaws. It had no power of national taxation, no power to control trade, and it provided for a comparatively weak executive. Therefore, it could not enforce legislation. It was a "league of friendship" which was opposed to any type of national authority.

41. Which president is noted for using the "spoils system"?

(A) Andrew Johnson

(B) Andrew Jackson

(C) Zachary Taylor

(D) George Washington

(E) Theodore Roosevelt

Answer: B.

Andrew Jackson. Andrew Jackson put many of his "Jacksonian Democrats" into political offices. His system of patronage was called the "spoils system".

42. Which is the trial court at the federal level?

(A) Circuit Court

(B) District Court

(C) Supreme Court

(D) Court of Claims

(E) Bankruptcy Court

Answer: B.

District Court. The U.S. District Court is the trial court at the federal level. East state has at least one District Court. The Circuit Court is an appellate court at the federal level. The Court of Claims and the Bankruptcy Court are special courts in the federal system.

43. **Which Amendment provides for a "two-term" president?**

    (A) Twenty-second

    (B) Twenty-third

    (C) Twenty-fourth

    (D) Twenty-fifth

    (E) Twenty-sixth

    Answer: A.

    Twenty-second. The Twenty-second Amendment provides that a president shall serve a maximum of two-terms. In the event a vice-president becomes president for more than two years of the term of the person being replaced, then the new president is only able to serve one term. If the time of replacement is less than two years, then the "two-term" applies.

44. **The United States legislature is bicameral, which means _____.**

    (A) It consists of several houses

    (B) It consists of two houses

    (C) The legislature meets twice a year

    (D) The legislature meets every other year

    (E) It has an upper house and a lower house

    Answer: B.

    It consists of two houses. Congress has two houses. "Bi" means "two" and "cameral" means chamber (house).

45. Before the Seventeenth Amendment, how were U.S. Senators chosen?

(A) By the House of Representatives

(B) By the people

(C) By the state legislatures

(D) By the courts

(E) By the President

Answer: C.

By the state legislatures. The Seventeenth Amendment provides for the popular election of U.S. Senators. Before the Seventeenth Amendment, senators were chosen by state legislatures.

46. A Supreme Court that shows a willingness to change public policy and alter judicial precedent is engaging in

(A) Due process

(B) Judicial restraint

(C) Judicial activism

(D) Judicial review

(E) Ex post facto lawmaking

Answer: C.

Judicial Activism. Due process refers to the protections of life, liberty, and property granted by the Fourteenth Amendment in the Constitution. Judicial review is the Supreme Court's power to overturn a law on the grounds that it is unconstitutional. Judicial activism is when a court alters or strikes down an executive or legislative branch decision. Often the court endeavors to change public policy this way.

47. **Which of the following institutions established in the Constitution make public policy?**

(A) The Senate, the president, and political parties.

(B) The Congress, the president, and the courts.

(C) The Congress, the courts, and the military.

(D) The Congress, the president, and the military.

(E) The Congress, the president, and the bureaucracy.

Answer: B.

The Congress, the president, and the courts. The only institutions granted the power to make policy (which means law or legislation) are the President, who can issue an Executive Order, Congress, which can pass a bill making legislation, or the Supreme Court, which can decide on a case and make their decision law. The military and the bureaucracy execute the law, not pass the law.

48. **Which of the following best defines a set of institutions linking government, politics, and public policy?**

(A) An educational system

(B) A political system

(C) A social system

(D) An economic system

(E) A socioeconomic system

Answer: B.

A political system. Only a political system fits government, public policy and politics. An educational system is irrelevant to the question. Social, economic, or socioeconomic systems do not concern politics. Therefore, the correct response is a political system.

49. Which of the following best illustrates a use of the "elastic clause"?

(A) The Supreme Court allows a lower court ruling to stand by refusing to hear an appeal.

(B) A congressional committee prevents the full chamber from voting on legislation by delaying its report.

(C) Congress passes legislation establishing a national speed limit.

(D) A member of the House of Representatives introduces a bill to increase federal income tax rates.

(E) A governor issues an executive order requiring all state employees to submit to drug testing.

Answer: C.

Congress passes legislation establishing a national speed limit. The "elastic clause" is a statement in the Constitution (Article I, Section 8) granting Congress the power to pass all laws necessary and proper for carrying out their enumerated list of powers.

50. The programs of the New Deal are examples of

(A) The safety net

(B) The state sponsored era

(C) The federal era

(D) Grant blocks to states

(E) The New Federalism

Answer: A.

The safety net. Safety net refers to government programs to provide support or financial assistance to low income families to prevent them from slipping into poverty.

51. The main purpose of the National Environmental Policy Act was to

(A) Require government agencies to issue environmental impact statements if their policies would have a negative impact on the environment.

(B) Require the Environmental Protection Agency to monitor clean air standards.

(C) Establish clean water standards.

(D) Establish a superfund to clean up environmental abuses.

(E) Require the Department of the Interior to establish criteria for ocean dumping.

Answer: A.

Require government agencies to issue environmental impact statements if their policies would have a negative impact on the environment. The National Environmental Policy Act passed in 1970 requires federal agencies to assess the environmental impacts of their proposed actions prior to making decisions. Agencies have to evaluate the environmental and related social and economic effects of their proposed actions. Agencies also provide opportunities for public review and comment on those evaluations.

52. All of the following choices represent features of the Clean Air Act of 1990 EXCEPT that

(A) It established standards to protect the ozone layer.

(B) It set overall carbon dioxide standards.

(C) It established standards to attack the acid rain problem.

(D) It directed factories to reduce emissions.

(E) It directed auto manufacturers to sell electric cars.

Answer: E.

It directed auto manufacturers to sell electric cars. The Clean Air Act did all the actions described in A, B, C and D. It did not mandate auto companies to sell electric cars.

53. The role of a conference committee in Congress is to

(A) Hold hearings on proposed legislation.

(B) Oversee the actions of the executive branch of the government.

(C) Decide which bills should be considered by the full Senate.

(D) Conduct hearings that make information available to the public.

(E) Reconcile differences in bills passed by the House and Senate.

Answer: E.

Reconcile differences in bills passed by the House and Senate. A conference committee meets to go over the differences between the versions of the bills passed by the House and the Senate. It is comprised of members of both the House and Senate, and once a bill goes through conference, it is presented back to be voted on in both chambers. Once both the chambers vote and pass the conferenced bill, it goes to the President for signature or veto.

54. Supreme Court justices were given tenure subject to good behavior by the framers of the Constitution in order to ensure that

(A) Justices are free from direct political pressures.

(B) Justices remain accountable to the public.

(C) Justices are encouraged to make politically popular decisions.

(D) Cooperation between the judicial and legislative branches is assured.

(E) Presidents are encouraged to seek younger nominees for the Supreme Court.

Answer: A.

Justices are free from direct political pressures. The Founding fathers believed it important to ensure that not only the branches of government remain separate with distinct responsibilities, but also that the judicial branch should remain isolated from the rigorous work of politicking for election or re-election. Therefore, Supreme Court justices, once confirmed as members of the court, have life tenure.

55. The committee system is more important in the House than in the Senate because

(A)   The seniority system plays no role in the House and therefore committees must play a larger role.

(B)   The Constitution mandates the committee structure in the House.

(C)   Committee members are appointed by the President.

(D)   The House is so large that more work can be accomplished in committees than on the floor.

(E)   The majority party in the House prefers to give priority to the work of the committees.

Answer: D.

The House is so large that more work can be accomplished in committees than on the floor. The House of Representatives has 435 members. It would be impossible for the Speaker of the House to oversee the work of so many members. So, all the work happens in committees, sub-committees, and in conference committees. Therefore, members vie to get prestigious committee assignments and leadership positions within the committees.

56. Which of the following is NOT true of the privilege of habeas corpus?

(A)   It is a right, which can prevent unlawful arrest.

(B)   It is a right that can be suspended in times of rebellion or threats to public safety.

(C)   It is a right, which can only be exercised after criminal conviction.

(D)   It is a right which can prevent ongoing unlawful imprisonment.

(E)   It is intended to safeguard individual freedom against arbitrary and lawless state action.

Answer: A.

It is a right, which can prevent unlawful arrest. Habeas corpus primarily relates to unlawful, ongoing detention, and does not prevent an initial arrest.

57. **Which of the following relates most directly to the admissibility of wrongly obtained evidence in court?**

    (A) The right against self-incrimination

    (B) The right against double jeopardy

    (C) Amicus curiae

    (D) The exclusionary rule

    (E) The Miranda warning

    Answer: D.
    The exclusionary rule. The exclusionary rule requires that evidence obtained in violation of constitutional standards cannot be used against the accused.

58. **The right of a convicted felon to vote in the United States is**

    (A) Guaranteed by the Fourteenth Amendment.

    (B) Denied by the Twenty-fourth Amendment.

    (C) A matter of state law, which varies from state to state.

    (D) Not addressed in either federal or state law.

    (E) Only allowed for "lesser" felonies.

    Answer: C.
    A matter of state law, which varies from state to state. Article 2 of the Fourteenth Amendment allows the states to decide whether a person has the right to vote if he has been found guilty of "participation in rebellion, or other crime." The states vary widely on what voting rights are allowed to convicted felons.

59. **Which of the following relates to making an action criminal after it was committed?**

    (A) A bill of attainder

    (B) Self incrimination

    (C) Ex post facto law

    (D) Double jeopardy

    (E) Cruel and unusual punishment

Answer: C.

Ex post facto law. An ex post facto law, which is prohibited by Article I, Sections 9 and 10 of the Constitution, is a law making an action criminal only after it occurred.

60. The "Lemon Test" is

(A) A test followed by the Supreme Court when reviewing legislation concerning free speech.

(B) A test followed by the Supreme Court when reviewing legislation concerning religion.

(C) A test followed by the Supreme Court when reviewing legislation concerning the right to bear arms.

(D) A test followed by the Supreme Court when reviewing legislation concerning government "takings."

(E) A test followed by the Supreme Court when reviewing whether to take a case regarding automobiles.

Answer: B.

A test followed by the Supreme Court when reviewing legislation concerning religion. The "Lemon Test" is derived from the 1971 case of *Lemon v. Kurtzman*, 403 U.S.602 (1971), and dealt with legislation regarding religion.

1. **Interest groups play political roles in the democratic process.**

   a. **How are interest groups formed? How are they structured?**

   b. **Discuss the outcome/result of different types of representation of interests.**

   c. **Describe some types of interest groups.**

   Sample Answers:

   a. Interest groups are formed around common interests. The group shares common objectives to influence political officials and the outcome of the efforts of an interest group depends upon the acceptance of their position by political officials. They focus on a single issue and usually have a fixed position on the issue. If a group changes its position, then the new position might change the composition of the group.

   Interest groups are often formed as the result of major changes in an historical period. For example, interest groups during the Progressive Era focused on the government regulation of business and immigration issues.

   Interest groups use lobbyists to promote their ideas and issues. Lobbyists try to get legislation passed that supports the positions of the interest groups. Lobbyists use methods to directly influence legislation. Lobbyists are professionals who work for firms or they are individuals within the interest group.

   b. Interest groups share common goals and try to influence those who make government policy. Interest groups are organized, work toward specific goals, raise money to meet their goals, and promote politicians. They do not work through government officials or suggest names of individuals for political office but they have specific issues and take specific positions relative to those issues. For example, an interest group may advocate improvement of air pollution and present specific ideas as how to accomplish that goal.

   c. The main types of interest groups focus on economic issues, public-interest issues, and issues involving foreign government. Interest groups have various strategies to accomplish their goals of passing legislation that is favorable to the group. They may lobby, offer assistance during campaigns, publish voting records, or engage in public protest demonstrations. Interest groups also align themselves with other groups that have similar goals. This effort concentrates the focus of the interest and eliminates, or lessens, duplication of efforts.

2. **Checks and balances serve an important purpose in government.**

   a. **Why did the framers of the Constitution include checks and balances?**

   b. **What are examples of checks each branch of government has on the other branch?**

   c. **What balance(s) result from the checks?**

Sample Answers:

The U.S. Constitution is very much a reaction to the events that came before it. The founding fathers had several goals. Foremost among those goals was to avoid tyranny. In order to do this several different systems were set up to prevent the abuse of power.

a. Checks and balances were identified by the framers of the Constitution in order to prevent one branch from becoming too powerful and to maintain the balance of power at the national level of government. The founding fathers did not want to repeat the "ills" of the British rule in the colonies and did not want one branch to become the "ruler" of the country. Therefore, careful thought was given to setting up the three branches and the specific role of each branch. Not only does each branch of the government have particular powers, but also, each branch has certain powers over the other branches. This is done to keep them balanced and to prevent one branch form ever gaining too much power.

b. Executive: veto legislation; suggest nominations.

   Judicial: judicial review; declare legislation unconstitutional.

   Legislative: override veto; approve nominations.

   For example, Congress may pass laws, but the President can veto them. If the President vetoes a law, Congress can override the veto with a two-thirds vote. The President and Congress may agree on a law, but the Supreme Court can declare a law unconstitutional.

c. As a result of the checks, one branch does not become too powerful. In order for laws to pass and become policy, all three branches of government must come to agreement. The final balance is that of the people. If the President or Congress pass laws not popular with the people, then during reelection time, the citizens can let their opinions be known, acting as another balance.

3. Assume for a moment that you are from the state of _____, the year is 1789, and you have been given the task of creating a list of proposed rights to be sent to James Madison, who will be taking suggestions from all the states and compiling a single list of rights to be proposed to Congress. However, also assume that you have the benefit of knowing the history (especially of Supreme Court decisions) that has taken place in the United States between 1789 and the present day.

a. Please describe the rights you would include on your list. Which would you list first?

b. Please indicate any added descriptive terminology or definitions you would give to your listed rights based on the history of the U.S. since 1789. Specifically, are there words you would use to clarify your intended meaning, words you would avoid using, or that you would define differently if you did use them? Where possible, give reasons for your changes in wording.

Sample Answers:

a. The basic rights listed in the original Bill of Rights continue to be valuable to this day, and should be included. First and foremost among these would be rights very similar to the First Amendment, protecting free speech, freedom of the press, free exercise of religion and the freedom of the people to assemble.

The Universal Declaration of Human Rights from 1948 would also be a valuable guide in creating a list of rights. It includes both positive rights (such as those found in the U.S. Bill of rights, as well as rights to life and liberty) and rights prohibitions, or statements of things that a person should NOT ever be subjected to (such as slavery or torture).

Also important to include on the list would be the right against search and seizure in the Fourth Amendment, and the many rights related to the criminally accused, which are found in the Fifth, Sixth and Eighth Amendments. These include due process and the right to counsel, to confront witnesses, to a speedy trial, against double jeopardy, and that no cruel or unusual punishments are allowed.

Some rights are more controversial, and represent the personal opinion of the person proposing them. Among these is the right to bear arms. Whether this right should be included is a hotly contested and highly emotional matter in which opinions differ in legitimate ways. Another controversial right is the right of privacy, and as it related to sexual orientation and to email and social media presence.

b. It would certainly be best to define or clarify some of the rights, in light of the history since 1789. For example, "due process" continues to be a somewhat vague and evasive concept to this day. Perhaps it could be clarified to mean "fair and just terms and conditions."

The term "equal protection" was not in the original bill of rights but could be included in this new list, and perhaps could be expanded to mean "equal and fair protection regardless of race, gender, age or disability," similar to the Civil Rights Act of 1964, the ADA, etc. and to the Universal Declaration of Human Rights.

The right to bear arms could also be clarified, given the large number of school and civilian shootings in the last decade. For example, maybe wording that bans certain types of guns from being sold to the public and which requires registration of all guns.

Finally, the "right of privacy" could well be expanded upon. Indeed, rather than using this broad term, perhaps a right to abortion, right to gay marriage, or the right to "own your social presence," (instead of it being available to everyone) could be listed. Again, the Internet is so new, that we are only now starting to think of what it means to have rights in the information age.

4. **The U.S. Congress and the President together have the power to enact federal law. Federal bureaucratic agencies have the responsibility to execute federal law. However, in the carrying out of these laws, federal agencies have policy-making discretion.**

   a. **Explain two reasons why Congress gives federal agencies policy-making discretion in executing federal laws.**

   b. **Choose one of the bureaucratic agencies listed below. Identify the policy area over which it exercises policy-making discretion AND give one specific example of how it exercises that discretion.**

      Environmental Protection Agency (EPA)
      Federal Communications Commission (FCC)
      Federal Reserve Board

   c. **Describe two ways in which Congress ensures that federal agencies follow legislative intent.**

Sample Answers:

a. Congress gives federal agencies policy-making discretion in executing federal laws for several reasons as follows. Congress lacks the expertise to manage specific programs. Government agencies can hire experts with the specific expertise and knowledge to manage the programs. It is time consuming to manage policies. Congressional members have too many duties, including re-elections, to give policy oversight the time it deserves. In executing federal laws, it is important to ensure that the overseers can reach the citizens impacted or benefiting from the law. Again, federal agencies can conduct the outreach and manage citizen interaction on the law. Thus, overall, it is more efficient for government agencies to manage and execute federal law.

b. EPA: The EPA exercises oversight over air standards, clean water standards, endangered species, wilderness areas, hazardous waste, and pesticide use. Several laws passed since the agency was created in 1970, allow the EPA to administer its functions. The Clean Air Act and the Clean Water Act are two examples of specific legislation that the EPA enforces.

FCC: The FCC is an independent government agency responsible for regulating the radio, television and phone industries. The FCC regulates all interstate communications, such as wire, satellite and cable, and international communications originating or terminating in the United States. Most recently, the issue of Net Neutrality (the idea that consumers should have a choice in their internet services), is an important new issue on their agenda.

Federal Reserve Board: The Federal Reserve System, often referred to as the Federal Reserve or simply "the Fed," is the central bank of the United States. It was created by the Congress to provide the nation with a safer, more flexible, and more stable monetary and financial system. The system is overseen by a Board of Governors (thus the term—Federal Reserve Board), and is considered a prestigious and influential appointment that influences economic policy.

c. Ways by which Congress insures that federal agencies follow legislative intent include: committee hearings where agency officials are invited to testify on progress, appropriations (tweaking the budget of the agency if it doesn't follow intent), investigative hearings, asking the General Accounting Office to do an audit, change the law, or create sunset clauses to dissolve agencies.

SECTION VI:
Practice Test Two

Section I: Multiple Choice _____

Instructions

Section I of this examination contains 60 multiple-choice questions. Fill in only the ovals for numbers 1 through 60 on your answer sheet.

Indicate all your answers to the multiple-choice questions on the answer sheet. No credit will be given for anything written in this exam booklet, but you may use the booklet for notes or scratch work. After you have decided which of the suggested answers is best, completely fill in the corresponding oval on the answer sheet. Give only one answer to each question. If you change an answer, be sure that the previous mark is erased completely. Here is a sample question and answer.

Sample Question   **Sample Answer**

1. **Washington is a**   Ⓐ ● Ⓒ Ⓓ Ⓔ

    (A) City

    (B) State

    (C) Country

    (D) Continent

    (E) Bourough

Use your time effectively, working as quickly as you can without losing accuracy. Do not spend too much time on any one question. Go on to other questions and come back to the ones you have not answered if you have time. It is not expected that everyone will know the answers to all the multiple-choice questions.

About Guessing

Many candidates wonder whether or not to guess the answers to questions about which they are not certain. Multiple-choice scores are based on the number of questions answered correctly. Points are not deducted for incorrect answers, and no points are awarded for unanswered questions. Because points are not deducted for incorrect answers, you are encouraged to answer all multiple-choice questions. On questions you do not know the answer to, you should eliminate as many choices as you can, and then select the best answer among the remaining choices.

Time – 45 minutes
60 Questions

Directions: Each of the questions or incomplete statements below is followed by five suggested answers or explanations. Select the one that is BEST in each case.

1. **What was one reason a bill of rights was not included in the original constitution of 1787?**

   (A) Because the founders were too tired after the numerous debates to draft a bill of rights.

   (B) Because the majority of delegates thought a bill of rights was worthless.

   (C) Because many delegates feared that a bill of rights could be dangerous.

   (D) Because the delegates could not agree on which rights to include.

   (E) Because the delegates knew that every state already had a bill of rights.

2. **All of the following are examples of checks and balances in the Constitution EXCEPT:**

   (A) The president's veto power

   (B) "Judicial review" by the Supreme Court

   (C) The power to impeach

   (D) The authority to amend the Constitution

   (E) All of the above

3. **The Constitution alludes to which group holding the greatest power in the new government?**

   (A) The federal government

   (B) The states

   (C) The people

   (D) The courts

   (E) None of the above

4. **Which of the following could be said to be an expression of federalism?**

   (A) The desire by western states to gain control of public lands held by the federal government.

   (B) State constitutional amendments about the definition of marriage.

   (C) The decision by an aggrieved party about whether to sue in state or federal court.

   (D) All of the above.

   (E) None of the above.

5. **The Twelfth Amendment modified Article II, Section 1 of the Constitution regarding electors for president in what way?**

   (A) It increased the number of electors per state from 5 to 10.

   (B) It changed the time electors were to meet from the last Tuesday in October to the first Tuesday in November.

   (C) It increased the number of votes an elector could cast for President and Vice President to two votes for each, for a total of four votes.

   (D) It forced electors for the first time to vote separately for President and Vice President.

   (E) It stated for the first time that if no presidential candidate received a majority of votes, the House of Representatives would decide who would be president.

6. **The nurturing process through which people acquire knowledge, have feelings, and evaluations about the political world is called**

   (A) Political socialization

   (B) Political efficacy

   (C) Propaganda acquisition

   (D) Political ideology

   (E) Public opinion

7. **Political participation in the government is an essential component of**

(A) Freedom

(B) Independence

(C) Free enterprise

(D) Self-expression

(E) Self-government

8. **Which of the following is a random sample?**

(A) Interviewing people in a nonsystematic fashion.

(B) A selection mechanism that gives each person an equal chance of being selected.

(C) Going up to people on the street asking for their opinions.

(D) Asking every student in the Introduction to Psychology course to fill out a survey.

(E) Putting a survey on the web and asking people to take it.

9. **Which of the following polls is most likely to help a candidate evaluate the short-term effect of a certain campaign event?**

(A) An exit poll

(B) A tracking poll

(C) A push poll

(D) A stratified sample

(E) A cross-sectional poll

10. **A conservative friend of yours avoids watching MSNBC because she believes it to be a liberal news network. Your friend is engaging in**

(A) Prejudice questioning

(B) Selective exposure

(C) Infotainment

(D) Stereotype challenging

(E) Narrowcasting

11. **In general, public opinion**

(A) Has no relation to government action at all

(B) Has an impact on government action only during elections

(C) Constrains only the actions of incumbents in government

(D) Constrains the actions of government

(E) Has very little impact on government action

12. **Most political scientists and political observers assess public opinion primarily through**

(A) Polls

(B) Social media blogs

(C) Letters to the editor

(D) Voter registration rolls

(E) Reports from interest groups

13. **All of the following are functions of political parties EXCEPT:**

(A) Recruiting candidates for public office.

(B) Gaining control of the government.

(C) Gathering volunteers to register voters.

(D) Presenting alternative policies to the electorate.

(E) Opposing the winning party by putting forth its own policies.

14. **Which of the following statements is correct about mass media?**

(A) Mass media is limited to newspapers, television, and the Internet.

(B) Broadcasts relating to political advertisement is the least valuable asset for politicians.

(C) In the United States, corporations control most mass media.

(D) Another name for mass media in the United States is "state media."

(E) The focus of mass media is to reach a specific audience.

Practice Test Two

15. **All of the following are thought to be advantages of a two-party system EXCEPT:**

    (A) Lack of third choice

    (B) More efficient government

    (C) More stability

    (D) Moderate views

    (E) Less disagreement

16. **Which of the following is an example of the media shaping a political attitude?**

    (A) A television newscaster reporting on a terrorist bombing in a foreign city.

    (B) A radio broadcast describing a presidential inauguration.

    (C) An Internet story of the reasons why a person should vote or not vote for a specific candidate.

    (D) A newsletter providing telephone numbers and other contact information for discussing an issue with the chairperson of an interest group.

    (E) A newspaper article about an upcoming presidential debate and the topics that will be covered during the debate.

17. **Which system of nominating a presidential candidate involves a local gathering where voters discuss and then decide openly which candidate they will support?**

    (A) Caucus

    (B) Primary

    (C) General election

    (D) Convention

    (E) Committee hearing

18. **What is the purpose of a Political Action Committee?**

    (A) To approve actions of the House and Senate

    (B) To raise money to defeat or elect candidates

    (C) To monitor political spending

    (D) To nominate candidates for office

    (E) To lobby for legislation

19. **Who choses whether there will be a caucus or primary election?**

    (A) Political parties

    (B) Local governments

    (C) The head of the National Committee of a political party

    (D) States

    (E) Presidential candidates

20. **Why did the framers of the Constitution establish a national bicameral legislature?**

    (A) To appease the large states

    (B) To eliminate the law-making body from becoming too powerful

    (C) To appease the leaders of the Constitutional Convention

    (D) To create the three-fifths compromise

    (E) To eliminate checks and balances between Congress and the other branches

21. **What is the term for drawing or connecting voting districts in odd shapes so that a candidate can easily win that district?**

    (A) Mal-apportionment

    (B) Gerrymandering

    (C) Reallocation

    (D) Caucusing

    (E) Reorganization

22. **In the United States, who (or which body) has the power to declare war?**

(A) The President

(B) Congress

(C) The Executive Branch

(D) The Supreme Court

(E) The states

23. **Which of the following statements is true about political parties in the United States?**

(A) The Constitution never actually mentions them.

(B) They are called "a necessary part of the political process."

(C) They are most effective if there are only two major parties.

(D) They are harmful to the political process.

(E) To be identified as a political party, the group must have at least 100 members.

24. **What term refers to the situation when the president's party is not the same as the party controlling either the Senate of the House?**

(A) Neutral government

(B) Unified government

(C) Divided government

(D) Contested government

(E) Adversarial government

25. **Competition between the president and Congress exists because of**

(A) Inequality of bargaining power

(B) Checks and balances

(C) Separation of powers

(D) Separation of powers and checks and balances

(E) Judicial review

26. **Which of the following statements are true about gridlock?**

    (A) Gridlock rarely protects the interests of many.

    (B) Gridlock only occurs when many diverse sides are present.

    (C) Gridlock is an unnecessary part of the democratic process.

    (D) Gridlock was exemplified by Congressional action during the presidency of Franklin Roosevelt.

    (E) Gridlock is good because if there is more diverse thinking, there will be more people represented.

27. **All of the following statements about the presidency are correct EXCEPT**

    (A) The framers feared anarchy.

    (B) The framers feared a monarchy.

    (C) Some of the framers wanted a legislature to check all actions of the president.

    (D) The framers wanted a president who could dominate the legislative branch.

    (E) The framers gave the president broad powers to create a balance of power.

28. **All of the following are powers of the President EXCEPT**

    (A) Serve as commander-in-chief of the Armed Forces

    (B) Grant pardons in impeachment cases

    (C) Convene Congress in special sessions

    (D) Grant reprieves in cases other than impeachment

    (E) Receive ambassadors

29. **If a Cabinet member were to become president, which cabinet position is the first in the line of succession?**

    (A) State

    (B) Treasury

    (C) Defense

    (D) Justice

    (E) Interior

30. **When may a president use a "pocket veto"?**

(A) At any time during the Congressional session.

(B) When the president forgets to sign a bill into law.

(C) When the president is unable to return the bill to Congress while it is in session.

(D) When the president cannot return the bill to Congress within ten days because Congress has adjourned.

(E) When the president is away from the White House and has been told Congress will be sending a bill for signature.

31. **Which Constitutional amendment allows a Vice-President who becomes President to nominate a new vice-president?**

(A) Nineteenth

(B) Twenty-first

(C) Twenty-third

(D) Twenty-fourth

(E) Twenty-fifth

32. **The ability of the president to veto an act of Congress is an example of**

(A) Separation of powers

(B) Checks and balances

(C) Judicial review

(D) Presidential prerogative

(E) Presidential right

33. **Which is an example of a case of original jurisdiction heard by the U.S. Supreme Court?**

    (A) Diversity jurisdiction case

    (B) Bankruptcy case

    (C) Dispute between states

    (D) Cases arising under the Constitution

    (E) A patent infringement case

34. **What does "diversity jurisdiction" mean?**

    (A) The parties are from different states.

    (B) The issues involve federal and state issues.

    (C) The issues involve two courts.

    (D) There are multiple parties from the same state.

    (E) The amount required to be involved is $75,000.00.

35. **Which of the following describes a body of non-elected government staff that makes government decisions?**

    (A) Federal government

    (B) State government

    (C) Bureaucracy

    (D) Agency

    (E) Congress

36. **Which branch of government controls the majority of the federal bureaucracy?**

    (A) Executive

    (B) Legislative

    (C) Judicial

    (D) Agencies

    (E) Courts

37. **Cabinet departments and independent regulatory agencies are a type of _____.**

   (A) Government corporation

   (B) Presidential commission

   (C) Method of oversight

   (D) Organization in the federal bureaucracy

   (E) Government employee

38. **What is the system called of rewarding friends and political allies with government jobs in exchange for their support?**

   (A) Civil service

   (B) Regulation

   (C) Patronage

   (D) Appointments

   (E) Merit system

39. **What is the significance of the Pendleton Act?**

   (A) It created the bureaucracy.

   (B) It was passed after the assassination of James A. Garfield.

   (C) It created the patronage system.

   (D) It required a person desiring to be a federal employee to take a competitive exam.

   (E) It created the first agency within the federal bureaucracy.

40. **Why is the Constitution called a 'living document'?**

   (A) It has the ability to change at different times.

   (B) It was created by the people.

   (C) It is a static document.

   (D) Anyone can change.

   (E) It can be destroyed if there is excessive reliance on it.

41. **Common law refers mostly to which of the following?**

(A) Precedents and traditions that have been accepted in society for so long that they have become accepted norms

(B) The laws dealing with common people

(C) Laws that are written and codified

(D) Law that is decided by the House of Commons in Great Britain

(E) Law that is common among different nations

42. **How is Congress different from the parliament of most European nations?**

(A) In parliamentary elections, any person can run for office.

(B) In Congress, legislators determine whether new leaders must be elected.

(C) In Congress, the members are less worried than members of parliaments about losing future elections.

(D) In parliamentary situations, the legislators don't have to worry about losing their positions when new elections take place.

(E) Parliamentary legislators have much independent power.

43. **What is the difference between cloture and filibuster?**

(A) Filibuster is prohibited if 25% of the Representatives oppose legislation and cloture means talking to encourage passage of a bill.

(B) Filibuster is a method senators use to veto a bill where cloture is used to continue a debate.

(C) Filibuster is used by Representatives to end debate and cloture is used to call for a vote.

(D) Cloture is used to begin a congressional debate and filibuster is used by Representatives to oppose legislation.

(E) Filibuster is used by senators to stall a debate and cloture is used to end a debate.

44. **Bills that give tangible benefits to people are called _____.**

   (A) Pork-barrel legislation

   (B) Franking privilege

   (C) Loopholes

   (D) Oversight

   (E) Entertainment spending

45. **What is the term for sending free information by mail to constituents?**

   (A) Gerrymandering

   (B) Loophole

   (C) Checks and balances

   (D) Bribery

   (E) Franking

46. **Policy "gridlock" refers to _____.**

   (A) Ideas about reforming Congress

   (B) The slow manner in which Congress functions

   (C) Failing to serve the public interest

   (D) Local prejudices shown by legislators

   (E) The decisiveness of Congress

47. **In the process and structure of public policymaking, "iron triangles" refer to the**

(A) Bargaining and negotiating process between the President and Congress about the direction of domestic policy.

(B) Dominance of corporate power in setting the national policy agenda for economic expansion.

(C) Interrelationship among federal, state, and local levels of government in the policy process .

(D) Networks of congressional committees, bureaucratic agencies, and interest groups that strongly influence the policy process.

(E) Group of presidential advisers who formulate the President's foreign policy agenda.

48. **Which of the following best describes the concept of political efficacy?**

(A) It is the belief that the average citizen can make little or no difference in an election.

(B) It is the belief that an intelligent voting decision cannot be made without information.

(C) It is the belief that the media must provide unbiased information for citizens to be able to make well-informed choices.

(D) It is the belief that one can make a difference in politics by expressing an opinion and acting politically.

(E) It is the belief that politicians must keep the electorate well-informed if they are to govern efficiently.

49. **Cooperative federalism can best be described by which of the following statements?**

    (A) Different levels of government are involved in common policy areas.

    (B) Government must have cooperation from the people in order to make legislative decisions.

    (C) Local levels of government can make decisions on issues more efficiently than state and national governments can.

    (D) The federal government must make regulations that can be applied across every state in the same way.

    (E) Business and government can work together to more effectively accomplish shared goals.

50. **Which of the following describes a consequence of the growing concentration of ownership of the news media?**

    (A) Newspaper prices have gone down.

    (B) Coverage of political events has gotten more liberal over time.

    (C) Prices for televised campaign ads have gone down.

    (D) Candidates get greater free airtime than in the past.

    (E) There is increased similarity of network news coverage.

51. **Interest groups engage in all of the following activities EXCEPT**

    (A) Testifying before congressional committees.

    (B) Sponsoring issue advocacy advertisements.

    (C) Lobbying federal agencies.

    (D) Filing federal lawsuits.

    (E) Using the franking privilege.

52. **Which of the following is NOT part of the Miranda warning typically given to suspects when they are arrested for a crime?**

   (A) You have the right to remain silent.

   (B) You have the right to an attorney.

   (C) Anything you say may be used against you in a court of law.

   (D) If you answer questions now without an attorney present, you have the right to stop answering at any time.

   (E) All of the above are part of the Miranda warning.

53. **Which of the following is not covered by the Civil Rights Act of 1964?**

   (A) Discrimination on the basis of gender.

   (B) Discrimination on the basis of age.

   (C) Discrimination on the basis of race.

   (D) Discrimination on the basis of national origin.

   (E) Discrimination on the basis of religion.

54. **The right to a jury trial is**

   (A) Only stated in the Constitution and its amendments as a right in criminal cases, not in civil cases.

   (B) Not stated in the Constitution, but was first granted in the Judiciary Act of 1789.

   (C) Stated in the Constitution as a guarantee of twelve jurors, who must be taken from the local community.

   (D) Guaranteed in the Constitution for all federal crimes except impeachment.

   (E) The same as indictment by a Grand Jury.

55. **The 1973 *Roe v. Wade* decision found a "right of privacy" primarily based on**

(A) The Fourth Amendment's prohibition of search and seizure.

(B) The Fourteenth Amendment's due process clause.

(C) The Ninth Amendment's reference to rights not listed in the Constitution.

(D) The First Amendment's guarantee of free speech.

(E) The ex-post facto clause in Article 1, Sections 9 and 10 of the Constitution.

56. **In the landmark case of *Brown v. Board of Education* the Supreme Court ruled that**

(A) Segregation of blacks from whites in private schools was illegal.

(B) States were required to bus black students to white schools.

(C) The "separate but equal" standard from the 1896 case of *Plessy v. Ferguson* was overturned.

(D) Segregation in higher education state schools (universities and colleges) was banned, but it was allowed to continue in public schools.

(E) Segregation in buses, restaurants, and other public places was banned, not just in schools.

57. **Which of the following is NOT true regarding flag burning, as interpreted by the Supreme Court?**

(A) It is a protected form of speech under the First Amendment.

(B) State governments can pass laws to regulate the time, place and manner of flag burning.

(C) While burning is protected under the First Amendment, other forms of flag desecration are strictly prohibited.

(D) The court applies "strict scrutiny" when reviewing flag burning cases.

(E) Old, worn out flags are legitimately destroyed by burning.

58. **Which of the following would NOT be considered a violation of the Family Medical Leave Act or laws which prevent gender discrimination?**

    (A) A fire department paying women differently than men for the same job.

    (B) An airline refusing to hire men as stewards.

    (C) A man taking up to twelve weeks off without pay after his wife has a baby.

    (D) A state university, which only allows men in its engineering programs.

    (E) A state hospital, which only hires female nurses.

59. **Which of the following would NOT be considered illegal sexual harassment?**

    (A) A female boss fires a male employee for refusing her advances.

    (B) Reassigning a woman to a different department and reducing her pay because she refused male advances.

    (C) A male cashier in a hair salon who is continuously subjected to put-downs and anti-male talk by the female employees.

    (D) Simple teasing, offhand comments, or isolated incidents of a sexual nature that are not considered serious.

    (E) All of the above are considered illegal sexual harassment.

60. **In the *Roe v. Wade* decision the "point of viability" at which a state could prohibit abortion by state law was**

    (A) The point at which a fetal heartbeat could be detected, at approximately 25 days after conception.

    (B) The point at which DNA tests would identify a fetus as distinctly human when compared to the DNA of other living organisms.

    (C) The point at which the mother first felt the fetus move.

    (D) The point at which the infant could live outside the womb with artificial aid.

    (E) The moment of conception.

Section II: Free Response Questions

1. Public opinion polls are a way to link the public with elected officials. Members of Congress often use polls to understand the views of their constituents, but they must also pay attention to other political considerations.

   a. Identify two characteristics of a valid, scientific, public opinion poll.

   b. Explain why each of the following enhances the influence of public opinion on the voting decisions of members of Congress.

      i. Strong public opinion as expressed in polling results

      ii. Competitive re-elections

   c. Explain why each of the following limits the influence of public opinion on the voting decisions of members of Congress.

      i. Legislators' voting records

      ii. Party leadership

2. **Federalism is the co-existence of different levels of government (such as state and federal governments), each holding power within its sphere, but unable to fully control the other levels of government.**

   a. Discuss how federalism was viewed differently prior to the Civil War, particularly by the states. As part of your discussion, explain the degree to which the Fourteenth Amendment contributed to a new and changed view of federal power versus state power.

   b. In the last 100 years we have seen a tremendous growth in the power and influence of government agencies, which deal with issues ranging from taxation to the environment. Discuss where federal and state agencies fit into the scheme of federalism, with particular emphasis on the degree to which federal agencies may alter the traditional view of federalism of the founders.

   c. Discuss the idea of federalism within a state; i.e., is the "top down" relationship of the state government to the counties and cities. It is roughly the same as the relationship between the federal government and the states?

3. **Third parties have played a role in America's political system.**

   a. Identify the purposes of third parties.

   b. Discuss the ways third parties are formed.

   c. Describe two specific third parties and third-party movements in American history and include information about the following:

   i. The candidates and their views.

   ii. The parties' platforms and their contributions to the political process and/or society.

   iii. Impact on the United States in later years.

4. **The organization of Congress is instrumental to the functioning of the legislative branch.**

   a. Describe the roles of parties and caucuses.

   b. Explain the role of committees.

   c. Discuss the legislative function of Congressional staff and specialized offices.

1. Ⓐ Ⓑ Ⓒ Ⓓ Ⓔ
2. Ⓐ Ⓑ Ⓒ Ⓓ Ⓔ
3. Ⓐ Ⓑ Ⓒ Ⓓ Ⓔ
4. Ⓐ Ⓑ Ⓒ Ⓓ Ⓔ
5. Ⓐ Ⓑ Ⓒ Ⓓ Ⓔ
6. Ⓐ Ⓑ Ⓒ Ⓓ Ⓔ
7. Ⓐ Ⓑ Ⓒ Ⓓ Ⓔ
8. Ⓐ Ⓑ Ⓒ Ⓓ Ⓔ
9. Ⓐ Ⓑ Ⓒ Ⓓ Ⓔ
10. Ⓐ Ⓑ Ⓒ Ⓓ Ⓔ
11. Ⓐ Ⓑ Ⓒ Ⓓ Ⓔ
12. Ⓐ Ⓑ Ⓒ Ⓓ Ⓔ
13. Ⓐ Ⓑ Ⓒ Ⓓ Ⓔ
14. Ⓐ Ⓑ Ⓒ Ⓓ Ⓔ
15. Ⓐ Ⓑ Ⓒ Ⓓ Ⓔ
16. Ⓐ Ⓑ Ⓒ Ⓓ Ⓔ
17. Ⓐ Ⓑ Ⓒ Ⓓ Ⓔ
18. Ⓐ Ⓑ Ⓒ Ⓓ Ⓔ
19. Ⓐ Ⓑ Ⓒ Ⓓ Ⓔ
20. Ⓐ Ⓑ Ⓒ Ⓓ Ⓔ

21. Ⓐ Ⓑ Ⓒ Ⓓ Ⓔ
22. Ⓐ Ⓑ Ⓒ Ⓓ Ⓔ
23. Ⓐ Ⓑ Ⓒ Ⓓ Ⓔ
24. Ⓐ Ⓑ Ⓒ Ⓓ Ⓔ
25. Ⓐ Ⓑ Ⓒ Ⓓ Ⓔ
26. Ⓐ Ⓑ Ⓒ Ⓓ Ⓔ
27. Ⓐ Ⓑ Ⓒ Ⓓ Ⓔ
28. Ⓐ Ⓑ Ⓒ Ⓓ Ⓔ
29. Ⓐ Ⓑ Ⓒ Ⓓ Ⓔ
30. Ⓐ Ⓑ Ⓒ Ⓓ Ⓔ
31. Ⓐ Ⓑ Ⓒ Ⓓ Ⓔ
32. Ⓐ Ⓑ Ⓒ Ⓓ Ⓔ
33. Ⓐ Ⓑ Ⓒ Ⓓ Ⓔ
34. Ⓐ Ⓑ Ⓒ Ⓓ Ⓔ
35. Ⓐ Ⓑ Ⓒ Ⓓ Ⓔ
36. Ⓐ Ⓑ Ⓒ Ⓓ Ⓔ
37. Ⓐ Ⓑ Ⓒ Ⓓ Ⓔ
38. Ⓐ Ⓑ Ⓒ Ⓓ Ⓔ
39. Ⓐ Ⓑ Ⓒ Ⓓ Ⓔ
40. Ⓐ Ⓑ Ⓒ Ⓓ Ⓔ

41. Ⓐ Ⓑ Ⓒ Ⓓ Ⓔ
42. Ⓐ Ⓑ Ⓒ Ⓓ Ⓔ
43. Ⓐ Ⓑ Ⓒ Ⓓ Ⓔ
44. Ⓐ Ⓑ Ⓒ Ⓓ Ⓔ
45. Ⓐ Ⓑ Ⓒ Ⓓ Ⓔ
46. Ⓐ Ⓑ Ⓒ Ⓓ Ⓔ
47. Ⓐ Ⓑ Ⓒ Ⓓ Ⓔ
48. Ⓐ Ⓑ Ⓒ Ⓓ Ⓔ
49. Ⓐ Ⓑ Ⓒ Ⓓ Ⓔ
50. Ⓐ Ⓑ Ⓒ Ⓓ Ⓔ
51. Ⓐ Ⓑ Ⓒ Ⓓ Ⓔ
52. Ⓐ Ⓑ Ⓒ Ⓓ Ⓔ
53. Ⓐ Ⓑ Ⓒ Ⓓ Ⓔ
54. Ⓐ Ⓑ Ⓒ Ⓓ Ⓔ
55. Ⓐ Ⓑ Ⓒ Ⓓ Ⓔ
56. Ⓐ Ⓑ Ⓒ Ⓓ Ⓔ
57. Ⓐ Ⓑ Ⓒ Ⓓ Ⓔ
58. Ⓐ Ⓑ Ⓒ Ⓓ Ⓔ
59. Ⓐ Ⓑ Ⓒ Ⓓ Ⓔ
60. Ⓐ Ⓑ Ⓒ Ⓓ Ⓔ

Practice Test Two

Section I: Multiple Choice Answer Key

Question Number	Correct Answer
1.	C
2.	D
3.	C
4.	D
5.	D
6.	A
7.	E
8.	B
9.	B
10.	B
11.	D
12.	A
13.	B
14.	C
15.	A
16.	C
17.	A
18.	B
19.	D
20.	B

Question Number	Correct Answer
21.	B
22.	B
23.	A
24.	C
25.	D
26.	E
27.	D
28.	B
29.	A
30.	D
31.	E
32.	B
33.	C
34.	A
35.	C
36.	A
37.	D
38.	C
39.	D
40.	A

Question Number	Correct Answer
41.	A
42.	C
43.	E
44.	A
45.	E
46.	B
47.	D
48.	D
49.	E
50.	E
51.	E
52.	E
53.	B
54.	D
55.	B
56.	C
57.	C
58.	C
59.	D
60.	D

Section I: Multiple Choice Explanations

1. **What was one reason a bill of rights was not included in the original constitution of 1787?**

   (A) Because the founders were too tired after the numerous debates to draft a bill of rights.

   (B) Because the majority of delegates thought a bill of rights was worthless.

   (C) Because many delegates feared that a bill of rights could be dangerous.

   (D) Because the delegates could not agree on which rights to include.

   (E) Because the delegates knew that every state already had a bill of rights.

   Answer: C.

   Because many delegates feared that a bill of rights could be dangerous. While most states had a bill of rights, some did not. Some delegates, like Madison and Hamilton, felt a bill of rights could be dangerous since the federal government might assume it had power over rights not listed.

2. **All of the following are examples of checks and balances in the Constitution EXCEPT:**

   (A) The president's veto power

   (B) "Judicial review" by the Supreme Court

   (C) The power to impeach

   (D) The authority to amend the Constitution

   (E) All of the above

   Answer: D.

   The authority to amend the Constitution. Choices A, B and C represent direct methods provided in the Constitution by which one branch of government may directly check the actions of another branch of government. D on the other hand relates to Article V of the Constitution, which gives either the states or Congress the power to amend the Constitution.

3. **The Constitution alludes to which group holding the greatest power in the new government?**

   (A)   The federal government

   (B)   The states

   (C)   The people

   (D)   The courts

   (E)   None of the above

   Answer: C.
   The people. The text begins with "We the People ..." not "We the States." The very essence of the structure created by the constitution is that all aspects of its operation as well as the possibility of amendment are to be controlled by the people, through their elected representatives.

4. **Which of the following could be said to be an expression of federalism?**

   (A)   The desire by western states to gain control of public lands held by the federal government.

   (B)   State constitutional amendments about the definition of marriage.

   (C)   The decision by an aggrieved party about whether to sue in state or federal court.

   (D)   All of the above.

   (E)   None of the above.

   Answer: D.
   All of the above. Choices A, B and C each represent a different aspect of the division of power between the states and the federal government which essentially constitutes federalism.

5. **The Twelfth Amendment modified Article II, Section 1 of the Constitution regarding electors for president in what way?**

(A) It increased the number of electors per state from 5 to 10.

(B) It changed the time electors were to meet from the last Tuesday in October to the first Tuesday in November.

(C) It increased the number of votes an elector could cast for President and Vice President to two votes for each, for a total of four votes.

(D) It forced electors for the first time to vote separately for President and Vice President.

(E) It stated for the first time that if no presidential candidate received a majority of votes, the House of Representatives would decide who would be president.

Answer: D.

It forced electors for the first time to vote separately for President and Vice President. Article II, Section 1 originally provided that the person with the second highest number of votes would become the Vice President. This resulted in Thomas Jefferson becoming Vice President under President John Adams in the election of 1796, even though the two were rivals at the time.

6. **The nurturing process through which people acquire knowledge, have feelings, and evaluations about the political world is called**

(A) Political socialization

(B) Political efficacy

(C) Propaganda acquisition

(D) Political ideology

(E) Public opinion

Answer: A.

Political socialization. Socialization is a slow evolving process of learning about one's response to politics. Over time, people accumulate their feelings, responses, and information to have a good understanding about their "politics."

7. **Political participation in the government is an essential component of**

(A) Freedom

(B) Independence

(C) Free enterprise

(D) Self-expression

(E) Self-government

Answer: E.
Self-government. Self-government is a key tenet of representative democracy, requiring political participation by the electorate and the citizens.

8. **Which of the following is a random sample?**

(A) Interviewing people in a nonsystematic fashion.

(B) A selection mechanism that gives each person an equal chance of being selected.

(C) Going up to people on the street asking for their opinions.

(D) Asking every student in the Introduction to Psychology course to fill out a survey.

(E) Putting a survey on the web and asking people to take it.

Answer: B.
A selection mechanism that gives each person an equal chance of being selected.
The meaning of random sampling is that every person has an equal probability of being selected for the sample.

9. **Which of the following polls is most likely to help a candidate evaluate the short-term effect of a certain campaign event?**

(A) An exit poll

(B) A tracking poll

(C) A push poll

(D) A stratified sample

(E) A cross-sectional poll

Answer: B.

A tracking poll. A tracking poll enables a campaign to follow its daily rise or fall in support.

10. **A conservative friend of yours avoids watching MSNBC because she believes it to be a liberal news network. Your friend is engaging in**

   (A) Prejudice questioning

   (B) Selective exposure

   (C) Infotainment

   (D) Stereotype challenging

   (E) Narrowcasting

Answer: B.

Selective exposure. Selective exposure is the process by which people consciously choose to get the news from information sources that have viewpoints compatible with their own.

11. **In general, public opinion**

   (A) Has no relation to government action at all

   (B) Has an impact on government action only during elections

   (C) Constrains only the actions of incumbents in government

   (D) Constrains the actions of government

   (E) Has very little impact on government action

Answer: D.

Constrains the actions of government. Public opinion constrains the actions of government, and not just during elections. It makes government responsive to the citizens when making policy, allocating budgets, or passing legislation.

12. **Most political scientists and political observers assess public opinion primarily through**

(A) Polls

(B) Social media blogs

(C) Letters to the editor

(D) Voter registration rolls

(E) Reports from interest groups

Answer: A.
Polls. Polls are still the most statistical method by which to gather data and engage a representative sample population. The other methods tend to be single-point representations of opinions.

13. **All of the following are functions of political parties EXCEPT:**

(A) Recruiting candidates for public office.

(B) Gaining control of the government.

(C) Gathering volunteers to register voters.

(D) Presenting alternative policies to the electorate.

(E) Opposing the winning party by putting forth its own policies.

Answer: B.
Gaining control of the government. Gaining control of the government is a goal of political parties but not a function or purpose.

14. **Which of the following statements is correct about mass media?**

(A) Mass media is limited to newspapers, television, and the Internet.

(B) Broadcasts relating to political advertisement is the least valuable asset for politicians.

(C) In the United States, corporations control most mass media.

(D) Another name for mass media in the United States is "state media."

(E) The focus of mass media is to reach a specific audience.

Answer: C.

In the United States, corporations control most mass media. Mass media consists of many types of communication. Its purpose is to reach a large, general audience rather than a smaller, specific audience. State media refers to countries such as Russia where the government controls the media.

15. **All of the following are thought to be advantages of a two-party system EXCEPT:**

    (A) Lack of third choice

    (B) More efficient government

    (C) More stability

    (D) Moderate views

    (E) Less disagreement

Answer: A.

Lack of a third choice. Moderate views, which lead to less disagreement, more stability, and a more efficient government, are thought to be advantages of a two-party system. One disadvantage of the two-party system is that a third-choice candidate is not usually a viable option.

16. **Which of the following is an example of the media shaping a political attitude?**

    (A) A television newscaster reporting on a terrorist bombing in a foreign city.

    (B) A radio broadcast describing a presidential inauguration.

    (C) An Internet story of the reasons why a person should vote or not vote for a specific candidate.

    (D) A newsletter providing telephone numbers and other contact information for discussing an issue with the chairperson of an interest group.

    (E) A newspaper article about an upcoming presidential debate and the topics that will be covered during the debate.

Answer: C.

An Internet story of the reasons why a person should vote or not vote for a specific candidate. A political attitude is the way a person feels about political issues, a person involved in government, or the government. All of choices, other than C, provide facts. Option C attempts to influence thinking about a candidate.

17. **Which system of nominating a presidential candidate involves a local gathering where voters discuss and then decide openly which candidate they will support?**

(A) Caucus

(B) Primary

(C) General election

(D) Convention

(E) Committee hearing

Answer: A.
Caucus. Primaries and caucuses are methods of voting for presidential candidates. In states where caucuses are held, voters gather to discuss and then vote for the candidate they favor.

18. **What is the purpose of a Political Action Committee?**

(A) To approve actions of the House and Senate.

(B) To raise money to defeat or elect candidates.

(C) To monitor political spending.

(D) To nominate candidates for office.

(E) To lobby for legislation.

Answer: B.
To raise money to defeat or elect candidates. Political action committees are referred to as "PACs," and their purpose is to raise money and spend it to elect or defeat candidates who are running for office.

19. **Who choses whether there will be a caucus or primary election?**

(A) Political parties

(B) Local governments

(C) The head of the National Committee of a political party

(D) States

(E) Presidential candidates

Answer: D.

States. Each state determines whether they will hold a caucuses or primary elections.

20. **Why did the framers of the Constitution establish a national bicameral legislature?**

    (A) To appease the large states

    (B) To eliminate the law-making body from becoming too powerful

    (C) To appease the leaders of the Constitutional Convention

    (D) To create the 3/5 compromise

    (E) To eliminate checks and balances between Congress and the other branches

Answer: B.

To eliminate the law-making body from becoming too powerful. The framers established a two-house legislature so one house would be based on population and the other would have an equal number from each state. The compromise was the result of the wishes of both large and small states. The Three-fifths Compromise related to how the population was counted.

21. **What is the term for drawing or connecting voting districts in odd shapes so that a candidate can easily win that district?**

    (A) Mal-apportionment

    (B) Gerrymandering

    (C) Reallocation

    (D) Caucusing

    (E) Reorganization

Answer: B.

Gerrymandering. Mal-apportionment is where districts are unequally sized. Gerrymandering is drawing districts in ways so a candidate can easily win that district. One example is connecting districts that represent opposing political parties where one party has a slight difference in strength.

22. **In the United States, who (or which body) has the power to declare war?**

    (A) The President

    (B) Congress

    (C) The Executive Branch

    (D) The Supreme Court

    (E) The states

    Answer: B.
    Congress. Although the president can recommend declaring war, only Congress has the power to declare war.

23. **Which of the following statements is true about political parties in the United States?**

    (A) The Constitution never actually mentions them.

    (B) They are called "a necessary part of the political process."

    (C) They are most effective if there are only two major parties.

    (D) They are harmful to the political process.

    (E) To be identified as a political party, the group must have at least 100 members.

    Answer: A.
    The Constitution never actually mentions them. Political parties are not referred to in the Constitution.

24. **What term refers to the situation when the president's party is not the same as the party controlling either the Senate of the House?**

    (A) Neutral government

    (B) Unified government

    (C) Divided government

    (D) Contested government

    (E) Adversarial government

Answer: C.

Divided government. A unified government is when the party of the president is the same as one that controls the House of the Senate. A divided government exists when the parties are not the same

25. **Competition between the president and Congress exists because of**

(A) Inequality of bargaining power

(B) Checks and balances

(C) Separation of powers

(D) Separation of powers and checks and balances

(E) Judicial review

Answer: D.

Separation of powers and checks and balances. Separation of powers and checks and balances result in the executive and legislative branches competing for power.

26. **Which of the following statements are true about gridlock?**

(A) Gridlock rarely protects the interests of many.

(B) Gridlock only occurs when many diverse sides are present.

(C) Gridlock is an unnecessary part of the democratic process.

(D) Gridlock was exemplified by Congressional action during the presidency of Franklin Roosevelt.

(E) Gridlock is good because if there is more diverse thinking, there will be more people represented.

Answer: E.

Gridlock is good because if there is more diverse thinking, there will be more people represented. Gridlock occurs when there are many diverse thoughts and ideas. Gridlock is a necessary and important part of representative democracy and even though it causes delays, it is an event that forces compromise.

27. **All of the following statements about the presidency are correct EXCEPT**

    (A) The framers feared anarchy.

    (B) The framers feared a monarchy.

    (C) Some of the framers wanted a legislature to check all actions of the president.

    (D) The framers wanted a president who could dominate the legislative branch.

    (E) The framers gave the president broad powers to create a balance of power.

    Answer: D.
    The framers wanted a president who could dominate the legislative branch. The framers of the Constitution did not want the executive officer to become a monarch. They also feared the possibility of anarchy. They gave the president broad powers to create a balance between branches of government.

28. **All of the following are powers of the President EXCEPT**

    (A) Serve as commander-in-chief of the Armed Forces

    (B) Grant pardons in impeachment cases

    (C) Convene Congress in special sessions

    (D) Grant reprieves in cases other than impeachment

    (E) Receive ambassadors

    Answer: B.
    Grant pardons in impeachment cases. A president may not grant pardons or reprieves in cases involving impeachment.

29. **If a Cabinet member were to become president, which cabinet position is the first in the line of succession?**

    (A) State

    (B) Treasury

    (C) Defense

    (D) Justice

    (E) Interior

Answer: A.

State. The Secretary of State is the first Cabinet officer in line of Cabinet members to become president.

30. **When may a president use a "pocket veto"?**

(A) At any time during the Congressional session.

(B) When the president forgets to sign a bill into law.

(C) When the president is unable to return the bill to Congress while it is in session.

(D) When the president cannot return the bill to Congress within ten days because Congress has adjourned.

(E) When the president is away from the White House and has been told Congress will be sending a bill for signature.

Answer: D.

When the president cannot return the bill to Congress within ten days because Congress has adjourned. Article I, Section 7, of the Constitution provides that "If any Bill shall not be returned by the President within ten days (Sundays excepted) after it shall have been presented to him, the same shall be a Law, in like manner as if he had signed it, unless the Congress by their Adjournment prevent its return, in which case it shall not be a Law."

31. **Which Constitutional amendment allows a Vice-President who becomes President to nominate a new vice-president?**

(A) Nineteenth

(B) Twenty-first

(C) Twenty-third

(D) Twenty-fourth

(E) Twenty-fifth

Answer: E.

Twenty-fifth. Section 1 of the Twenty-fifth Amendment provides that in case of the removal of the President from office or of his death or resignation, the Vice President shall become President. Section 2 provides that whenever there is a vacancy in the office of the Vice President, the President shall nominate a Vice President who shall take office upon confirmation by a majority vote of both Houses of Congress.

32. **The ability of the president to veto an act of Congress is an example of**

   (A) Separation of powers

   (B) Checks and balances

   (C) Judicial review

   (D) Presidential prerogative

   (E) Presidential right

   Answer: B.
   Checks and balances. A president can limit the powers of Congress by vetoing legislation. The act of vetoing operates to maintain a balance among the branches and keep the legislature from becoming dominant.

33. **Which is an example of a case of original jurisdiction heard by the U.S. Supreme Court?**

   (A) Diversity jurisdiction case

   (B) Bankruptcy case

   (C) Dispute between states

   (D) Cases arising under the Constitution

   (E) A patent infringement case

   Answer: C.
   Dispute between states. All of the case types listed can be heard by a federal court. Cases that involve disputes between states can only be heard by the U.S. Supreme Court. Therefore, original jurisdiction in state-dispute cases is in the U.S. Supreme Court.

34. **What does "diversity jurisdiction" mean?**

   (A) The parties are from different states.

   (B) The issues involve federal and state issues.

   (C) The issues involve two courts.

   (D) There are multiple parties from the same state.

   (E) The amount required to be involved is $75,000.00.

Answer: A.

The parties are from different states. Diversity jurisdiction requires a certain amount of money that is involved and parties to be from different states. The way the question is worded, the meaning relates to the parties, not the requirement of a threshold level of money being sought for damages.

35. **Which of the following describes a body of non-elected government staff that makes government decisions?**

   (A)   Federal government

   (B)   State government

   (C)   Bureaucracy

   (D)   Agency

   (E)   Congress

Answer: C.

Bureaucracy. A government bureaucracy works to administer the law.

36. **Which branch of government controls the majority of the federal bureaucracy?**

   (A)   Executive

   (B)   Legislative

   (C)   Judicial

   (D)   Agencies

   (E)   Courts

Answer: A.

Executive. The executive branch controls the majority of the federal bureaucracy even though the legislative and judicial branches are also involved.

Practice Test Two

37. **Cabinet departments and independent regulatory agencies are a type of _____.**

   (A) Government corporation

   (B) Presidential commission

   (C) Method of oversight

   (D) Organization in the federal bureaucracy

   (E) Government employee

   Answer: D.
   Organization in the federal bureaucracy. Both the Cabinet departments and independent regulatory agencies are examples of organizations in the federal bureaucracy. Other examples include: independent executive agencies, government corporations, and presidential commissions

38. **What is the system called of rewarding friends and political allies with government jobs in exchange for their support?**

   (A) Civil service

   (B) Regulation

   (C) Patronage

   (D) Appointments

   (E) Merit system

   Answer: C.
   Patronage. Civil service reform called for awarding jobs based on merit. Patronage is the system of awarding friends and political supporters with jobs. Another name for patronage is the "spoils system".

39. **What is the significance of the Pendleton Act?**

   (A) It created the bureaucracy.

   (B) It was passed after the assassination of James A. Garfield.

   (C) It created the patronage system.

   (D) It required a person desiring to be a federal employee to take a competitive exam.

   (E) It created the first agency within the federal bureaucracy.

Answer: D.

It required a person desiring to be a federal employee to take a competitive exam. The Pendleton Act was passed after an unhappy federal job seeker, who was not given the job, killed President James A. Garfield. The Pendleton Act requires people seeking federal government jobs to take a competitive exam. The awarding of federal jobs is made on the basis of merit.

40. **Why is the Constitution called a 'living document'?**

    (A) It has the ability to change at different times.

    (B) It was created by the people.

    (C) It is a static document.

    (D) Anyone can change.

    (E) It can be destroyed if there is excessive reliance on it.

    Answer: A.

    It has the ability to change at different times. A 'living document' is flexible and can change with time, as needed.

41. **Common law refers mostly to which of the following?**

    (A) Precedents and traditions that have been accepted in society for so long that they have become accepted norms

    (B) The laws dealing with common people

    (C) Laws that are written and codified

    (D) Law that is decided by the House of Commons in Great Britain

    (E) Law that is common among different nations

    Answer: A.

    Precedents and traditions that have been accepted in society for so long that they have become accepted norms. Common law refers to precedents and traditions that have become accepted norms in society. Laws that are written and codified are statutes, legislative enactments, and Codes.

42. How is Congress different from the parliament of most European nations?

(A) In parliamentary elections, any person can run for office.

(B) In Congress, legislators determine whether new leaders must be elected.

(C) In Congress, the members are less worried than members of parliaments about losing future elections.

(D) In parliamentary situations, the legislators don't have to worry about losing their positions when new elections take place.

(E) Parliamentary legislators have much independent power.

Answer: C.

In Congress, the members are less worried than members of parliaments about losing future elections. In Congress, anyone can run for office but in a parliamentary system, the candidate must usually have the approval of his political party. Congressional elections are held every two years but a leader's support or non-support determines the times for elections in parliamentary systems. Because parliamentary members depend on the success of their parties, they are more worried about winning in future elections.

43. What is the difference between cloture and filibuster?

(A) Filibuster is prohibited if 25% of the Representatives oppose legislation and cloture means talking to encourage passage of a bill.

(B) Filibuster is a method senators use to veto a bill where cloture is used to continue a debate.

(C) Filibuster is used by Representatives to end debate and cloture is used to call for a vote.

(D) Cloture is used to begin a congressional debate and filibuster is used by Representatives to oppose legislation.

(E) Filibuster is used by senators to stall a debate and cloture is used to end a debate.

Answer: E.

Filibuster is used by senators to stall a debate and cloture is used to end a debate. The filibuster is a method used by Senators to stall for time. The result is usually the prevention of discussion or passage of a bill because stalling usually takes the form of continued talking. If 60 senators vote to end the debate (cloture), then the filibuster is ended.

44. Bills that give tangible benefits to people are called _____.

(A) Pork-barrel legislation

(B) Franking privilege

(C) Loopholes

(D) Oversight

(E) Entertainment spending

Answer: A.

Pork-barrel legislation. Pork-barrel legislation gives tangible benefits to a specific district. For example, funding for a new dam or highway in a specific Congressional district is made available in an appropriations bill.

45. What is the term for sending free information by mail to constituents?

(A) Gerrymandering

(B) Loophole

(C) Checks and balances

(D) Bribery

(E) Franking

Answer: E.

Franking. When members of Congress use free postage to mail constituents information, the use is called franking. Franking also applies to placing signatures on faxes. Sometimes, franking is used in greater quantities before an election.

46. Policy "gridlock" refers to _____.

(A) Ideas about reforming Congress

(B) The slow manner in which Congress functions

(C) Failing to serve the public interest

(D) Local prejudices shown by legislators

(E) The decisiveness of Congress

Answer: B.

The slow manner in which Congress functions. A gridlock is a deadlock or "traffic jam" that derails progress. The slow manner in which Congress functions in relation to creating and developing policy is often referred to as a "gridlock."

47. **In the process and structure of public policymaking, "iron triangles" refer to the**

    (A) Bargaining and negotiating process between the President and Congress about the direction of domestic policy.

    (B) Dominance of corporate power in setting the national policy agenda for economic expansion.

    (C) Interrelationship among federal, state, and local levels of government in the policy process .

    (D) Networks of congressional committees, bureaucratic agencies, and interest groups that strongly influence the policy process.

    (E) Group of presidential advisers who formulate the President's foreign policy agenda.

Answer: D.

Networks of congressional committees, bureaucratic agencies, and interest groups that strongly influence the policy process. The key players in creating public policy are Congress—which passes the policy legislation, government agencies that have oversight of execution over any law or legislation passed by Congress, and interest groups that act on behalf of citizens or companies that are affected by the policy. So, the three groups comprise the corners of the triangle. Therefore, the iron triangle is a unique relationship between the bureaucracy, congressmen, and lobbyists that results in the mutual benefit of all three of them.

48. **Which of the following best describes the concept of political efficacy?**

(A) It is the belief that the average citizen can make little or no difference in an election.

(B) It is the belief that an intelligent voting decision cannot be made without information.

(C) It is the belief that the media must provide unbiased information for citizens to be able to make well-informed choices.

(D) It is the belief that one can make a difference in politics by expressing an opinion and acting politically.

(E) It is the belief that politicians must keep the electorate well-informed if they are to govern efficiently.

Answer: D.

It is the belief that one can make a difference in politics by expressing an opinion and acting politically. Political efficacy refers to the citizens' belief that they can understand and "influence" political actions of their governments. It is important in establishing faith and trust in any form of representative government.

49. **Cooperative federalism can best be described by which of the following statements?**

(A) Different levels of government are involved in common policy areas.

(B) Government must have cooperation from the people in order to make legislative decisions.

(C) Local levels of government can make decisions on issues more efficiently than state and national governments can.

(D) The federal government must make regulations that can be applied across every state in the same way.

(E) Business and government can work together to more effectively accomplish shared goals.

Answer: E.

Business and government can work together to more effectively accomplish shared goals. Federalism refers to the relationship between two governmental roles. In large policy domains, for example like climate change, education, etc., one can see all levels of government engage to develop a cooperative solution.

50. **Which of the following describes a consequence of the growing concentration of ownership of the news media?**

(A)   Newspaper prices have gone down.

(B)   Coverage of political events has gotten more liberal over time.

(C)   Prices for televised campaign ads have gone down.

(D)   Candidates get greater free airtime than in the past.

(E)   There is increased similarity of network news coverage.

Answer: E.

There is increased similarity of network news coverage. Newspaper prices have gone up, since subscriptions have dropped. Coverage of political events has become ideology-specific, so there's more of both conservative and liberal oriented coverage. Prices for televised ads have gone up, with huge sums being paid for primetime advertising. And, while there are more debates and candidate airtime, it is not a consequence of concentration of ownership. The direct consequence has been that there is more similarity of stories covered.

51. **Interest groups engage in all of the following activities EXCEPT**

(A)   Testifying before congressional committees.

(B)   Sponsoring issue advocacy advertisements.

(C)   Lobbying federal agencies.

(D)   Filing federal lawsuits.

(E)   Using the franking privilege.

Answer: E.

Using the franking privilege. The franking privilege is only available to Congressional members to send mail under their signature without postage. The privilege has its roots in 17th century Great Britain. Congress is considered to reimburse the U.S. Postal Service for the cost of the mail by the appropriations it gives the Postal Agency.

52. **Which of the following is NOT part of the Miranda warning typically given to suspects when they are arrested for a crime?**

(A) You have the right to remain silent.

(B) You have the right to an attorney.

(C) Anything you say may be used against you in a court of law.

(D) If you answer questions now without an attorney present, you have the right to stop answering at any time.

(E) All of the above are part of the Miranda warning.

Answer: E.

All of the above are part of the Miranda warning. The "Miranda warning" derived from *Miranda v. Arizona*, 384 U.S. 436 (1966) includes all of the above statements. Later cases have not changed this.

53. **Which of the following is not covered by the Civil Rights Act of 1964?**

(A) Discrimination on the basis of gender.

(B) Discrimination on the basis of age.

(C) Discrimination on the basis of race.

(D) Discrimination on the basis of national origin.

(E) Discrimination on the basis of religion.

Answer: B.

Discrimination on the basis of age. Age discrimination is covered by entirely different acts, namely the Age Discrimination in Employment Act of 1967 (ADEA) and the Age Discrimination Act of 1975.

54. The right to a jury trial is

(A) Only stated in the Constitution and its amendments as a right in criminal cases, not in civil cases.

(B) Not stated in the Constitution, but was first granted in the Judiciary Act of 1789.

(C) Stated in the Constitution as a guarantee of twelve jurors, who must be taken from the local community.

(D) Guaranteed in the Constitution for all federal crimes except impeachment.

(E) The same as indictment by a Grand Jury.

Answer: D.

Guaranteed in the Constitution for all federal crimes except impeachment. Article III section 2 of the Constitution states that "the trial of all crimes, except in cases of impeachment, shall be by jury ..." Juries in civil cases are guaranteed by the Seventh Amendment. The number of jurors is not given in the Constitution. The Grand Jury mentioned in the Fifth Amendment is an entirely separate body organized for a different reason (indictment of crime only).

55. The 1973 *Roe v. Wade* decision found a "right of privacy" primarily based on

(A) The Fourth Amendment's prohibition of search and seizure.

(B) The Fourteenth Amendment's due process clause.

(C) The Ninth Amendment's reference to rights not listed in the Constitution.

(D) The First Amendment's guarantee of free speech.

(E) The ex-post facto clause in Article 1, Sections 9 and 10 of the Constitution.

Answer: B.

The Fourteenth Amendment's due process clause. The primary reliance was on the Fourteenth Amendment's due process clause, which states: "No State shall deprive any person of life, liberty or property, without due process of law..."

56. **In the landmark case of *Brown v. Board of Education* the Supreme Court ruled that**

   (A) Segregation of blacks from whites in private schools was illegal.

   (B) States were required to bus black students to white schools.

   (C) The "separate but equal" standard from the 1896 case of *Plessy v. Ferguson* was overturned.

   (D) Segregation in higher education state schools (universities and colleges) was banned, but it was allowed to continue in public schools.

   (E) Segregation in buses, restaurants, and other public places was banned, not just in schools.

   Answer: C.

   The "separate but equal" standard from the 1896 case of *Plessy v. Ferguson* was overturned. Segregation in private schools was not banned until the 1976 case of *Runyon v. McRary*. Enforcement by busing was not addressed by the court in its ruling in *Brown*. The main goal of the opinion was to overturn the precedent of *Plessy v. Ferguson*. Desegregation on buses was not banned until the 1956 case of *Browder v. Gayle*, which was brought about due to the Montgomery, Alabama bus boycott

57. **Which of the following is NOT true regarding flag burning, as interpreted by the Supreme Court?**

   (A) It is a protected form of speech under the First Amendment.

   (B) State governments can pass laws to regulate the time, place and manner of flag burning.

   (C) While burning is protected under the First Amendment, other forms of flag desecration are strictly prohibited.

   (D) The court applies "strict scrutiny" when reviewing flag burning cases.

   (E) Old, worn out flags are legitimately destroyed by burning.

   Answer: C.

   While burning is protected under the First Amendment, other forms of flag desecration are strictly prohibited. The Supreme Court in *Texas v. Johnson*, 491 U.S. 397 (1989) found that a Texas law which prohibited flag desecration, including burning, was unconstitutional. Burning is not the only method of desecration, which is allowed as part of the free speech guarantee.

58. Which of the following would NOT be considered a violation of the Family Medical Leave Act or laws which prevent gender discrimination?

(A) A fire department paying women differently than men for the same job.

(B) An airline refusing to hire men as stewards.

(C) A man taking up to twelve weeks off without pay after his wife has a baby.

(D) A state university, which only allows men in its engineering programs.

(E) A state hospital, which only hires female nurses.

Answer: C.

A man taking up to twelve weeks off without pay after his wife has a baby. The Family Medical Leave Act allows a man or woman to take up to twelve weeks off without pay each year for a variety of family related events, including birth of a new baby.

59. Which of the following would NOT be considered illegal sexual harassment?

(A) A female boss fires a male employee for refusing her advances.

(B) Reassigning a woman to a different department and reducing her pay because she refused male advances.

(C) A male cashier in a hair salon who is continuously subjected to put-downs and anti-male talk by the female employees.

(D) Simple teasing, offhand comments, or isolated incidents of a sexual nature that are not considered serious.

(E) All of the above are considered illegal sexual harassment.

Answer: D.

Simple teasing, offhand comments, or isolated incidents of a sexual nature that are not considered serious. The Equal Employment Opportunity Commission website provides an exception for D. And states that "harassment is illegal when it is so frequent or severe that it creates a hostile or offensive work environment or when it results in an adverse employment decision (such as the victim being fired or demoted)."

60. In the *Roe v. Wade* decision the "point of viability" at which a state could prohibit abortion by state law was

(A) The point at which a fetal heartbeat could be detected, at approximately 25 days after conception.

(B) The point at which DNA tests would identify a fetus as distinctly human when compared to the DNA of other living organisms.

(C) The point at which the mother first felt the fetus move.

(D) The point at which the infant could live outside the womb with artificial aid.

(E) The moment of conception.

Answer: D.

The point at which the infant could live outside the womb with artificial aid. The court described viability as the point at which the infant could "live outside the mother's womb, albeit with artificial aid." *Roe v. Wade*, 410 U.S. 113, 160 (1973). This was identified by the court as the third trimester, and was the point at which states could ban abortion. In the later case of *Planned Parenthood v. Casey*, 505 U.S. 833 (1992), the court abandoned the trimester approach, finding that the date of viability was pushed back from the 28th week to approximately 22nd week, due to medical advances. This new period is in the second half of the second trimester.

Section II: Free Response Sample Answers

1. **Public opinion polls are a way to link the public with elected officials. Members of Congress often use polls to understand the views of their constituents, but they must also pay attention to other political considerations.**

   a. **Identify two characteristics of a valid, scientific, public opinion poll.**

   b. **Explain why each of the following enhances the influence of public opinion on the voting decisions of members of Congress.**

      i. Strong public opinion as expressed in polling results

      ii. Competitive re-elections

   c. **Explain why each of the following limits the influence of public opinion on the voting decisions of members of Congress.**

      i. Legislators' voting records

      ii. Party leadership

Sample Answers:

A public opinion poll is used to understand what the public thinks about an issue or a set of issues at a point in time. The polls consist of interviews or surveys with a sample group of citizens or individuals and then extrapolated to the larger population.

   a. Four characteristics of a valid public opinion poll are (1) it must be a random sample, (2) it must be clearly worded so that there is no ambiguity in understanding the question, (3) It must try to attain a sample representation of the entire population, and (4) it must be a large enough sample size to allow for extrapolation.

   b. i. Strong public opinion on an issue is an indicator of how a sample subset of a population feels, thinks, and wants to act on the issue. Members of Congress are representatives of the citizens of their District or State, therefore, it is important for them to consider the sentiments expressed in the polling.

      ii. Congressional member are up for re-election every two years in the House of Representatives and every six years in the Senate. For the shorter election cycle, elected member of Congress have to answer to their District or State citizens on their voting record. They are elected to represent their District or State, therefore, a strong poll result on a key issue, will suggest that they vote the same way as the public opinion from their District or State shows.

   c. i. Legislator voting records can also be correlated with public opinion polls. If the polls point to one decision and the voting records to another, then the voting public might perceive the legislator as being too independent and not responsive to their opinions. Also, if a legislator does not vote on an issue, that the public cares about, then they can be perceived as being indecisive by their voters.

ii. Party leadership limits the influence of public opinion by delegating party vote-counters (called whips) to determine the vote count and to influence a member to support their side. So, in order to avoid the risk of losing party support or to gain party support and maybe a leadership position in a committee, sometimes, legislators might vote against the outcome suggested by a public opinion poll.

2. **Federalism is the co-existence of different levels of government (such as state and federal governments), each holding power within its sphere, but unable to fully control the other levels of government.**

a. **Discuss how federalism was viewed differently prior to the Civil War, particularly by the states. As part of your discussion, explain the degree to which the Fourteenth Amendment contributed to a new and changed view of federal power versus state power.**

b. **In the last 100 years we have seen a tremendous growth in the power and influence of government agencies, which deal with issues ranging from taxation to the environment. Discuss where federal and state agencies fit into the scheme of federalism, with particular emphasis on the degree to which federal agencies may alter the traditional view of federalism of the founders.**

c. **Discuss the idea of federalism within a state; i.e., is the "top down" relationship of the state government to the counties and cities. It is roughly the same as the relationship between the federal government and the states?**

Sample Answers:

a. Prior to the Civil War, the states were considered to have a great deal of power. The state governments held nearly unlimited power within their territory, while the federal government was an entity of limited powers. The federal government only had authority over those things specifically granted to it by the Constitution. This concept of greater state power contributed greatly to the sectional debates, which led to the Civil War.

After the war, the passage of the Civil Rights Act of 1966, allowed for the first time in the history of the nation, the preservation and protection of civil rights to rest firmly in the hands of the federal government. But more fundamentally, the Civil Rights Act of 1866 marked an unprecedented reorientation of the relationship between federal oversight and individual and states' rights. The Act was codified in 1968 as the Fourteenth Amendment.

The Supreme Court, through its decisions, began to technically "incorporate" many of the federal government's rights through the Fourteenth Amendment as being directly applicable to the states. The federal courts could therefore enforce rights protections more completely than they ever could before in the nation. This led to a more homogenous interpretation of rights across the whole country and a new view of federalism.

b. The founders did not contemplate the large federal and state agencies, which exist today. This has led to concern by many that agencies are not sufficiently limited in their powers, and may be denying principles of separation of powers and federalism because they have become too powerful.

The genius of the Constitutional plan set forth by the founders has nevertheless helped to deal with this problem. The people, through their elected representatives, have created laws, which provide for accountability, transparency and oversight of government agencies. Likewise the courts are often called on to step in and review the actions and decisions of agencies, thereby protecting individuals in their rights. This is the new norm, where federalism at the federal and state level is managed through public opinion and the courts.

c. There are differences between federalism at the federal/state level, and federalism at the state/local level. At the federal level, when the original constitution was formed, it was understood to have limited powers over the existing states. Local governments on the other hands—cities, towns and counties—are usually creations of the state, and have tight connections to the State for funding and limited self-power.

States meanwhile are not considered to have limited powers like the federal government. States tax their cities and have their own revenue for expenditure and pass their own legislation for their governing. The Constitution, the foundational document for the federal government expresses what the federal government is allowed to do, but state constitutions are seen as expressions of what the states are NOT allowed to do. Anything not limited by the state constitution is presumed to be a power retained by the states.

In conclusion, federalism at the federal/state level is limited in terms of federal oversight of the state government while at the state/local levels there is greater federal oversight of local governments by state governments.

3. **Third parties have played a role in America's political system.**

a. **Identify the purposes of third parties.**

b. **Discuss the ways third parties are formed.**

c. **Describe two specific third parties and third-party movements in American history and include information about the following:**

i. **The candidates and their views.**

ii. **The parties' platforms and their contributions to the political process and/or society.**

iii. **Impact on the United States in later years.**

Sample Answers:

a. Third parties serve the purpose of providing voters with a third choice for an office, usually the presidency. They also provide the voters with alternative ideas that members of the party believe should be accepted as part of the government process or adopted for the benefit of society, in general.

b. Third parties are formed by individuals who believe in a certain issue or philosophy. Sometimes they are formed because of a division within one of the major political parties. The division may be the result of disagreement with the choice of candidate or the result of a difference in belief about the party's policies. The groups that are formed as the result of a division within a party are called splinter parties.

c. Several third parties have formed over the last 100 years. Several examples are listed here.

The Freesoil Party: The party came into existence in 1848 and its primary purpose was opposing the extension of slavery into the new territories and the western states. Martin Van Buren was the party's candidate and most of the party's members were in the state of New York, Ohio, and the Northeast. Van Buren did not have enough votes to win any electoral votes.

The Southern Democratic Party and the Constitutional Union Party: In the 1860 election two third parties had candidates running for the presidency. The Southern Democrats, a party that had split from the Democrats, selected John Breckenridge and gained 72 electoral votes. This party defended slavery and opposed the ideas of the Freesoil party. John Bell was the presidential candidate for the Constitutional Union party. This party opposed secession based on the slavery issue, consisted of conservatives, and former Whigs. This third party gained 39 electoral votes.

The Populist Party: One of the more successful third parties, was the Populist Party. This party chose James Weaver as its candidate in the 1892 election. The party was

Practice Test Two

244 AP US Government and Politics

made up of farmers' alliances and labor groups that represented the "common" person. They were successful in western states and won 22 electoral votes. They urged the adoption of silver and gold for currency and the free coinage of silver. They also favored a graduated income tax.

The Progressive Party: A split from the Republican party, the Progressive Party, had as its candidate Theodore Roosevelt in the 1912 election. Roosevelt ran as a third-party candidate because he found the views of William Howard Taft too conservative. This party wanted to promote reform and progressivism. The party's platform focused on ideas such as registration of lobbyists, social insurance for the elderly, minimum wage laws for women, an eight-hour work day, workers' compensation for job-related injuries, direct election of senators, the referendum, recall, and initiative. The party received the most electoral votes of any third-party in the country's history.

In 1924 the Progressive Party, a new party with the name of the former party, supported Robert LaFallotte for president. Its main basis of support was in the state of Wisconsin. One of its planks supported the public ownership of railroads. Lafollette's support in Wisconsin gained the party 13 electoral votes.

States Right Party: In 1948, the State's Right party had Strom Thurmond as its candidate. He won 39 electoral votes, and the party was formed from anti-semitic and racist elements. It opposed integration of the military and President Truman's support of a civil rights plank in the Democratic Party's platform. Thurmond, who was governor of South Carolina, and others walked out of the Democratic convention to protest the party's position on civil rights.

Another Progressive Party was formed the same year and this party nominated Henry Wallace, former Secretary of Agriculture for President Truman. The Progressive Party opposed Truman's policies in the Cold War and objected to the Marshall Plan and the Truman Doctrine.

The American Independent Party: In 1968, during the civil rights movement, the American Independent Party emerged with George Wallace, former governor of Alabama, as its candidate. The party won 46 electoral votes and opposed integration.

The Reform Party: No third party since that time has won electoral votes. The Reform Party of the 1990s and early 2000s supported the belief that government was corrupt. The party was created as a split from the Republican Party and had Ross Perot and Ralph Nader as its candidates. The party elected Jesse Ventura, a former wrestler, as governor of Minnesota.

The Green Party: The Green Party ran Ralph Nader for President in 2004. The party supports and promotes environmentalism, LGBT rights, feminism, and social justice.

4. **The organization of Congress is instrumental to the functioning of the legislative branch.**

    a. **Describe the roles of parties and caucuses.**

    b. **Explain the role of committees.**

    c. **Discuss the legislative function of Congressional staff and specialized offices.**

Sample Answers:

a. Roles of parties and caucuses. The majority party chooses the Speaker of the House and President Pro tem of the Senate. The majority leader of the Senate has much power in the areas of negotiating and scheduling the business of the Senate. The minority leader and whip are also important leaders. The parties assign senators to committees. The Speaker of the House controls who speaks, and the rules to be followed and the bills to be debated. Caucuses are associations of legislators who advocate interests and ideology. Caucuses are usually, but not always, intraparty associations.

b. Committees are where most of the work of Congress is done. There are standing committees, select committees, and joint committees. Each type of committee has different functions. The conference committee is a type of joint committee. The conference committee is composed of members of each chamber who resolve differences between House and Senate bills before final passage. Each house limits the number of committees that a member can serve on.

c. Staff members are important to the functioning of Congress. The Staff responds to requests from constituents and helps in the re-election efforts of the legislators. Most staffers work in the local districts from which the legislators are elected, rather than inform Washington. Staff also reviews proposals and works with lobbyists. Staff agencies work within Congress. The research service looks up policy information and presents summaries (for and against) of arguments for each policy. The General Accounting Office investigates agencies and policies. The budget office provides information on costs and analyzes the president's proposed budget.

SECTION VII:
Practice Test Three

Section I: Multiple Choice _____

Instructions

Section I of this examination contains 60 multiple-choice questions. Fill in only the ovals for numbers 1 through 60 on your answer sheet.

Indicate all your answers to the multiple-choice questions on the answer sheet. No credit will be given for anything written in this exam booklet, but you may use the booklet for notes or scratch work. After you have decided which of the suggested answers is best, completely fill in the corresponding oval on the answer sheet. Give only one answer to each question. If you change an answer, be sure that the previous mark is erased completely. Here is a sample question and answer.

Sample Question   **Sample Answer**

1. **Washington is a**   Ⓐ ⬤ Ⓒ Ⓓ Ⓔ

    (A) City

    (B) State

    (C) Country

    (D) Continent

    (E) Bourough

Use your time effectively, working as quickly as you can without losing accuracy. Do not spend too much time on any one question. Go on to other questions and come back to the ones you have not answered if you have time. It is not expected that everyone will know the answers to all the multiple-choice questions.

About Guessing

Many candidates wonder whether or not to guess the answers to questions about which they are not certain. Multiple-choice scores are based on the number of questions answered correctly. Points are not deducted for incorrect answers, and no points are awarded for unanswered questions. Because points are not deducted for incorrect answers, you are encouraged to answer all multiple-choice questions. On questions you do not know the answer to, you should eliminate as many choices as you can, and then select the best answer among the remaining choices.

Time – 45 minutes
60 Questions

Directions: Each of the questions or incomplete statements below is followed by five suggested answers or explanations. Select the one that is BEST in each case.

1. The Constitution replaced the _____ as the form of government for the United States.

   (A) Albany Plan of Union

   (B) First Continental Congress

   (C) Second Continental Congress

   (D) Articles of Confederation

   (E) Declaration of Independence

2. A congressional vote to override a veto is an example of _____.

   (A) Federalism

   (B) Checks and balances

   (C) Separation of Powers

   (D) An implied power

   (E) The Supreme Law of the Land

3. An example of separation of powers is _____.

   (A) Congress approving appointments

   (B) The Supreme Court interpreting the laws

   (C) The president making a treaty

   (D) The Supreme Court Chief Justice presiding at a president's impeachment trial

   (E) The president vetoing an act of Congress

4. The concept of a central government sharing powers with state governments is _____.

(A) Sovereignty

(B) The Shared Power Doctrine

(C) The Reserved Powers Doctrine

(D) Democracy

(E) Federalism

5. The belief that government exists to protect the rights of individual citizens is an example of the _____ theory of democratic government.

(A) Protective

(B) Pluralist

(C) Developmental

(D) Participatory

(E) Federalist

6. All of the following were considerations in adopting the Constitution EXCEPT _____.

(A) Slavery

(B) Uninformed citizens

(C) Distance between settlements

(D) History of rule under England

(E) Strengths of a central government

7. **Which of the following statements is INCORRECT about the beliefs that citizens hold regarding their government and leaders?**

(A) Young people tend to be more apathetic toward government

(B) Young people tend to be less educated about politics

(C) The elderly tend to be less educated about politics

(D) Young people tend to have a lack of interest in foreign affairs

(E) Elderly people tend to have more of an interest in political issues

8. **After which time period did the people begin to have a greater distrust in government?**

(A) World War I

(B) World War II

(C) Korean War

(D) Vietnam War

(E) Iraq War

9. **How do most people develop their political attitudes?**

(A) By voting

(B) Listening to campaign ads

(C) At home

(D) Listening to political leaders

(E) By participating in government

10. **Which group has undergone the most political socialization?**

(A) Pre-school age children

(B) Elementary and middle school age children

(C) Teens

(D) Young voters

(E) Elderly

11. **Which of the following statements about polls is INCORRECT?**

(A) They measure public opinion

(B) Random sampling helps keep polls unbiased

(C) Random sampling selects participants at random

(D) Polls can be conducted so there is no sampling error

(E) A sampling error means that people can vote for a candidate for various reasons

12. **When might a candidate alter his/her policy on a certain issue?**

(A) When a poll shows the public has had a major swing in opinion

(B) When there is a sampling error of under five percent

(C) When he/she realizes that public opinion is not the same as voting opinion

(D) When people write letters to the editor of the local newspaper

(E) When citizens stage a protest outside the candidate's rally

13. **Which of the following is an example of an unconventional method of participating in politics?**

(A) Filing a lawsuit

(B) Attending a political meeting

(C) Protesting

(D) Writing a letter to a government official

(E) Voting

14. **Which of the following statements is CORRECT about a primary election?**

(A) Non-registered voters may vote in primary elections

(B) A primary election takes place after a caucus

(C) A primary election takes place after a general election

(D) A single winner for the city, state, or country is chosen at a primary election

(E) Voters at a primary election select candidates to run for election in a general election.

15. **Why do most voters vote the way they do?**

(A) They have a party affiliation

(B) They agree with a specific policy of the candidate

(C) They approve of the candidate's past action

(D) They agree with most of the candidate's views

(E) They believe the candidate has benefited them the most.

16. **Voting in a primary election is an example of which function of a political party?**

(A) Running campaigns

(B) Picking candidates

(C) Making voters aware of who is running for office

(D) Articulating party policy

(E) Coordinating party policies

17. **Which group organizes a political party?**

(A) National Committee

(B) State Committee

(C) Local Committee

(D) Candidates selected by the party

(E) Voters in each locale

18. **The development of political parties began early in our country's history. Which of the following was the earliest?**

(A) Republican

(B) Democrat

(C) Bull Moose

(D) Whig

(E) Federalist

19. **Which of the following is an example of an effect on political processes made by a political party?**

    (A) Prohibition

    (B) Women's suffrage

    (C) Direct election of Senators

    (D) Creation of the Interstate Commerce Commission

    (E) Trust Busting

20. **Political parties affected the Electoral College by _____.**

    (A) Proposing a Constitutional amendment to change the way vice presidents were elected

    (B) Creating it

    (C) Eliminating it

    (D) Adding more members to the college

    (E) Requiring each state to have one vote for the election of the president and one for the vice president

21. **A collection of people who share a common attitude and seek to influence government is called a(n) _____.**

    (A) Political party

    (B) Third party

    (C) Lobbyist

    (D) Interest group

    (E) Legislature

22. **Which statement is correct about interest groups?**

(A) They work outside the political process to accomplish their goals.

(B) They have varying goals with policies.

(C) Political parties and interest groups are the same thing.

(D) Political parties are policy specialists, while interest groups are policy generalists.

(E) Interest groups use different tactics to get their policies known.

23. **The U.S. Chamber of Commerce is an example of which type of interest group?**

(A) Environmental

(B) Economic

(C) Consumer

(D) Equality

(E) Public interest

24. **What is the political arm of an interest group that raises funds to contribute to candidates?**

(A) Political party

(B) Political action committee

(C) Caucus

(D) Bureaucracy

(E) Agency

25. **Which of the following is an example of a way a presidency is most likely to become too powerful?**

(A) Use of the veto power

(B) Use of the power of commander-in-chief

(C) Making appointments

(D) Issuing executive orders

(E) Drafting legislation

26. **Which is an example of a specific role of the House of Representatives that is integral to lawmaking?**

   (A) Confirming appointments

   (B) Introducing a revenue bill

   (C) Ratifying a treaty

   (D) Trying impeachment proceedings

   (E) Enforcing the law

27. **Which of the following is NOT an oversight responsibility of the Senate?**

   (A) Confirming appointments

   (B) Ratifying a treaty

   (C) Introducing a bill to require mud flaps on semi-trucks involved in interstate commerce

   (D) Holding debates to vote whether or not to override a presidential veto

   (E) Trying cases of impeachment

28. **"To coin money" is an example of what type of Congressional power?**

   (A) Necessary and proper

   (B) Implied

   (C) Shared

   (D) Reserved

   (E) Enumerated

29. **Which of the following is an example of an implied power of the federal government?**

   (A) Creating inferior courts

   (B) Creating the Supreme Court

   (C) Punishing piracies

   (D) Establishing a national bank

   (E) Establishing a post office

30. "Oversight of the federal budget" is an example of what type of Congressional power?

(A) Necessary and proper

(B) Shared

(C) Reserved

(D) Enumerated

(E) Legislative

31. Which of the following is an example of Congressional use of the "elastic clause?"

(A) Lay and collect duties and import and excise taxes

(B) Borrow money

(C) Investigate government wrong-doing

(D) Issue patents and copyrights

(E) Regulate commerce with foreign nations

32. How many states have a bicameral legislature?

(A) One

(B) Twenty

(C) Thirty

(D) Forty-nine

(E) Fifty

33. Federal judges serve _____.

(A) For a limited number of years

(B) For a specific number of terms

(C) For life

(D) At the pleasure of the President

(E) During good behavior

34. The "separate but equal" doctrine was overturned by _____.

   (A) *McCulloch v. Maryland*

   (B) *Marbury v. Madison*

   (C) *Plessy v. Ferguson*

   (D) *Brown v. Board of Education*

   (E) *Gibbons v. Ogden*

35. A U.S. Representative must be at least _____ years old.

   (A) 18

   (B) 20

   (C) 25

   (D) 30

   (E) 35

36. A U.S. Senator must have been a U.S. citizen for at least _____ years.

   (A) 5

   (B) 7

   (C) 9

   (D) 11

   (E) 15

37. Who has the power to impeach?

   (A) The President

   (B) The House of Representatives

   (C) The Senate

   (D) The Supreme Court

   (E) Both houses of Congress must agree to impeach

38. What does the term "impeach" mean?

(A) To convict

(B) To charge with a wrong doing

(C) To remove from office

(D) To allege treason

(E) To speak at length to stop the passage of a bill

39. What is the reapportionment of Congressional districts to gain election wins for the party in power?

(A) Spoils system

(B) Cloture

(C) Gerrymandering

(D) Filibuster

(E) Oversight

40. Which member of Congress keeps close contact with all members of his/her political party, acts a link to the political party, and keeps track of all key votes?

(A) Speaker of the House

(B) Majority Leader

(C) President pro tempore

(D) Whip

(E) Minority Leader

41. To what extent do the voters have influence on the federal judiciary?

(A) A great deal

(B) A limited amount

(C) An average amount

(D) Sporadic amounts

(E) No influence

42. If a U.S. Representative obtains passage of a bill to build a military base in his/her state, that legislation is called _____.

   (A) Oversight

   (B) Domestic

   (C) Pork barrel

   (D) Entitlement

   (E) Earmarks

43. The money or funds that an appropriations bill that designates for specific use within a state is called _____.

   (A) Earmarks

   (B) Spoils

   (C) Entitlement

   (D) Pork barrel

   (E) Revenue

44. The franking privilege is _____.

   (A) Overseeing the bureaucracy

   (B) Voting on pork barrel legislation

   (C) Approving presidential appointments

   (D) Sending mail without stamps

   (E) Acknowledging "most favored nation" status for trade

45. Congressional "logrolling" means _____.

   (A) Gaining support through the Whip's efforts to pass a bill favorable to a political party

   (B) Gathering adequate votes to approve or confirm a nominee for a federal office

   (C) Granting entitlements to a group of people

   (D) Debating a bill through the filibuster process so the bill will not be voted upon

   (E) Voting for a colleague's bill so he/she will vote for yours

46. **Which committee in the House of Representatives determines when a bill will be heard, which bills may have amendments attached, and whether the floor debate for a bill will be limited?**

(A) Committee of the Whole

(B) Committee on Rules

(C) Joint committee

(D) Subcommittee

(E) Ways and Means Committee

47. **What vote is needed to override a presidential veto?**

(A) Simple majority

(B) 51%

(C) Two-thirds

(D) Three-fourths

(E) 100%.

48. **What is a major way an interest group links to Congress?**

(A) Through the bureaucracy

(B) Through lobbyists

(C) By winning elections

(D) By protesting

(E) By litigating

49. **What is public policy based on?**

(A) History

(B) Theory

(C) Law

(D) Belief

(E) Values

50. **At what stage of policymaking do researchers and task forces take part?**

   (A) Recognizing the problem

   (B) Setting the agenda

   (C) Formulating the policy

   (D) Adopting the policy

   (E) Implementing the policy

51. **Promoting human rights is an example of what kind of policy?**

   (A) Economic

   (B) Defense

   (C) Foreign

   (D) Domestic

   (E) Public

52. **What role do the courts have in policymaking?**

   (A) Adopting the policy

   (B) Evaluating the policy

   (C) Formulating the policy

   (D) Implementing the policy

   (E) Setting the agenda

53. **Which policy involves federalism?**

   (A) World peace

   (B) Hurricane relief

   (C) National security

   (D) Participating in the United Nations

   (E) A trade agreement with Mexico

54. George Washington's advice to avoid tangling alliances shaped _____ policy for nearly 100 years.

(A) Domestic

(B) National

(C) Defense

(D) Foreign

(E) Economic

55. In what part of the Constitution are civil liberties protected?

(A) Article I

(B) Article II

(C) Article III

(D) Article IV

(E) Bill of Rights

56. The Fifteenth Amendment to the Constitution protects which right for former slaves?

(A) Citizenship

(B) Voting

(C) Equality

(D) Freedom

(E) Due process

57. The Heart of Atlanta case extended rights of blacks in _____.

(A) Education

(B) Politics

(C) Interstate commerce

(D) Naturalization

(E) Religion

58. **What protections are guaranteed by the Fourth Amendment?**

(A) The right to an attorney

(B) Due process

(C) Trial by jury

(D) Equal protection

(E) Freedom from unreasonable searches and seizures

59. **Which Amendment guarantees the right to an attorney in a criminal case?**

(A) Second

(B) Fifth

(C) Sixth

(D) Seventeenth

(E) Nineteenth

60. **The Civil Rights Act of 1964 was signed by President _____.**

(A) Kennedy

(B) Johnson

(C) Eisenhower

(D) Carter

(E) Nixon

Section II: Free Response Questions

1. The Constitution includes the concepts of federalism, separation of powers, and checks and balances.

   a. Define the term "federalism."

      • Explain the reasons federalism was embodied in the newly organized government.

      • Explain how federalism functions in today's society.

   b. Describe how the framers viewed the concept of "separation of powers."

      • Discuss separation of powers in relation to today's government.

   c. What purpose(s) do checks and balances serve?

      • Identify checks that are present in the government.

      • Explain how "balance" results when "checks" are implemented.

Practice Test Three

2. Political beliefs form the foundation of the U.S. political culture.

   a. Identify several political beliefs about today's government.

   b. Identify several political beliefs about government leaders.

   c. Identify several political beliefs about the U.S. political system, in general.

   d. Compare and contrast how beliefs are formed, how they evolve, and how they are transmitted.

3. Political mechanisms allow for citizens to organize and communicate their interests and concerns.

   a. Identify (and define / explain) two of the mechanisms.

   b. How have campaign strategies and financing in the age of the Internet affected these mechanisms?

   c. Describe areas of politics that help citizens to better understand the nature of party behavior and individual voting behavior.

   d. Describe the role of lobbyists and their relation to the political mechanisms.

4. Congress is a major political institution in the United States.

   a. Discuss the powers held by this institution.

   b. Describe the functions performed by Congress.

   c. Explain whether, and to what extent, the power balance between Congress and the other two branches of government has changed over the years.

   d. Identify and describe the ties between Congress and state and local governments.

Section I: Multiple Choice Answer Sheet

1. Ⓐ Ⓑ Ⓒ Ⓓ Ⓔ
2. Ⓐ Ⓑ Ⓒ Ⓓ Ⓔ
3. Ⓐ Ⓑ Ⓒ Ⓓ Ⓔ
4. Ⓐ Ⓑ Ⓒ Ⓓ Ⓔ
5. Ⓐ Ⓑ Ⓒ Ⓓ Ⓔ
6. Ⓐ Ⓑ Ⓒ Ⓓ Ⓔ
7. Ⓐ Ⓑ Ⓒ Ⓓ Ⓔ
8. Ⓐ Ⓑ Ⓒ Ⓓ Ⓔ
9. Ⓐ Ⓑ Ⓒ Ⓓ Ⓔ
10. Ⓐ Ⓑ Ⓒ Ⓓ Ⓔ
11. Ⓐ Ⓑ Ⓒ Ⓓ Ⓔ
12. Ⓐ Ⓑ Ⓒ Ⓓ Ⓔ
13. Ⓐ Ⓑ Ⓒ Ⓓ Ⓔ
14. Ⓐ Ⓑ Ⓒ Ⓓ Ⓔ
15. Ⓐ Ⓑ Ⓒ Ⓓ Ⓔ
16. Ⓐ Ⓑ Ⓒ Ⓓ Ⓔ
17. Ⓐ Ⓑ Ⓒ Ⓓ Ⓔ
18. Ⓐ Ⓑ Ⓒ Ⓓ Ⓔ
19. Ⓐ Ⓑ Ⓒ Ⓓ Ⓔ
20. Ⓐ Ⓑ Ⓒ Ⓓ Ⓔ

21. Ⓐ Ⓑ Ⓒ Ⓓ Ⓔ
22. Ⓐ Ⓑ Ⓒ Ⓓ Ⓔ
23. Ⓐ Ⓑ Ⓒ Ⓓ Ⓔ
24. Ⓐ Ⓑ Ⓒ Ⓓ Ⓔ
25. Ⓐ Ⓑ Ⓒ Ⓓ Ⓔ
26. Ⓐ Ⓑ Ⓒ Ⓓ Ⓔ
27. Ⓐ Ⓑ Ⓒ Ⓓ Ⓔ
28. Ⓐ Ⓑ Ⓒ Ⓓ Ⓔ
29. Ⓐ Ⓑ Ⓒ Ⓓ Ⓔ
30. Ⓐ Ⓑ Ⓒ Ⓓ Ⓔ
31. Ⓐ Ⓑ Ⓒ Ⓓ Ⓔ
32. Ⓐ Ⓑ Ⓒ Ⓓ Ⓔ
33. Ⓐ Ⓑ Ⓒ Ⓓ Ⓔ
34. Ⓐ Ⓑ Ⓒ Ⓓ Ⓔ
35. Ⓐ Ⓑ Ⓒ Ⓓ Ⓔ
36. Ⓐ Ⓑ Ⓒ Ⓓ Ⓔ
37. Ⓐ Ⓑ Ⓒ Ⓓ Ⓔ
38. Ⓐ Ⓑ Ⓒ Ⓓ Ⓔ
39. Ⓐ Ⓑ Ⓒ Ⓓ Ⓔ
40. Ⓐ Ⓑ Ⓒ Ⓓ Ⓔ

41. Ⓐ Ⓑ Ⓒ Ⓓ Ⓔ
42. Ⓐ Ⓑ Ⓒ Ⓓ Ⓔ
43. Ⓐ Ⓑ Ⓒ Ⓓ Ⓔ
44. Ⓐ Ⓑ Ⓒ Ⓓ Ⓔ
45. Ⓐ Ⓑ Ⓒ Ⓓ Ⓔ
46. Ⓐ Ⓑ Ⓒ Ⓓ Ⓔ
47. Ⓐ Ⓑ Ⓒ Ⓓ Ⓔ
48. Ⓐ Ⓑ Ⓒ Ⓓ Ⓔ
49. Ⓐ Ⓑ Ⓒ Ⓓ Ⓔ
50. Ⓐ Ⓑ Ⓒ Ⓓ Ⓔ
51. Ⓐ Ⓑ Ⓒ Ⓓ Ⓔ
52. Ⓐ Ⓑ Ⓒ Ⓓ Ⓔ
53. Ⓐ Ⓑ Ⓒ Ⓓ Ⓔ
54. Ⓐ Ⓑ Ⓒ Ⓓ Ⓔ
55. Ⓐ Ⓑ Ⓒ Ⓓ Ⓔ
56. Ⓐ Ⓑ Ⓒ Ⓓ Ⓔ
57. Ⓐ Ⓑ Ⓒ Ⓓ Ⓔ
58. Ⓐ Ⓑ Ⓒ Ⓓ Ⓔ
59. Ⓐ Ⓑ Ⓒ Ⓓ Ⓔ
60. Ⓐ Ⓑ Ⓒ Ⓓ Ⓔ

Practice Test Three

Section I: Multiple Choice Answer Key _____

Question Number	Correct Answer
1.	D
2.	B
3.	B
4.	E
5.	A
6.	C
7.	C
8.	D
9.	C
10.	E
11.	D
12.	A
13.	C
14.	E
15.	D
16.	B
17.	A
18.	E
19.	C
20.	A

Question Number	Correct Answer
21.	D
22.	E
23.	B
24.	B
25.	D
26.	B
27.	C
28.	E
29.	D
30.	A
31.	C
32.	D
33.	E
34.	D
35.	C
36.	C
37.	B
38.	B
39.	C
40.	D

Question Number	Correct Answer
41.	E
42.	C
43.	A
44.	D
45.	E
46.	B
47.	C
48.	B
49.	C
50.	C
51.	C
52.	C
53.	B
54.	D
55.	E
56.	B
57.	C
58.	E
59.	C
60.	B

Section I: Multiple Choice Explanations _____

1. **The Constitution replaced the _____ as the form of government for the United States.**

   (A)   Albany Plan of Union

   (B)   First Continental Congress

   (C)   Second Continental Congress

   (D)   Articles of Confederation

   (E)   Declaration of Independence

   Answer: D.
   Articles of Confederation. The Albany Plan of Union was proposed by Benjamin Franklin before independence. The Declaration of Independence explained why the colonists would separate from England. The First and Second Continental Congresses met to govern. The form of government the Constitution replaced was the Articles of Confederation.

2. **A congressional vote to override a veto is an example of _____.**

   (A)   Federalism

   (B)   Checks and balances

   (C)   Separation of Powers

   (D)   An implied power

   (E)   The Supreme Law of the Land

   Answer: B.
   Checks and balances. The Constitution gives Congress the power to override a presidential veto. It is a method used by the legislative branch to check on the powers of the executive branch and to maintain balance among the branches of government.

3. **An example of separation of powers is _____.**

   (A) Congress approving appointments

   (B) The Supreme Court interpreting the laws

   (C) The president making a treaty

   (D) The Supreme Court Chief Justice presiding at a president's impeachment trial

   (E) The president vetoing an act of Congress

   Answer: B.

   The Supreme Court interpreting the laws. Each branch of government has its functions, thus separating powers among the branches. The judicial branch has the duty of interpreting the laws. Congress makes the laws and the executive branch enforces the laws.

4. **The concept of a central government sharing powers with state governments is _____.**

   (A) Sovereignty

   (B) The Shared Power Doctrine

   (C) The Reserved Powers Doctrine

   (D) Democracy

   (E) Federalism

   Answer: E.

   Federalism. Federalism is a system of government that has a central government and shares powers with state governments. The Constitution provides for shared powers and also reserves certain powers for the states. Sovereignty means there is a supreme power over someone or some group. Democracy is a system of government by all the people or by the people through their representatives.

5. **The belief that government exists to protect the rights of individual citizens is an example of the _____ theory of democratic government.**

(A) Protective

(B) Pluralist

(C) Developmental

(D) Participatory

(E) Federalist

Answer: A.
Protective. The pluralist theory focuses on power held by special interests. The developmental theory is based on what is best for the society as a whole. The participatory theory attempts to get more people involved in government. The federalist system of government involves a central government with branches, such as states.

6. **All of the following were considerations in adopting the Constitution EXCEPT _____.**

(A) Slavery

(B) Uninformed citizens

(C) Distance between settlements

(D) History of rule under England

(E) Strengths of a central government

Answer: C.
Distance between settlements. The remoteness of some settlements, not the distance between settlements, was a concern. All of the other choices were concerns, either in creating the legislative branch or the executive branch of the federal government.

7. **Which of the following statements is INCORRECT about the beliefs that citizens hold regarding their government and leaders?**

(A) Young people tend to be more apathetic toward government

(B) Young people tend to be less educated about politics

(C) The elderly tend to be less educated about politics

(D) Young people tend to have a lack of interest in foreign affairs

(E) Elderly people tend to have more of an interest in political issues

Answer: C.

The elderly tend to be less educated about politics. Older people tend to have more of an interest in political issues and are more educated about politics. Younger people tend to be more apathetic toward government, less educated about politics, and have less of an interest in foreign affairs.

8. **After which time period did the people begin to have a greater distrust in government?**

(A) World War I

(B) World War II

(C) Korean War

(D) Vietnam War

(E) Iraq War

Answer: D.

Vietnam War. After the Watergate scandal, the resignation of President Nixon, and during the Vietnam War, people began to have more of a general distrust of government. The Iraq War took place after the Vietnam War, and many people doubted the government's reasons for going into Iraq.

9. **How do most people develop their political attitudes?**

(A) By voting

(B) Listening to campaign ads

(C) At home

(D) Listening to political leaders

(E) By participating in government

Answer: C.
At home. Although all of the options are ways that people learn about politics, the primary way is through the political socialization processes at home and in the schools that most people develop their political attitudes.

10. **Which group has undergone the most political socialization?**

(A) Pre-school age children

(B) Elementary and middle school age children

(C) Teens

(D) Young voters

(E) Elderly

Answer: E.
Elderly. The elderly have gone through the earlier processes, such as beginning to take an interest in politics, learning about politics in school, and voting. As people become older, they tend to pay more attention to political activities, issues, and attitudes of political leaders.

11. **Which of the following statements about polls is INCORRECT?**

(A) They measure public opinion

(B) Random sampling helps keep polls unbiased

(C) Random sampling selects participants at random

(D) Polls can be conducted so there is no sampling error

(E) A sampling error means that people can vote for a candidate for various reasons

Answer: D.

Polls can be conducted so there is no sampling error. Polls always have a sampling error because a poll only involves selected individuals. Without the complete picture of all the voters, no poll will be totally accurate. Therefore, a sampling error must be included to give any validation to the results of a poll.

12. **When might a candidate alter his/her policy on a certain issue?**

    (A) When a poll shows the public has had a major swing in opinion

    (B) When there is a sampling error of under five percent

    (C) When he/she realizes that public opinion is not the same as voting opinion

    (D) When people write letters to the editor of the local newspaper

    (E) When citizens stage a protest outside the candidate's rally

    Answer: A.

    When a poll shows the public has had a major swing in opinion. A candidate usually has a platform or series of ideas he/she wants to promote. If there is a major shift by the citizens as to whether or not those ideas are favorable, then the candidate is likely to alter positions or policy making decisions to keep the support of the public.

13. **Which of the following is an example of an unconventional method of participating in politics?**

    (A) Filing a lawsuit

    (B) Attending a political meeting

    (C) Protesting

    (D) Writing a letter to a government official

    (E) Voting

    Answer: C.

    Protesting. All of the choices are conventional methods of participating in politics except protesting.

14. **Which of the following statements is CORRECT about a primary election?**

(A) Non-registered voters may vote in primary elections

(B) A primary election takes place after a caucus

(C) A primary election takes place after a general election

(D) A single winner for the city, state, or country is chosen at a primary election

(E) Voters at a primary election select candidates to run for election in a general election.

Answer: E.

Voters at a primary election select candidates to run for election in a general election. Voters must be registered to vote in a primary election. Primary elections are party elections and at a primary election, voters select candidates for a particular political party to run against candidates from another political party in a general election.

15. **Why do most voters vote the way they do?**

(A) They have a party affiliation

(B) They agree with a specific policy of the candidate

(C) They approve of the candidate's past action

(D) They agree with most of the candidate's views

(E) They believe the candidate has benefited them the most.

Answer: D.

They agree with most of the candidate's views. All of the choices provide valid reasons why voters might vote for a candidate. However, most people vote for a candidate because they favor the candidate's views on a variety of subjects.

16. **Voting in a primary election is an example of which function of a political party?**

(A) Running campaigns

(B) Picking candidates

(C) Making voters aware of who is running for office

(D) Articulating party policy

(E) Coordinating party policies

Answer: B.

Picking candidates. A primary election is a party election. A primary election decides which party member will be chosen to run against the candidate selected by the other political party or parties.

17. **Which group organizes a political party?**

    (A) National Committee

    (B) State Committee

    (C) Local Committee

    (D) Candidates selected by the party

    (E) Voters in each locale

    Answer: A.

    National Committee. The National Committee organizes the political party. There are representatives from the state party on the National Committee, but it is the National Committee that sets policy and organizes the convention every four years in which a candidate is chosen to represent that specific political party in the presidential election.

18. **The development of political parties began early in our country's history. Which of the following was the earliest?**

    (A) Republican

    (B) Democrat

    (C) Bull Moose

    (D) Whig

    (E) Federalist

    Answer: E.

    Federalist. The first Federalist president was John Adams. The other parties either evolved from early parties or were formed later.

19. **Which of the following is an example of an effect on political processes made by a political party?**

(A) Prohibition

(B) Women's suffrage

(C) Direct election of Senators

(D) Creation of the Interstate Commerce Commission

(E) Trust Busting

Answer: C.

Direct election of Senators. As part of its platform, the Populist Party had the direct election of senators. Referendum and recall were two other results of a third party's effects on the political process. President Theodore Roosevelt was the "trust buster" and he broke up the Standard Oil monopoly. Congress created the Interstate Commerce Commission. Prohibition and women's suffrage were the results of amendments to the U.S. Constitution.

20. **Political parties affected the Electoral College by _____.**

(A) Proposing a Constitutional Amendment to change the way vice presidents were elected

(B) Creating it

(C) Eliminating it

(D) Adding more members to the college

(E) Requiring each state to have one vote for the election of the president and one for the vice president

Answer: A.

Proposing a Constitutional Amendment to change the way vice presidents were elected. The election of 1800 changed the way the Electoral College voted for the President and Vice President. Thomas Jefferson and Aaron Burr were running mates and each had the same number of votes because the candidates for president and vice president were not listed separately. Therefore, the House of Representatives had to break the tie. As a result, the political parties, through their elected officials in Congress proposed a new method for the Electoral College. The Seventeenth Amendment was the result.

21. **A collection of people who share a common attitude and seek to influence government is called a(n) _____.**

    (A) Political party

    (B) Third party

    (C) Lobbyist

    (D) Interest group

    (E) Legislature

    Answer: D.
    Interest group. Interest groups are made up of people with common interests or attitudes. They try to accomplish their goals through lobbying.

22. **Which statement is correct about interest groups?**

    (A) They work outside the political process to accomplish their goals.

    (B) They have varying goals with policies.

    (C) Political parties and interest groups are the same thing.

    (D) Political parties are policy specialists, while interest groups are policy generalists.

    (E) Interest groups use different tactics to get their policies known.

    Answer: E.
    Interest groups use different tactics to get their policies known. Interest groups use lobbying and political action committees. They also use litigation. Interest groups are policy specialists and work within the government to accomplish their goals.

23. **The U.S. Chamber of Commerce is an example of which type of interest group?**

    (A) Environmental

    (B) Economic

    (C) Consumer

    (D) Equality

    (E) Public interest

Answer: B.

Economic. The Chamber of Commerce is an economic interest group and represents business interests.

24. **What is the political arm of an interest group that raises funds to contribute to candidates?**

    (A) Political party

    (B) Political action committee

    (C) Caucus

    (D) Bureaucracy

    (E) Agency

    Answer: B.

    Political action committee. A political action committee raises funds to contribute to candidates or political parties. It is the political arm of an interest group.

25. **Which of the following is an example of a way a presidency is most likely to become too powerful?**

    (A) Use of the veto power

    (B) Use of the power of commander-in-chief

    (C) Making appointments

    (D) Issuing executive orders

    (E) Drafting legislation

    Answer: D.

    Issuing executive orders. A veto is subject to being overridden. Congress must approve the country's entry into war and the Senate must confirm appointments. Drafting legislation may or may not be what Congress wants to pass. Issuing executive orders can give the presidency a great deal of power without adequate checks to balance the power.

Practice Test Three

26. **Which is an example of a specific role of the House of Representatives that is integral to lawmaking?**

    (A) Confirming appointments

    (B) Introducing a revenue bill

    (C) Ratifying a treaty

    (D) Trying impeachment proceedings

    (E) Enforcing the law

    Answer: B.

    Introducing a revenue bill. The Senate confirms appointments, ratifies treaties, and tries persons who have been impeached. The executive branch of government enforces the law. Introducing a revenue bill is the first step in the legislative process.

27. **Which of the following is NOT an oversight responsibility of the Senate?**

    (A) Confirming appointments

    (B) Ratifying a treaty

    (C) Introducing a bill to require mud flaps on semi-trucks involved in interstate commerce

    (D) Holding debates to vote whether or not to override a presidential veto

    (E) Trying cases of impeachment

    Answer: C.

    Introducing a bill to require mud flaps on semi-trucks involved in interstate commerce. Ratifying treaties, confirming appointments, and holding debates to decide whether to override a veto are examples of powers integral to oversight. Introducing bills is an example of the lawmaking role of Congress.

28. "To coin money" is an example of what type of Congressional power?

(A) Necessary and proper

(B) Implied

(C) Shared

(D) Reserved

(E) Enumerated

Answer: E.

Enumerated. A "necessary and proper" power is an implied power. A shared power is a power of the states and federal government. A reserved power is a power of the states. Enumerated powers are listed in Article I of the Constitution.

29. Which of the following is an example of an implied power of the federal government?

(A) Creating inferior courts

(B) Creating the Supreme Court

(C) Punishing piracies

(D) Establishing a national bank

(E) Establishing a post office

Answer: D.

Establishing a national bank. All of the choices listed except "creating a national bank" are examples of enumerated or listed powers of Congress. Establishing a national bank is an implied power because Congress has the power to coin money.

30. "Oversight of the federal budget" is an example of what type of Congressional power?

(A) Necessary and proper

(B) Shared

(C) Reserved

(D) Enumerated

(E) Legislative

Answer: A.

Necessary and proper. A "necessary and proper" power is an implied power. The "elastic clause" gives Congress the power to pass laws that are necessary and proper to execute the powers granted to it in Article I of the Constitution. A shared power is a power of the states and federal government. A reserved power is a power of the states. Enumerated powers are listed in Article I of the Constitution.

31. **Which of the following is an example of Congressional use of the "elastic clause?"**

    (A) Lay and collect duties and import and excise taxes

    (B) Borrow money

    (C) Investigate government wrong-doing

    (D) Issue patents and copyrights

    (E) Regulate commerce with foreign nations

    Answer: C.

    Investigate government wrong-doing. All of the choices except C are examples of enumerated powers set out in Article I of the Constitution.

32. **How many states have a bicameral legislature?**

    (A) One

    (B) Twenty

    (C) Thirty

    (D) Forty-nine

    (E) Fifty

    Answer: D.

    Forty-nine. All states except Nebraska have a bicameral legislature.

33. Federal judges serve _____.

(A) For a limited number of years

(B) For a specific number of terms

(C) For life

(D) At the pleasure of the President

(E) During good behavior

Answer: E.

During good behavior. Although most federal judges serve for life, the Constitution states they shall serve during good behavior.

34. The "separate but equal" doctrine was overturned by _____.

(A) *McCulloch v. Maryland*

(B) *Marbury v. Madison*

(C) *Plessy v. Ferguson*

(D) *Brown v. Board of Education*

(E) *Gibbons v. Ogden*

Answer: D.

Brown v. Board of Education. The McCulloch case involved issues about taxing the national bank. *Marbury v. Madison* established the doctrine of judicial review. Gibbons involved steamships and interstate commerce. Plessy established the "separate but equal doctrine" and Brown overturned the "separate but equal" doctrine as it related to education.

35. A U.S. Representative must be at least _____ years old.

(A) 18

(B) 20

(C) 25

(D) 30

(E) 35

Answer: C.

25. A representative must be at least 25 years old.

36. A U.S. Senator must have been a U.S. citizen for at least _____ years.

(A) 5

(B) 7

(C) 9

(D) 11

(E) 15

Answer: C.

9. A Senator must have been a U.S. citizen for at least nine years.

37. Who has the power to impeach?

(A) The President

(B) The House of Representatives

(C) The Senate

(D) The Supreme Court

(E) Both houses of Congress must agree to impeach

Answer: B.

The House of Representatives. Impeach means to charge with an offense. The Constitution gives the House of Representatives the authority to impeach. The constitution authorizes the senate to try cases of impeachment.

38. What does the term "impeach" mean?

(A) To convict

(B) To charge with a wrong doing

(C) To remove from office

(D) To allege treason

(E) To speak at length to stop the passage of a bill

Answer: B.

To charge with a wrong doing. If the person is found to have committed a wrong doing, he/she can be convicted by the Senate and removed from office. To filibuster is to speak at length to stop the passage of a bill.

39. **What is the reapportionment of Congressional districts to gain election wins for the party in power?**

    (A) Spoils system

    (B) Cloture

    (C) Gerrymandering

    (D) Filibuster

    (E) Oversight

Answer: C.

Gerrymandering. Cloture is a procedure for ending a debate in the legislature and taking a vote on a bill. Oversight is the overseeing of projects and programs. Filibuster means to "speak a bill to death." Gerrymandering is not legal today. It was legal in the past.

40. **Which member of Congress keeps close contact with all members of his/her political party, acts a link to the political party, and keeps track of all key votes?**

    (A) Speaker of the House

    (B) Majority Leader

    (C) President pro tempore

    (D) Whip

    (E) Minority Leader

Answer: D.

Whip. The Whip is the link between Congress and his/her political party. Each party has a Whip.

41. **To what extent do the voters have influence on the federal judiciary?**

    (A) A great deal

    (B) A limited amount

    (C) An average amount

    (D) Sporadic amounts

    (E) No influence

    Answer: E.
    No influence. The judiciary is independent and not affected by public opinion because judges at the federal level are not elected or subject to removal, unless they are impeached.

42. **If a U.S. Representative obtains passage of a bill to build a military base in his/her state, that legislation is called _____.**

    (A) Oversight

    (B) Domestic

    (C) Pork barrel

    (D) Entitlement

    (E) Earmarks

    Answer: C.
    Pork barrel. To "bring home the pork" means to "bring home the bacon" or money. It is assumed the money would have been put into a barrel. Thus, "pork barrel legislation" is bringing something to one's home state that will benefit the state, such as a military base.

43. **The money or funds that an appropriations bill that designates for specific use within a state is called _____.**

    (A) Earmarks

    (B) Spoils

    (C) Entitlement

    (D) Pork barrel

    (E) Revenue

Answer: A.
Earmarks. The money is "ear marked", meaning it is allocated for a specific purpose.

44. **The franking privilege is _____.**

    (A) Overseeing the bureaucracy

    (B) Voting on pork barrel legislation

    (C) Approving presidential appointments

    (D) Sending mail without stamps

    (E) Acknowledging "most favored nation" status for trade

    Answer: D.
    Sending mail without stamps. Franking is placing marks (franks) on postage that Congressmen and women send to their constituents without having to pay for the postage.

45. **Congressional "logrolling" means _____.**

    (A) Gaining support through the Whip's efforts to pass a bill favorable to a political party

    (B) Gathering adequate votes to approve or confirm a nominee for a federal office

    (C) Granting entitlements to a group of people

    (D) Debating a bill through the filibuster process so the bill will not be voted upon

    (E) Voting for a colleague's bill so he/she will vote for yours

    Answer: E.
    Voting for a colleague's bill so he/she will vote for yours. Logrolling is a term that is used when one legislator gathers support for a bill he/she is presenting by promising to vote for a bill that is going to be introduced by the person who has promised to vote for the current bill.

46. **Which committee in the House of Representatives determines when a bill will be heard, which bills may have amendments attached, and whether the floor debate for a bill will be limited?**

    (A) Committee of the Whole

    (B) Committee on Rules

    (C) Joint committee

    (D) Subcommittee

    (E) Ways and Means Committee

Answer: B.

Committee on Rules. A subcommittee does research on a bill to decide whether it is necessary to hold hearings on the bill. A joint committee is made up of members of both houses in a bicameral legislature. Revenue bills come from the Ways and Means Committee. A Committee of the Whole is where the whole legislative body debates a bill as a whole. The Committee on Rules decides when (and if) bills will be heard, whether amendments will be attached, and whether debate will be limited.

47. **What vote is needed to override a presidential veto?**

    (A) Simple majority

    (B) 51%

    (C) Two-thirds

    (D) Three-fourths

    (E) 100%.

Answer: C.

Two-thirds. To override a presidential veto, Congress must have a two-thirds majority in each house. A two-thirds majority is called a super majority.

48. What is a major way an interest group links to Congress?

(A) Through the bureaucracy

(B) Through lobbyists

(C) By winning elections

(D) By protesting

(E) By litigating

Answer: B.

Through lobbyists. All of the choices are used by interest groups to link to the government, however the use of lobbyists is the major way interest groups link to Congress.

49. What is public policy based on?

(A) History

(B) Theory

(C) Law

(D) Belief

(E) Values

Answer: C.

Law. All of the choices can be used to formulate a policy, but the public policy must be based on law.

50. At what stage of policymaking do researchers and task forces take part?

(A) Recognizing the problem

(B) Setting the agenda

(C) Formulating the policy

(D) Adopting the policy

(E) Implementing the policy

Answer: C.

Formulating the policy. Each of the choices is a step in policymaking. However, researchers and task forces take part at the formulation stage.

51. **Promoting human rights is an example of what kind of policy?**

   (A) Economic

   (B) Defense

   (C) Foreign

   (D) Domestic

   (E) Public

   Answer: C.
   Foreign. Protecting human rights involves working with other nations. Therefore, it is part of foreign policy.

52. **What role do the courts have in policymaking?**

   (A) Adopting the policy

   (B) Evaluating the policy

   (C) Formulating the policy

   (D) Implementing the policy

   (E) Setting the agenda

   Answer: C.
   Formulating the policy. The Supreme Court becomes involved in adopting policies when it makes decisions in cases involving policy.

53. **Which policy involves federalism?**

   (A) World peace

   (B) Hurricane relief

   (C) National security

   (D) Participating in the United Nations

   (E) A trade agreement with Mexico

   Answer: B.
   Hurricane relief. Federalism involves the central government and state governments. Hurricane relief is an example of where both work together to resolve an issue.

54. **George Washington's advice to avoid tangling alliances shaped _____ policy for nearly 100 years.**

    (A) Domestic

    (B) National

    (C) Defense

    (D) Foreign

    (E) Economic

    Answer: D.
    Foreign. George Washington believed that the U.S. would grow and be successful if the country avoided becoming involved with foreign nations and the problems of foreign nations.

55. **In what part of the Constitution are civil liberties protected?**

    (A) Article I

    (B) Article II

    (C) Article III

    (D) Article IV

    (E) Bill of Rights

    Answer: E.
    Bill of Rights. The first amendment to the Bill of Rights, for example, protects the liberties of speech, assembly, press, and religion.

56. **The Fifteenth Amendment to the Constitution protects which right for former slaves?**

    (A) Citizenship

    (B) Voting

    (C) Equality

    (D) Freedom

    (E) Due process

Answer: B.

Voting. The right of freedom was granted in the Thirteenth Amendment. Citizenship was granted in the Fourteenth Amendment. The right to vote was granted in the Fifteenth Amendment.

57. **The Heart of Atlanta case extended rights of blacks in _____.**

    (A)   Education

    (B)   Politics

    (C)   Interstate commerce

    (D)   Naturalization

    (E)   Religion

Answer: C.

Interstate commerce. The case involved interstate travel and the right to have access to public facilities.

58. **What protections are guaranteed by the Fourth Amendment?**

    (A)   The right to an attorney

    (B)   Due process

    (C)   Trial by jury

    (D)   Equal protection

    (E)   Freedom from unreasonable searches and seizures

Answer: E.

Freedom from unreasonable searches and seizures. The Fourth Amendment protects individuals from unreasonable searches and seizures. The other choices are also protections guaranteed by other amendments in the Constitution.

59. Which Amendment guarantees the right to an attorney in a criminal case?

(A) Second

(B) Fifth

(C) Sixth

(D) Seventeenth

(E) Nineteenth

Answer: C.
Sixth. The Second Amendment provides the right to bear arms. The Fifth Amendment ensures due process. The Seventeenth provides for jury trials, and the Nineteenth Amendment gave women the right to vote.

60. The Civil Rights Act of 1964 was signed by President _____.

(A) Kennedy

(B) Johnson

(C) Eisenhower

(D) Carter

(E) Nixon

Answer: B.
Johnson. President Lyndon Johnson signed the first major civil rights legislation, the Civil Rights Act of 1964.

Section II: Free Response Sample Answers

1. The Constitution includes the concepts of federalism, separation of powers, and checks and balances.

    a. Define the term "federalism."

        • Explain the reasons federalism was embodied in the newly organized government.

        • Explain how federalism functions in today's society.

    b. Describe how the framers viewed the concept of "separation of powers."

        • Discuss separation of powers in relation to today's government.

    c. What purpose(s) do checks and balances serve?

        • Identify checks that are present in the government.

        • Explain how "balance" results when "checks" are implemented.

Sample Answers:

a. Federalism has one central government, and branch or state governments. The framers decided on a system of federalism because of the problems with the Articles of Confederation. Under the Articles, there was a legislature but a central executive branch of government did not exist. The states were more powerful than the central government. Today, federalism functions with the central government (in Washington, D.C.) and each state government. Both state governments and the federal government have three separate branches and each has powers. Some are powers that held only by the federal government and other powers are shared. Some powers are reserved for the states.

b. The framers viewed separation of powers as a necessary organization for the new government. They did not want any one branch to become too powerful. In the early years of our country, the legislative branch was dominant over the other two branches. Today, if there is one branch that is more dominant, it is the executive branch—an example that is demonstrated by the President's use of the executive order. Many feel that executive orders are matters that should be addressed by Congress and presented as legislation after votes by both houses of Congress.

c. Checks and balances help maintain the separation of powers and ensure that one branch does not become too powerful. To maintain the necessary balance of power, the framers created the checks that each branch has on the other branches. When the Senate does not confirm an appointment of the president, that "check" on the president keeps the executive branch from becoming too powerful. The Supreme Court's power of judicial review is a check on the legislative enactments of Congress. The "check" prevents Congress from passing laws that are in violation of the Constitution, and as a possible result, becoming too powerful by passing any legislation it wants, without regard to whether the law is constitutional.

2. **Political beliefs form the foundation of the U.S. political culture.**

   a. **Identify several political beliefs about today's government.**

   b. **Identify several political beliefs about government leaders.**

   c. **Identify several political beliefs about the U.S. political system, in general.**

   d. **Compare and contrast how beliefs are formed, how they evolve, and how they are transmitted.**

   Sample Answers:

   a. Political beliefs about the government will depend upon a person's philosophy about government. Most people believe that the government is not as trustworthy as it was several years ago. The changes in thinking began after the Watergate break-ins and the events that happened during the administration of President Nixon that led to his resignation. Another belief, for example, is that the government is not concerned about the common person.

   b. The beliefs about government leaders also depend upon a person's political beliefs. Some beliefs include: not caring about the debt levels; not focusing on the economy to help the common person; favoring the wealthy by implementing tax benefits; losing control of business strength because of the trade agreements that appear to favor manufacturing outside the U.S.; and a weakness because we have not taken a stronger stand on terrorist acts.

   c. The political system of democracy is usually not criticized, but some people believe that we need to accept more liberal ideas, such as national healthcare, a national minimum wage, and support lower cost education. Others, who favor more conservative ideas, believe the government is advancing policies that are too liberal, such as gay rights, abortion rights, and government involvement in education.

   d. Political beliefs, whether regarding the system, the parties, or the candidate are formed from childhood. Most beliefs are formed in the home or as the result of family members' thinking. Listening to television and viewing news items on the Internet forms some ideas. In the past, the printed media served as a major source of forming political beliefs. However, not as many people read newspapers and news magazines today.

3. **Political mechanisms allow for citizens to organize and communicate their interests and concerns.**

   a. **Identify (and define / explain) two of the mechanisms.**

   b. **How have campaign strategies and financing in the age of the Internet affected these mechanisms?**

   c. **Describe areas of politics that help citizens to better understand the nature of party behavior and individual voting behavior.**

   d. **Describe the role of lobbyists and their relation to the political mechanisms.**

Sample Answers:

   a. Two examples of political mechanisms are political parties and interest groups. Both include people with specific interests. A political party has the function of electing people to government offices. Interest groups can have focuses other than politics. An interest group such as the humane society focuses on treatment of animals that do not have homes, for example. An environmental interest group may be concerned about toxic waste or greenhouse emissions. The legislature is also considered a political mechanism. Whether at the state or federal level, this political mechanism affects the public with every law that is passed.

   b. The Internet has affected campaign strategies and financing because millions of people have access to the information o the Internet. The Internet serves as a media source for candidates and also provides an easy way for people to contribute to candidates' campaign funds.

   c. Areas of politics that help citizens to better understand the nature of the party might include working on a candidate's campaign or becoming a delegate to a party's convention or working at the polling places. Each of these situations provides a first-hand experience to observe the inner working of grassroots politics.

   d. The role of a lobbyist is to convince someone with influence that the lobbyist's position should be adopted. Legislators and candidates are examples of people a lobbyist would want to convince.

Practice Test Three

4. **Congress is a major political institution in the United States.**

   a. **Discuss the powers held by this institution.**

   b. **Describe the functions performed by Congress.**

   c. **Explain whether, and to what extent, the power balance between Congress and the other two branches of government has changed over the years.**

   d. **Identify and describe the ties between Congress and state and local governments.**

   Sample Answers:

   a. Congress has enumerated and implied powers. An example of an enumerated power is the power to declare war or coin money. An implied power flows from the "necessary and proper" clause. The chartering of a national bank, for example, was considered to be an implied power that flowed from the right of Congress to coin money. The establishment of the Interstate Commerce Commission was implied from the right of Congress to control trade between the states.

   b. Congress performs a legislative function when it passes laws. Its oversight function includes monitoring federal agencies and their programs. Congress also has the function of educating the public and representing the people.

   c. The balance of power between Congress and the other two branches has changed over the years. When the Constitution was ratified, Congress continued to be the strongest branch of government, as it had been under the Articles of Confederation. When the Supreme Court declared it had the right to review acts of Congress, the Court became more powerful than Congress. When Franklin D. Roosevelt began forming agencies to help the country get out of the Great Depression, the executive branch of government became more powerful. Today, President Obama has extended the power of the presidency by issuing executive orders. Throughout history, the legislative branch of government has become less powerful.

   d. There are several ties between Congress and the state and local governments. Caring for highways and roads is one example. Taxing is another. Congress enacts interstate commerce regulations, but states legislate on intrastate commerce. Both the federal government and state and local governments deal with environmental concerns.

SECTION VIII:
Practice Test Four

Section I: Multiple Choice _____

Instructions

Section I of this examination contains 60 multiple-choice questions. Fill in only the ovals for numbers 1 through 60 on your answer sheet.

Indicate all your answers to the multiple-choice questions on the answer sheet. No credit will be given for anything written in this exam booklet, but you may use the booklet for notes or scratch work. After you have decided which of the suggested answers is best, completely fill in the corresponding oval on the answer sheet. Give only one answer to each question. If you change an answer, be sure that the previous mark is erased completely. Here is a sample question and answer.

Sample Question   **Sample Answer**

1. **Washington is a**   Ⓐ ⬤ Ⓒ Ⓓ Ⓔ

   (A) City

   (B) State

   (C) Country

   (D) Continent

   (E) Bourough

Use your time effectively, working as quickly as you can without losing accuracy. Do not spend too much time on any one question. Go on to other questions and come back to the ones you have not answered if you have time. It is not expected that everyone will know the answers to all the multiple-choice questions.

About Guessing

Many candidates wonder whether or not to guess the answers to questions about which they are not certain. Multiple-choice scores are based on the number of questions answered correctly. Points are not deducted for incorrect answers, and no points are awarded for unanswered questions. Because points are not deducted for incorrect answers, you are encouraged to answer all multiple-choice questions. On questions you do not know the answer to, you should eliminate as many choices as you can, and then select the best answer among the remaining choices.

Time – 45 minutes
60 Questions

Directions: Each of the questions or incomplete statements below is followed by five suggested answers or explanations. Select the one that is BEST in each case.

1. Which plan presented at the Constitutional Convention provided for two houses of Congress with each house being based on population?

   (A)   The Sherman Plan

   (B)   The Randolph Plan

   (C)   The New Jersey Plan

   (D)   The 3/5 Compromise

   (E)   The Great Compromise

2. Declaration of a law as unconstitutional by the Supreme Court is an example of _____.

   (A)   Federalism

   (B)   Checks and balances

   (C)   Separation of Powers

   (D)   An implied power

   (E)   The Supreme Law of the Land

3. The theory of separation of powers is the idea that _____.

   (A)   The branches of government have checks on each other

   (B)   The branches of government are balanced by the checks they have on each other

   (C)   There are branches of government with separate functions

   (D)   There are state governments in addition to the federal government

   (E)   The government and its people have a contract to govern and be governed

4. **Which theory of democracy assumes the best about the people?**

   (A) Protective

   (B) Pluralist

   (C) Participatory

   (D) Developmental

   (E) Federalist

5. **The Senate's failure to confirm a President's nomination for a federal court judgeship is an example of _____.**

   (A) Separation of Powers

   (B) Federalism

   (C) Checks and balances

   (D) Participatory government

   (E) An implied power

6. **What did the framers of the Constitution believe was the weakness of the Articles of Confederation?**

   (A) The states had too little power

   (B) The Executive branch was too strong

   (C) The legislative branch was too strong

   (D) There was no court system

   (E) The legislative branch was weak and the states had too much power

7. **Which group has the most apathy toward politics and government?**

   (A) Elderly

   (B) Teens

   (C) Young adults

   (D) 40-50 years olds

   (E) All of the above

8. **Which ideas promote a strong central government?**

   (A) Neutral

   (B) Conservative

   (C) Republican

   (D) Democratic

   (E) Liberal

9. **Which group is considered more liberal?**

   (A) Elderly

   (B) Teens

   (C) Young adults

   (D) Middle-aged

   (E) Young children

10. **Which group of voters tends to be in the least conservative group?**

    (A) Young adults

    (B) Men

    (C) Teens

    (D) Women

    (E) Middle-aged

11. **Where does the first formal part of political socialization take place?**

    (A) The home

    (B) Places of worship

    (C) Schools

    (D) Jobs

    (E) Family gathering

12. **Which statement is correct about informal socialization?**

(A) It is structured

(B) It is purposeful

(C) It is learned at an early age

(D) It is accidental

(E) It is insignificant

13. **How do polls best help politicians?**

(A) They do not help

(B) Polls show who support the candidate

(C) Polls show the eventual winner

(D) Polls create interest in elections

(E) Polls show the preferences of the people

14. **Which group is most likely to participate in government?**

(A) Lower income groups

(B) Teens

(C) Young adults

(D) Conservatives

(E) Wealthy individuals

15. **Voting on a candidate's past behavior is an example of _____.**

(A) Respective voting

(B) Agreeing with the candidate's views

(C) Policy voting

(D) Party-line voting

(E) Party-identification voting

16. Mass media has an impact on politics because _____.

(A) It is neutral in campaigns

(B) It is subjective in its approach to politics

(C) It is biased toward candidates

(D) It has a narrow area of influence

(E) Its bias may show despite its goal of objectiveness

17. Which of the following is the most widespread use of media in today's society?

(A) Newspapers

(B) Books

(C) Internet

(D) Television

(E) Radio

18. How have third parties influenced voting changes?

(A) They have elected presidents, legislators, and presented platforms.

(B) They have urged people not to vote, have urged the adoption of women's suffrage, and elected state officials.

(C) They have elected state but not federal officials.

(D) They have presented candidates at state and federal levels, promoted progressive ideas, and elected officials at state and federal levels.

(E) They have not influenced voting changes.

19. Primary elections are an example of _____.

(A) Running campaigns

(B) Articulating policies

(C) Coordinating policy making

(D) Presenting platforms for voters

(E) Selecting candidates

20. **Which of the following has been a major party in the history of the United States?**

   (A) Bull Moose

   (B) Democratic-Republican

   (C) People's Party

   (D) Green Party

   (E) Libertarian Party

21. **A voter who casts votes for members of each political party in a general election is said to _____.**

   (A) Split his/her ticket

   (B) Vote a straight ticket

   (C) Vote in a primary election

   (D) Vote in a state caucus

   (E) Be an independent voter

22. **How are candidates nominated for president and vice-president?**

   (A) At state caucuses

   (B) In primary elections

   (C) At party conventions

   (D) By voters

   (E) In general elections

23. **What is a major difference between political parties and interest groups?**

   (A) Interest groups express policies but political parties do not.

   (B) Political parties enter the political process to accomplish goals but interest groups do not.

   (C) Interest groups are more successful in achieving goals than political parties.

   (D) Political parties choose candidates for office and interest groups support them.

   (E) Political parties campaign to make changes while interest groups lobby.

24. Which is a correct statement about lobbyists?

(A) Interest groups use lobbyists to promote their causes

(B) Lobbyists are a negative influence on government

(C) Lobbyists are a positive influence on government

(D) Lobbyists were used in the early years of our country but fell into disfavor in recent years

(E) Lobbyists are used in today's political system but were unknown before the 1960s.

25. What is the administrative group in government that makes policy?

(A) Congress

(B) The presidency

(C) Bureaucracy

(D) Judiciary

(E) Executive

26. In policymaking, the term "agenda setting" means _____.

(A) Scheduling dates to hear the issues

(B) Recognizing the problem

(C) Formulating the policy

(D) Implementing the policy

(E) Adopting the policy

27. During the late 1800s and early 1900s a group referred to as _____ wrote articles to condemn practices in the food industry, the formation of trusts, lack of sanitary conditions in the factories, and other unethical practices in society that resulted in the creation of the Food and Drug Administration and other legislative policies.

(A) Yellow journalists

(B) Captains of industry

(C) Robber barons

(D) Muckrakers

(E) Lobbyist

28. **How might Congress adopt new policy?**

(A) Share the problem with the courts

(B) Explain the problem to the president

(C) Pass a law

(D) Submit a cease and desist order

(E) Adopt policies without interaction of other government bodies

29. **If you saw the slogan, "Stop, Look, and Listen", who or which group would be interested in implementing the policy?**

(A) Chamber of Commerce

(B) Consumer Affairs Division

(C) Department of Transportation

(D) Department of Justice

(E) The National Park System

30. **Which statement about evaluating policy is INCORRECT?**

(A) Policy makers need to determine what the policy is going to accomplish.

(B) Policy makers need to decide whether the policy is being carried out efficiently.

(C) Evaluations rarely result in the need for policy modification.

(D) Evaluating is a continuous process.

(E) Many interacting sources evaluate policy.

31. **What is the process of allocating congressional districts to each state based upon population numbers after a decennial census?**

(A) Gerrymandering

(B) Filibustering

(C) Redistricting

(D) Apportionment

(E) Cloture

32. **Redrawing of congressional districts to reflect the increase or decrease in the number of seats and populations shifts within a state is called _____.**

(A) Gerrymandering

(B) Filibustering

(C) Redistricting

(D) Apportionment

(E) Cloture

33. **A bill is _____.**

(A) A proposed law

(B) A law that has been passed

(C) A law that has been vetoes

(D) A law that has been passed over a presidential veto

(E) A budget proposal

34. How many of the U.S. Senators are up for re-election every two years?

(A) None

(B) One-fourth

(C) One-third

(D) One-half

(E) All

35. How many members of the House of Representatives are there?

(A) 50

(B) 100

(C) 250

(D) 435

(E) 500

36. What does "impeach" mean?

(A) To convict a government official of a wrong doing

(B) To charge a government official with a wrong doing

(C) To challenge a statement of a government official

(D) To agree with a statement of a government official

(E) To persuade a government official to change a statement

37. Who tries impeachment cases?

(A) The Supreme Court

(B) The Executive Branch

(C) The House of Representatives

(D) The Senate

(E) Congress as a whole

38. Who brings charges of impeachment?

(A) The Supreme Court

(B) The Executive Branch

(C) The House of Representatives

(D) The Senate

(E) Congress as a whole

39. Which Presidents have been impeached?

(A) Richard Nixon and Andrew Johnson

(B) Andrew Johnson and Andrew Jackson

(C) William Clinton and Andrew Jackson

(D) Andrew Johnson and James Buchanan

(E) William Clinton and Andrew Johnson

40. How many members of the Senate must vote to approve a treaty?

(A) One-fourth

(B) One-third

(C) Simple majority

(D) Two-thirds

(E) Three-fourths

41. **What is the difference between a joint committee and a conference committee?**

(A) A joint committee is a temporary committee appointed for a specific purpose whereas a conference committee conducts investigations.

(B) A conference committee is a joint committee but a joint committee is appointed for special purposes.

(C) A conference committee is a temporary committee whereas a joint committee is appointed for a specific purpose.

(D) A joint committee irons out differences between versions of legislation whereas a conference committee conducts special investigations.

(E) A joint committee includes members from both houses and conducts investigations and a conference committee is a joint committee that is created to iron out differences in versions of legislation.

42. **Which of the following is a correct statement about the link between interest groups and federalism?**

(A) It discourages the formation of interest groups.

(B) Interest groups often begin at the national level and filter down to the states and cities.

(C) As a result of federalism, there are only a few types of interest groups.

(D) The decentralization of government in federalism results in a stronger party system for interest groups.

(E) Because of the national, state, and local levels of government, interest groups often spread from local interests to national interests.

43. **How can interest groups best achieve policy objectives in connections with the courts?**

(A) Protesting

(B) Litigating

(C) Promoting objectives that result from decisions involving litigation

(D) Lobbying

(E) Voting for Judges

44. Which of the following statements is correct about the links between interest groups, political parties, and the media?

(A) Unpopular positions taken by interest groups can be dismissed by political parties but cannot be ignored by the media.

(B) The Internet has opened access to more interest groups that may have objectives different than one or both of the political parties.

(C) Americans have unlimited freedom of expression and all views of interest groups are entitled to consideration on all issues.

(D) Interest groups have very limited success in getting political party leaders to listen to their views.

(E) The media is not interested in communicating ideas of interest groups.

45. A government program created by legislation that guarantees members of a group to some benefits is called a(n) _____.

(A) Expenditure

(B) Entitlement

(C) Deficit

(D) Resolution

(E) Budget

46. The concept of federalism would permit a state to _____.

(A) Set maximum driving speeds on state highways

(B) Coin money

(C) Establish a second Bankruptcy Court in the state

(D) Increase the federal income tax within the state

(E) Decide that only certain types of crimes entitled defendants to an attorney

47. **The Bureaucracy is considered as part of which branch of government?**

(A) Congress

(B) Legislative

(C) Judicial

(D) Supreme Court

(E) Executive

48. **Which of the following is an informal power of the executive officer of the country or a state?**

(A) Provide input about the budget

(B) Veto legislation

(C) Serve as commander-in-chief of the armed forces

(D) Make appointments

(E) Enforce the laws

49. **What does the term "original jurisdiction" mean in relation to the courts?**

(A) The first type of court jurisdiction in the nation after the Constitution was written

(B) Judicial review

(C) The court where the case is heard first

(D) The court where the case is heard last

(E) The decision by a court that it will hear a case

50. **Why does there tend to be continuity on the Supreme Court and in the judicial branch of government?**

(A) The judges serve during the period of good behavior.

(B) The judges become aware of how the others think about cases.

(C) The doctrine of judicial review has made consistency easier, and consistence provides continuity.

(D) The judges are all approved by Congress.

(E) The judges are all appointed by the President.

51. **How are the federal courts linked to the state and local governments?**

(A) The federal courts hear cases involving state laws.

(B) The federal court judges help with the appointment standards for state judges.

(C) State court judges may become federal court judges.

(D) State courts use the process of judicial review to decide whether acts of Congress are constitutional.

(E) Federal courts can only hear cases that are appealed to them after a party loses in state court.

52. **The Federal Trade Commission is an example of _____.**

(A) Congressional appointment

(B) Presidential appointment

(C) Supreme Court approval

(D) An agency in the Bureaucracy

(E) A state application for the creation of a commission

53. **Which of the following is an example of the Bureaucracy?**

(A) Congress

(B) President's Cabinet

(C) U.S. District Court

(D) The Vice President

(E) The Supreme Court justices

54. **Which president expanded the executive branch and made it more powerful?**

(A) Herbert Hoover

(B) Franklin Roosevelt

(C) Harry Truman

(D) William Clinton

(E) George Bush

55. **If a person yells "Fire" in an auditorium that is filled with people, is that person entitled to claim freedom of speech as a defense if he/she is arrested?**

(A) Yes, because civil liberties are unlimited.

(B) Yes, because the person may have been joking.

(C) No, because there are limitations on the freedom of speech.

(D) No, because anyone with common sense would know there might be panic as a result.

(E) Yelling fire in a crowded auditorium is not an infringement on a civil liberty nor is freedom of speech a civil liberty.

56. Which of the following statements is true about commercial speech?

(A) It enjoys complete protection under the First Amendment.

(B) It is usually in the form of expressive speech.

(C) It may be restricted if it furthers a substantial government interest and if the restriction actually furthers that interest.

(D) It may be restricted if it furthers a slight government interest but it is subject to strict scrutiny.

(E) Commercial speech falls under a different amendment than the First Amendment.

57. Which Amendment provides protections for persons convicted of crimes?

(A) Fourth

(B) Fifth

(C) Sixth

(D) Eighth

(E) Fourteenth

58. The U.S. Supreme Court expanded civil rights and liberties in the case of *Griswold v. Connecticut*, a case that involved _____ privacy.

(A) Personal

(B) Marital

(C) Group

(D) Business

(E) Religious

59. **The attempt to end and prevent discrimination is called _____.**

   (A) Title IX

   (B) Desegregation

   (C) Integration

   (D) Affirmative Action

   (E) Assimilation

60. **The Fourteenth Amendment was made applicable to the states through _____.**

   (A) Stare decisis

   (B) Judicial review

   (C) The incorporation doctrine

   (D) The Due Process clause

   (E) The Equal Protection clause

1. Public policy has multiple stages.

    a. Define public policy.

    b. Identify major public policies and the sources of public policy.

    c. Provide substantive examples of ways public policy is the results of interactions among individuals, interests, institutions, and processes.

    d. Discuss the differences between foreign and domestic foreign policy areas

      • Describe how these policy areas affect citizens.

      • State whether these policy areas overlap and explain why or why not.

2. It is necessary to understand the development of rights and liberties in order to understand American politics.

   a. Explain the role of the U.S. Supreme Court in developing rights and liberties.

   b. What important Supreme Court Cases support your explanation?

      • Explain the significant of these cases.

      • Identify current issues in which the Supreme Court has, or will likely play a role in, developing rights and liberties.

   c. Describe the effects, or lack of effects, on society after these Supreme Court decisions.

   d. Explain the role of the Fourteenth Amendment in the expansion of rights and liberties.

3. The framers of the Constitution drew on ideological and philosophical traditions to draft the new organization of American government.

   a. Identify the traditions the framers used.

   b. How do these traditions relate to the historical situation at the time of the Constitutional convention?

   c. Identify specific concerns of the framers.

   d. Explain the concerns that existed in determining whether the Constitution should be ratified.

   e. Explain why a Bill of Rights was added to the Constitution.

      • Identify the rights that were included.

      • Describe the reasons for the inclusion of some of those rights.

4. **Interest groups and the media play a role in politics.**

   a. **Define the term interest group.**

   b. **Define the term media.**

   c. **Explain the role of each in politics.**
      - **How does each group function?**
      - **How do the activities of each group affect the process of government?**
      - **How do the activities of each group affect public policy?**

Sample Answer

   a. Interest groups are organized groups that have a specific goal of influencing public policy or public opinion.

   b. Media is the method of transmitting news and information to the public through organized means, such as television, the Internet, and written materials. It also refers to the people communicating the news.

   c. The media has a role in politics by communicating the platforms of candidates and parties. It also interprets the statements of candidates. The media and interest groups can have a great deal of influence on the process of government because the media's interpretation of events can shift public opinion; and interest groups shape public opinion through advertisements, litigation, and conversations with legislators. Both groups affect public policy through communications and promoting their views, whether through newscasts, documentaries, litigation, or communications.

Section I: Multiple Choice Answer Sheet _____

1. Ⓐ Ⓑ Ⓒ Ⓓ Ⓔ
2. Ⓐ Ⓑ Ⓒ Ⓓ Ⓔ
3. Ⓐ Ⓑ Ⓒ Ⓓ Ⓔ
4. Ⓐ Ⓑ Ⓒ Ⓓ Ⓔ
5. Ⓐ Ⓑ Ⓒ Ⓓ Ⓔ
6. Ⓐ Ⓑ Ⓒ Ⓓ Ⓔ
7. Ⓐ Ⓑ Ⓒ Ⓓ Ⓔ
8. Ⓐ Ⓑ Ⓒ Ⓓ Ⓔ
9. Ⓐ Ⓑ Ⓒ Ⓓ Ⓔ
10. Ⓐ Ⓑ Ⓒ Ⓓ Ⓔ
11. Ⓐ Ⓑ Ⓒ Ⓓ Ⓔ
12. Ⓐ Ⓑ Ⓒ Ⓓ Ⓔ
13. Ⓐ Ⓑ Ⓒ Ⓓ Ⓔ
14. Ⓐ Ⓑ Ⓒ Ⓓ Ⓔ
15. Ⓐ Ⓑ Ⓒ Ⓓ Ⓔ
16. Ⓐ Ⓑ Ⓒ Ⓓ Ⓔ
17. Ⓐ Ⓑ Ⓒ Ⓓ Ⓔ
18. Ⓐ Ⓑ Ⓒ Ⓓ Ⓔ
19. Ⓐ Ⓑ Ⓒ Ⓓ Ⓔ
20. Ⓐ Ⓑ Ⓒ Ⓓ Ⓔ

21. Ⓐ Ⓑ Ⓒ Ⓓ Ⓔ
22. Ⓐ Ⓑ Ⓒ Ⓓ Ⓔ
23. Ⓐ Ⓑ Ⓒ Ⓓ Ⓔ
24. Ⓐ Ⓑ Ⓒ Ⓓ Ⓔ
25. Ⓐ Ⓑ Ⓒ Ⓓ Ⓔ
26. Ⓐ Ⓑ Ⓒ Ⓓ Ⓔ
27. Ⓐ Ⓑ Ⓒ Ⓓ Ⓔ
28. Ⓐ Ⓑ Ⓒ Ⓓ Ⓔ
29. Ⓐ Ⓑ Ⓒ Ⓓ Ⓔ
30. Ⓐ Ⓑ Ⓒ Ⓓ Ⓔ
31. Ⓐ Ⓑ Ⓒ Ⓓ Ⓔ
32. Ⓐ Ⓑ Ⓒ Ⓓ Ⓔ
33. Ⓐ Ⓑ Ⓒ Ⓓ Ⓔ
34. Ⓐ Ⓑ Ⓒ Ⓓ Ⓔ
35. Ⓐ Ⓑ Ⓒ Ⓓ Ⓔ
36. Ⓐ Ⓑ Ⓒ Ⓓ Ⓔ
37. Ⓐ Ⓑ Ⓒ Ⓓ Ⓔ
38. Ⓐ Ⓑ Ⓒ Ⓓ Ⓔ
39. Ⓐ Ⓑ Ⓒ Ⓓ Ⓔ
40. Ⓐ Ⓑ Ⓒ Ⓓ Ⓔ

41. Ⓐ Ⓑ Ⓒ Ⓓ Ⓔ
42. Ⓐ Ⓑ Ⓒ Ⓓ Ⓔ
43. Ⓐ Ⓑ Ⓒ Ⓓ Ⓔ
44. Ⓐ Ⓑ Ⓒ Ⓓ Ⓔ
45. Ⓐ Ⓑ Ⓒ Ⓓ Ⓔ
46. Ⓐ Ⓑ Ⓒ Ⓓ Ⓔ
47. Ⓐ Ⓑ Ⓒ Ⓓ Ⓔ
48. Ⓐ Ⓑ Ⓒ Ⓓ Ⓔ
49. Ⓐ Ⓑ Ⓒ Ⓓ Ⓔ
50. Ⓐ Ⓑ Ⓒ Ⓓ Ⓔ
51. Ⓐ Ⓑ Ⓒ Ⓓ Ⓔ
52. Ⓐ Ⓑ Ⓒ Ⓓ Ⓔ
53. Ⓐ Ⓑ Ⓒ Ⓓ Ⓔ
54. Ⓐ Ⓑ Ⓒ Ⓓ Ⓔ
55. Ⓐ Ⓑ Ⓒ Ⓓ Ⓔ
56. Ⓐ Ⓑ Ⓒ Ⓓ Ⓔ
57. Ⓐ Ⓑ Ⓒ Ⓓ Ⓔ
58. Ⓐ Ⓑ Ⓒ Ⓓ Ⓔ
59. Ⓐ Ⓑ Ⓒ Ⓓ Ⓔ
60. Ⓐ Ⓑ Ⓒ Ⓓ Ⓔ

Section I: Multiple Choice Answer Key

Question Number	Correct Answer
1.	B
2.	B
3.	C
4.	D
5.	C
6.	E
7.	C
8.	E
9.	C
10.	D
11.	C
12.	D
13.	E
14.	E
15.	A
16.	E
17.	C
18.	D
19.	E
20.	B

Question Number	Correct Answer
21.	A
22.	C
23.	D
24.	A
25.	C
26.	B
27.	D
28.	C
29.	C
30.	C
31.	D
32.	C
33.	A
34.	C
35.	D
36.	B
37.	D
38.	C
39.	E
40.	D

Question Number	Correct Answer
41.	E
42.	E
43.	C
44.	B
45.	B
46.	A
47.	E
48.	A
49.	C
50.	A
51.	A
52.	D
53.	B
54.	B
55.	C
56.	C
57.	C
58.	B
59.	D
60.	C

1. **Which plan presented at the Constitutional Convention provided for two houses of Congress with each house being based on population?**

    (A) The Sherman Plan

    (B) The Randolph Plan

    (C) The New Jersey Plan

    (D) The 3/5 Compromise

    (E) The Great Compromise

    Answer: B.
    The Randolph Plan. The Sherman Plan, also known as the Great Compromise refers to Connecticut Compromise. The New Jersey Plan proposed a bicameral legislature. The 3/5 Compromise dealt with population count for slaves. The Randolph Plan was also known as the Virginia Plan. This plan proposed a bicameral legislature with both houses of Congress being based on population.

2. **Declaration of a law as unconstitutional by the Supreme Court is an example of _____.**

    (A) Federalism

    (B) Checks and balances

    (C) Separation of Powers

    (D) An implied power

    (E) The Supreme Law of the Land

    Answer: B.
    Checks and balances. The doctrine of judicial review is the basis for the Supreme Court's power to declare acts of Congress unconstitutional. It is a method used by the judicial branch to check on the powers of the legislative branch and to maintain balance among the branches of government.

Practice Test Four

3. **The theory of separation of powers is the idea that _____.**

   (A) The branches of government have checks on each other

   (B) The branches of government are balanced by the checks they have on each other

   (C) There are branches of government with separate functions

   (D) There are state governments in addition to the federal government

   (E) The government and its people have a contract to govern and be governed

   Answer: C.
   There are branches of government with separate functions. A government contract aligns to the "social contract", and the branches have checks and balances. When there is a central government and state governments, there is federalism. Separation of powers refers to each branch of government having a different function.

4. **Which theory of democracy assumes the best about the people?**

   (A) Protective

   (B) Pluralist

   (C) Participatory

   (D) Developmental

   (E) Federalist

   Answer: D.
   Developmental. A protective democracy protects the people. A pluralist democracy believes special interests hold power. A participatory government encourages more people to become involved in government. A developmental government assumes the best about society.

5. **The Senate's failure to confirm a President's nomination for a federal court judgeship is an example of _____.**

   (A) Separation of Powers

   (B) Federalism

   (C) Checks and balances

   (D) Participatory government

   (E) An implied power

Answer: C.

Checks and balances. Separation of powers means there are different branches of government with different functions. Federalism means a government has a central authority and branches (states) of governments. A participatory government encourages people to become more involved in government. An implied power is one that Congress has as the result of the 'necessary and proper' clause. The Senate's decision not to confirm a presidential appointment is a check on the executive branch.

6. **What did the framers of the Constitution believe was the weakness of the Articles of Confederation?**

   (A) The states had too little power

   (B) The Executive branch was too strong

   (C) The legislative branch was too strong

   (D) There was no court system

   (E) The legislative branch was weak and the states had too much power

Answer: E.

The legislative branch was weak and the states had too much power. The weaknesses of the Articles of Confederation resulted from the states having too much power and the legislature not having enough power.

7. **Which group has the most apathy toward politics and government?**

   (A) Elderly

   (B) Teens

   (C) Young adults

   (D) 40-50 years olds

   (E) All of the above

Answer: C.

Young adults. The elderly have the most interest in government and politics and the young adults have the least interest. Young adults are considered most apathetic about politics.

8. **Which ideas promote a strong central government?**

   (A) Neutral

   (B) Conservative

   (C) Republican

   (D) Democratic

   (E) Liberal

   Answer: E.

   Liberal. Conservatives favor a weaker central government and stronger state governments. Liberals tend to favor a stronger central government.

9. **Which group is considered more liberal?**

   (A) Elderly

   (B) Teens

   (C) Young adults

   (D) Middle-aged

   (E) Young children

   Answer: C.

   Young adults. Older people tend to be more conservative and young adults tend to be more liberal in their political thinking.

10. **Which group of voters tends to be in the least conservative group?**

   (A) Young adults

   (B) Men

   (C) Teens

   (D) Women

   (E) Middle-aged

   Answer: D.

   Women. Women tend to be less conservative. Young adults tend to be more liberal but women have been categorized as less conservative than men.

11. **Where does the first formal part of political socialization take place?**

(A) The home

(B) Places of worship

(C) Schools

(D) Jobs

(E) Family gathering

Answer: C.
Schools. The first information about politics is learned in the home but the first formal political socialization takes place in schools, and it is usually on a limited basis.

12. **Which statement is correct about informal socialization?**

(A) It is structured

(B) It is purposeful

(C) It is learned at an early age

(D) It is accidental

(E) It is insignificant

Answer: D.
It is accidental. Informal socialization refers to places where people learn about society, politics, government, and similar subjects. It can take place at many places and it is accidental.

13. **How do polls best help politicians?**

(A) They do not help

(B) Polls show who support the candidate

(C) Polls show the eventual winner

(D) Polls create interest in elections

(E) Polls show the preferences of the people

Answer: E.
Polls show the preferences of the people. Polls may show the eventual winner but their main purpose is to show the preferences of the people to the candidates.

14. **Which group is most likely to participate in government?**

   (A)   Lower income groups

   (B)   Teens

   (C)   Young adults

   (D)   Conservatives

   (E)   Wealthy individuals

   Answer: E.
   Wealthy individuals. Wealthy people tend to participate more in government than people with lower incomes.

15. **Voting on a candidate's past behavior is an example of _____.**

   (A)   Respective voting

   (B)   Agreeing with the candidate's views

   (C)   Policy voting

   (D)   Party-line voting

   (E)   Party-identification voting

   Answer: A.
   Respective voting. When a person utilizes "respective voting", the voter is looking at the candidate's past record or actions and deciding which candidate has done the best for them in the past. That candidate will obtain the vote.

16. **Mass media has an impact on politics because _____.**

   (A)   It is neutral in campaigns

   (B)   It is subjective in its approach to politics

   (C)   It is biased toward candidates

   (D)   It has a narrow area of influence

   (E)   Its bias may show despite its goal of objectiveness

Answer: E.

Its bias may show despite its goal of objectiveness. Although the news media has the goal of being objective when reporting on elections, any bias that is present in interpreting the news may become apparent.

17. **Which of the following is the most widespread use of media in today's society?**

    (A) Newspapers

    (B) Books

    (C) Internet

    (D) Television

    (E) Radio

    Answer: C.

    Internet. The Internet has become the most widespread use of media communications today.

18. **How have third parties influenced voting changes?**

    (A) They have elected presidents, legislators, and presented platforms.

    (B) They have urged people not to vote, have urged the adoption of women's suffrage, and elected state officials.

    (C) They have elected state but not federal officials.

    (D) They have presented candidates at state and federal levels, promoted progressive ideas, and elected officials at state and federal levels.

    (E) They have not influenced voting changes

    Answer: D.

    They have presented candidates at state and federal levels, promoted progressive ideas, and elected officials at state and federal levels. Third parties have the ability to present and promote progressive ideas and candidates.

19. **Primary elections are an example of _____.**

   (A) Running campaigns

   (B) Articulating policies

   (C) Coordinating policy making

   (D) Presenting platforms for voters

   (E) Selecting candidates

   Answer: E.

   Selecting candidates. All of the choices are functions of political parties. Primary elections serve the purpose of selecting candidates.

20. **Which of the following has been a major party in the history of the United States?**

   (A) Bull Moose

   (B) Democratic-Republican

   (C) People's Party

   (D) Green Party

   (E) Libertarian Party

   Answer: B.

   Democratic-Republican. Thomas Jefferson belonged to the Democratic-Republican Party, which was a party that believed the states should have considerable power. It was called the Republican Party and eventually became the Democratic Party. It was a party that opposed the Federalists in the late 1790s and early 1800s.

21. **A voter who casts votes for members of each political party in a general election is said to _____.**

   (A) Split his/her ticket

   (B) Vote a straight ticket

   (C) Vote in a primary election

   (D) Vote in a state caucus

   (E) Be an independent voter

Answer: A.

Split his/her ticket. Voting for each party's candidates is splitting a ticket. One may belong to a party or be an independent voter to split a ticket in a general election.

22. **How are candidates nominated for president and vice-president?**

    (A) At state caucuses

    (B) In primary elections

    (C) At party conventions

    (D) By voters

    (E) In general elections

Answer: C.

At party conventions. Voters express their choices for a potential nominee at caucuses and in primary elections. Candidates for president and vice president are nominated at party conventions.

23. **What is a major difference between political parties and interest groups?**

    (A) Interest groups express policies but political parties do not.

    (B) Political parties enter the political process to accomplish goals but interest groups do not.

    (C) Interest groups are more successful in achieving goals than political parties.

    (D) Political parties choose candidates for office and interest groups support them.

    (E) Political parties campaign to make changes while interest groups lobby.

Answer: D.

Political parties choose candidates for office and interest groups support them. Political candidates campaign. Both political parties and interest groups may be successful in accomplishing goals, are involved in the political process, and express policies. One of the main differences is that political parties select candidates and interest groups support the candidates.

24. **Which is a correct statement about lobbyists?**

   (A)   Interest groups use lobbyists to promote their causes

   (B)   Lobbyists are a negative influence on government

   (C)   Lobbyists are a positive influence on government

   (D)   Lobbyists were used in the early years of our country but fell into disfavor in recent years

   (E)   Lobbyists are used in today's political system but were unknown before the 1960s.

Answer: A.

Interest groups use lobbyists to promote their causes. Lobbying interests have been present in government for years. Whether lobbyists are a positive or negative influence is an opinion. The correct statement is that interest groups used lobbyists to promote their causes.

25. **What is the administrative group in government that makes policy?**

   (A)   Congress

   (B)   The presidency

   (C)   Bureaucracy

   (D)   Judiciary

   (E)   Executive

Answer: C.

Bureaucracy. Bureaucrats make policy. They are a group of non-elected officials. The presidency and legislative branch are elected and the judiciary is appointed.

26. **In policymaking, the term "agenda setting" means _____.**

   (A)   Scheduling dates to hear the issues

   (B)   Recognizing the problem

   (C)   Formulating the policy

   (D)   Implementing the policy

   (E)   Adopting the policy

Answer: B.

Recognizing the problem. Recognizing the problem is the correct choice because the problems need to be identified before policies can be written or decided. The term "agenda" means the list of problems that the government wants to solve.

27. **During the late 1800s and early 1900s a group referred to as _____ wrote articles to condemn practices in the food industry, the formation of trusts, lack of sanitary conditions in the factories, and other unethical practices in society that resulted in the creation of the Food and Drug Administration and other legislative policies.**

   (A) Yellow journalists

   (B) Captains of industry

   (C) Robber barons

   (D) Muckrakers

   (E) Lobbyist

Answer: D.

Muckrakers. The Progressive Era had many writers who wanted to expose the evils of society. Ida Tarbell wrote about the negative aspects of the Standard Oil trust and others wrote about the unsanitary conditions in industries such as the meatpacking industry and in other food industries. There were also unethical practices described in other areas, such as the utilization of child labor. The writers who dug up "muck," or dirt, were known as muckrakers. Their work led to new government regulations and policies and the creation of new agencies, such as the Food and Drug Administration.

28. **How might Congress adopt new policy?**

   (A) Share the problem with the courts

   (B) Explain the problem to the president

   (C) Pass a law

   (D) Submit a cease and desist order

   (E) Adopt policies without interaction of other government bodies

Answer: C.

Pass a law. The President may issue an executive order or the courts may decide important cases to adopt new policy. Congress can adopt policy by passing legislation.

29. **If you saw the slogan, "Stop, Look, and Listen", who or which group would be interested in implementing the policy?**

(A) Chamber of Commerce

(B) Consumer Affairs Division

(C) Department of Transportation

(D) Department of Justice

(E) The National Park System

Answer: C.

Department of Transportation. Different types of slogans are implemented for different purposes. The slogan "Stop Look, and Listen" makes it clear that people should do each of those things before crossing a railroad track. The Department of Transportation is interested in implementing this policy to eliminate, or at least reduce, accidents at railroad crossings. Slogans are a way to make policy implementation easier for people to remember.

30. **Which statement about evaluating policy is INCORRECT?**

(A) Policy makers need to determine what the policy is going to accomplish.

(B) Policy makers need to decide whether the policy is being carried out efficiently.

(C) Evaluations rarely result in the need for policy modification.

(D) Evaluating is a continuous process.

(E) Many interacting sources evaluate policy.

Answer: C.

Evaluations rarely result in the need for policy modification. Most evaluation results in some modification or change of policy.

31. **What is the process of allocating congressional districts to each state based upon population numbers after a decennial census?**

(A) Gerrymandering

(B) Filibustering

(C) Redistricting

(D) Apportionment

(E) Cloture

Answer: D.

Apportionment. Gerrymandering is redistricting to favor one political party. Filibustering is "talking a bill to death." Cloture is a method used to close debate. Apportionment is the process of allocating congressional districts to states after the census that is taken every ten years. When there is apportionment, some states may lose representatives and other states, such as the Sunbelt states to where many people are moving, may gain in the number of representatives.

32. **Redrawing of congressional districts to reflect the increase or decrease in the number of seats and populations shifts within a state is called _____.**

(A) Gerrymandering

(B) Filibustering

(C) Redistricting

(D) Apportionment

(E) Cloture

Answer: C.

Redistricting. Gerrymandering is redistricting to favor one political party. Filibustering is "talking a bill to death." Cloture is a method used to close debate. Apportionment is the process of allocating congressional districts to states after the census that is taken every ten years. When there is apportionment, some states may lose representatives and other states, such as the Sunbelt states to where many people are moving, may gain in the number of representatives. Redistricting is redrawing boundaries within the state for congressional districts so the districts reflect population shifts within the state and also reflect the increase or decrease in seats overall.

33. A bill is _____.

(A) A proposed law

(B) A law that has been passed

(C) A law that has been vetoes

(D) A law that has been passed over a presidential veto

(E) A budget proposal

Answer: A.
A proposed law. A bill is a suggested or proposed law. Once the proposal has passed both houses of Congress the proposal becomes a law.

34. How many of the U.S. Senators are up for re-election every two years?

(A) None

(B) One-fourth

(C) One-third

(D) One-half

(E) All

Answer: C.
One-third. Senators are chosen for six-year terms. One-third of the Senators are elected every two years. The terms are staggered so there will be continuity.

35. How many members of the House of Representatives are there?

(A) 50

(B) 100

(C) 250

(D) 435

(E) 500

Answer: D.
435. There are 435 members of the House of Representatives. There are 100 Senators.

36. **What does "impeach" mean?**

   (A) To convict a government official of a wrong doing

   (B) To charge a government official with a wrong doing

   (C) To challenge a statement of a government official

   (D) To agree with a statement of a government official

   (E) To persuade a government official to change a statement

Answer: B.

To charge a government official with a wrong doing. The term "impeach" means to charge a government official of a wrong doing. It is the first step in the process of removing a person from office.

37. **Who tries impeachment cases?**

   (A) The Supreme Court

   (B) The Executive Branch

   (C) The House of Representatives

   (D) The Senate

   (E) Congress as a whole

Answer: D.
The Senate. The Senate tries cases of impeachment.

38. **Who brings charges of impeachment?**

   (A) The Supreme Court

   (B) The Executive Branch

   (C) The House of Representatives

   (D) The Senate

   (E) Congress as a whole

Answer: C.
The House of Representatives. The House of Representatives brings charges of impeachment.

39. **Which Presidents have been impeached?**

   (A) Richard Nixon and Andrew Johnson

   (B) Andrew Johnson and Andrew Jackson

   (C) William Clinton and Andrew Jackson

   (D) Andrew Johnson and James Buchanan

   (E) William Clinton and Andrew Johnson

   Answer: E.
   William Clinton and Andrew Johnson. William Clinton and Andrew Johnson were both impeached but were not convicted.

40. **How many members of the Senate must vote to approve a treaty?**

   (A) One-fourth

   (B) One-third

   (C) Simple majority

   (D) Two-thirds

   (E) Three-fourths

   Answer: D.
   Two-thirds. Although bills only need a simple majority vote to become a law, treaties must be approved by two-thirds of the members of the Senate.

41. What is the difference between a joint committee and a conference committee?

(A) A joint committee is a temporary committee appointed for a specific purpose whereas a conference committee conducts investigations.

(B) A conference committee is a joint committee but a joint committee is appointed for special purposes.

(C) A conference committee is a temporary committee whereas a joint committee is appointed for a specific purpose.

(D) A joint committee irons out differences between versions of legislation whereas a conference committee conducts special investigations.

(E) A joint committee includes members from both houses and conducts investigations and a conference committee is a joint committee that is created to iron out differences in versions of legislation.

Answer: E.

A joint committee includes members from both houses and conducts investigations and a conference committee is a joint committee that is created to iron out differences in versions of legislation. A conference committee is a type of joint committee that is created to iron out differences in legislation passed by the House and Senate. A select or special committee is a temporary committee appointed for a specific purpose. A joint committee includes members from the House and Senate and can conduct investigations and help focus on major issues.

42. Which of the following is a correct statement about the link between interest groups and federalism?

(A) It discourages the formation of interest groups.

(B) Interest groups often begin at the national level and filter down to the states and cities.

(C) As a result of federalism, there are only a few types of interest groups.

(D) The decentralization of government in federalism results in a stronger party system for interest groups.

(E) Because of the national, state, and local levels of government, interest groups often spread from local interests to national interests.

Answer: E.

Because of the national, state, and local levels of government, interest groups often spread from local interests to national interests. Many interest groups have their beginnings at a state or local level and then progress to a national level group.

43. **How can interest groups best achieve policy objectives in connections with the courts?**

(A) Protesting

(B) Litigating

(C) Promoting objectives that result from decisions involving litigation

(D) Lobbying

(E) Voting for Judges

Answer: C.

Promoting objectives that result from decisions involving litigation. The judiciary is an independent body. Interest groups can advance their beliefs as the result of court decisions. For example, the decision in *Brown v. Board* of Education held that equal facilities were inherently unequal facilities when it came to education. The decision opened the door to desegregation in many aspects of American life. Interest groups involved in promoting the desegregation (or integration) of various aspects of American life had, as a result of the Brown decision, a platform on which they could proceed to accomplish their objectives.

44. **Which of the following statements is correct about the links between interest groups, political parties, and the media?**

(A) Unpopular positions taken by interest groups can be dismissed by political parties but cannot be ignored by the media.

(B) The Internet has opened access to more interest groups that may have objectives different than one or both of the political parties.

(C) Americans have unlimited freedom of expression and all views of interest groups are entitled to consideration on all issues.

(D) Interest groups have very limited success in getting political party leaders to listen to their views.

(E) The media is not interested in communicating ideas of interest groups.

Answer: B.

The Internet has opened access to more interest groups that may have objectives different than one or both of the political parties. There are important links between interest groups, political parties, and the media. The Internet has become a source that interest groups can use to disseminate their views over a wide area.

45. **A government program created by legislation that guarantees members of a group to some benefits is called a(n) _____.**

    (A) Expenditure

    (B) Entitlement

    (C) Deficit

    (D) Resolution

    (E) Budget

    Answer: B.

    Entitlement. Entitlements can include benefits such as food stamps, health insurance, mortgage deductions, Social Security, and housing benefits based on income.

46. **The concept of federalism would permit a state to _____.**

    (A) Set maximum driving speeds on state highways

    (B) Coin money

    (C) Establish a second Bankruptcy Court in the state

    (D) Increase the federal income tax within the state

    (E) Decide that only certain types of crimes entitled defendants to an attorney

    Answer: A.

    Set maximum driving speeds on state highways. A state could create or increase the rates of existing state income taxes but coining money and establishing bankruptcy courts are powers granted to Congress. The U.S. Constitution's Bill of Rights guarantees the right to counsel and that provision is applied to the states through the Fourteenth Amendment. A state may set driving speeds for state highways.

47. The Bureaucracy is considered as part of which branch of government?

(A) Congress

(B) Legislative

(C) Judicial

(D) Supreme Court

(E) Executive

Answer: E.

Executive. The bureaus or agencies that form the government's bureaucracy are considered part of the executive branch of government.

48. Which of the following is an informal power of the executive officer of the country or a state?

(A) Provide input about the budget

(B) Veto legislation

(C) Serve as commander-in-chief of the armed forces

(D) Make appointments

(E) Enforce the laws

Answer: A.

Provide input about the budget. All of the choices except A are the formal powers that are given to the President in the Constitution and are similar powers that would be given to a state governor in a state constitution. Providing input about a budget that is being proposed to Congress or a state legislature is an informal power because it has resulted from the historical activities the executive has performed.

49. What does the term "original jurisdiction" mean in relation to the courts?

(A) The first type of court jurisdiction in the nation after the Constitution was written

(B) Judicial review

(C) The court where the case is heard first

(D) The court where the case is heard last

(E) The decision by a court that it will hear a case

Answer: C.

The court where the case is heard first. The Supreme Court has original jurisdiction over disputes between states. "Original" as used with "jurisdiction" means the first time. Therefore, original jurisdiction is the first place a case is heard.

50. **Why does there tend to be continuity on the Supreme Court and in the judicial branch of government?**

   (A) The judges serve during the period of good behavior.

   (B) The judges become aware of how the others think about cases.

   (C) The doctrine of judicial review has made consistency easier, and consistence provides continuity.

   (D) The judges are all approved by Congress.

   (E) The judges are all appointed by the President.

Answer: A.

The judges serve during the period of good behavior. Continuity tends to be the result of "lifetime" appointments. Although the judges are appointed during the term of their "good behavior", the appointment is usually for life.

51. **How are the federal courts linked to the state and local governments?**

   (A) The federal courts hear cases involving state laws.

   (B) The federal court judges help with the appointment standards for state judges.

   (C) State court judges may become federal court judges.

   (D) State courts use the process of judicial review to decide whether acts of Congress are constitutional.

   (E) Federal courts can only hear cases that are appealed to them after a party loses in state court.

Answer: A.

The federal courts hear cases involving state laws. Federal courts hear cases appealed to them from state court decisions. Federal courts can also hear cases for the first time, so choice E is incorrect. State courts may not decide whether Congressional acts are unconstitutional but can decide whether state legislative acts are unconstitutional.

52. The Federal Trade Commission is an example of _____.

(A) Congressional appointment

(B) Presidential appointment

(C) Supreme Court approval

(D) An agency in the Bureaucracy

(E) A state application for the creation of a commission

Answer: D.

An agency in the Bureaucracy. The Federal Trade Commission was created by an act of Congress in 1914. It is a U.S. government agency that protects consumers and competition. It is an example of the result of Congressional legislation, not appointment.

53. **Which of the following is an example of the Bureaucracy?**

(A) Congress

(B) President's Cabinet

(C) U.S. District Court

(D) The Vice President

(E) The Supreme Court justices

Answer: B.

President's Cabinet. Congress, the Vice-President, and "inferior" courts are provided for in the Constitution. Supreme Court justices are included in Article III of the Constitution. The President's Cabinet is a group of non-elected government advisors that make up the Bureaucracy.

54. **Which president expanded the executive branch and made it more powerful?**

(A) Herbert Hoover

(B) Franklin Roosevelt

(C) Harry Truman

(D) William Clinton

(E) George Bush

Answer: B.

Franklin Roosevelt. During the Great Depression, President Roosevelt was involved in creating agencies to help the country's economy rebound. It was this effort that expanded the power of the executive branch of government.

55. **If a person yells "Fire" in an auditorium that is filled with people, is that person entitled to claim freedom of speech as a defense if he/she is arrested?**

    (A) Yes, because civil liberties are unlimited.

    (B) Yes, because the person may have been joking.

    (C) No, because there are limitations on the freedom of speech.

    (D) No, because anyone with common sense would know there might be panic as a result.

    (E) Yelling fire in a crowded auditorium is not an infringement on a civil liberty nor is freedom of speech a civil liberty.

    Answer: C.

    No, because there are limitations on the freedom of speech. Freedom of speech is a civil liberty that is guaranteed by the First Amendment to the Constitution. That freedom, however, may be limited if, for example, the speech can be considered a danger.

56. **Which of the following statements is true about commercial speech?**

    (A) It enjoys complete protection under the First Amendment.

    (B) It is usually in the form of expressive speech.

    (C) It may be restricted if it furthers a substantial government interest and if the restriction actually furthers that interest.

    (D) It may be restricted if it furthers a slight government interest but it is subject to strict scrutiny.

    (E) Commercial speech falls under a different amendment than the First Amendment.

    Answer: C.

    It may be restricted if it furthers a substantial government interest and if the restriction actually furthers that interest. Commercial speech is usually in the form of advertising and does not enjoy complete protection under the First Amendment. If the restriction on commercial speech furthers the interest of the government and the government's interest is substantial, then there can be a restriction on commercial speech.

57. **Which Amendment provides protections for persons convicted of crimes?**

    (A) Fourth

    (B) Fifth

    (C) Sixth

    (D) Eighth

    (E) Fourteenth

    Answer: C.
    Sixth. The Fourth Amendment provides protection from unreasonable searches and seizures. The Fifth Amendment does not require self-incrimination and provides for due process. The Eighth Amendment prohibits cruel and unusual punishment, and the Fourteenth Amendment provides equal protection. The Sixth Amendment guarantees a right to a speedy, public trial, the right to an attorney, the right to confront witnesses, and the right to have witnesses on behalf of a defendant.

58. **The U.S. Supreme Court expanded civil rights and liberties in the case of *Griswold v. Connecticut*, a case that involved _____ privacy.**

    (A) Personal

    (B) Marital

    (C) Group

    (D) Business

    (E) Religious

    Answer: B.
    Marital. The Supreme Court decided that a state law that made the use of birth control subject to criminal liability was unconstitutional because the law violated the right to marital privacy.

59. **The attempt to end and prevent discrimination is called _____.**

   (A) Title IX

   (B) Desegregation

   (C) Integration

   (D) Affirmative Action

   (E) Assimilation

   Answer: D.

   Affirmative Action. Affirmative Action consists of government-approved programs, government-mandated programs, and voluntary programs that attempt to prevent and end discrimination. Many affirmative action programs have been implemented in the field of employment.

60. **The Fourteenth Amendment was made applicable to the states through _____.**

   (A) Stare decisis

   (B) Judicial review

   (C) The incorporation doctrine

   (D) The Due Process clause

   (E) The Equal Protection clause

   Answer: C.

   The incorporation doctrine. The provisions of the Fourteenth Amendment and other parts of the Bill of Rights are made applicable through the incorporation doctrine. Stare decisis means "let the decision stand". Judicial review is the power of the Supreme Court to review, and declare unconstitutional, the acts of Congress. Due process is a protection guaranteed by the Fifth Amendment, and the Fourteenth Amendment provides for equal protection under the law.

Section II: Free Response Sample Answers

1. **Public policy has multiple stages.**

   a. **Define public policy.**

   b. **Identify major public policies and the sources of public policy.**

   c. **Provide substantive examples of ways public policy is the results of interactions among individuals, interests, institutions, and processes.**

   d. **Discuss the differences between foreign and domestic foreign policy areas**

      • **Describe how these policy areas affect citizens.**

      • **State whether these policy areas overlap and explain why or why not.**

   Sample Answers:

   a. Public policy is a course of action that the government follows in order to deal with an issue. It is goal oriented and based on law. Public policy provides for penalties and is formulated by the legislature and other groups.

   b. Major public policies involve foreign policy, domestic policy, economic policy, defense policy, and social and regulatory policy. A variety of groups and people interact to make policy. All of the following groups make policy in the U.S.: legislatures, both Congress and state; the President and governors; federal and state courts; the Cabinet; advisers, bureaucrats; the media; political parties, and interest groups.

   c. Foreign policy, for example, is made by the President; his advisors, such as members of the State Department and the Foreign Service (ambassadors); and the Senate. Diplomacy is the objective of foreign policy, and the goal is to resolve differences peacefully rather than by war. The National Security Council also shapes foreign policy, and the Central Intelligence Agency (CIA) shapes policy by analyzing information received from and about other countries and individuals that may be important for the protection and security of our country.

   d. Foreign policy deals with the relationships between our government and governments of other countries. Domestic policy is policy that affects people within the United States and focuses on topics such as the economy and social policy, including welfare and Social Security.

   Both policies affect citizens. Foreign policy affects us because we need to feel secure about relationships between our country and others. Domestic policy affects us because economic policy, for example, deals with fiscal policy and monetary policy. Fiscal and monetary policy deal with how much money is in the economy, whether there is inflation or stagnation of the economy and how to solve the problems, tax cuts, spending and other matters relating to the country's money and finances.

Many public policies overlap. The cost of living can affect whether Social Security recipients will be given a "cost of living" adjustment in their monthly checks. Cost of living and oil prices can affect monetary policy and foreign policy.

2. **It is necessary to understand the development of rights and liberties in order to understand American politics.**

   a. **Explain the role of the U.S. Supreme Court in developing rights and liberties.**

   b. **What important Supreme Court Cases support your explanation?**

      • **Explain the significant of these cases.**

      • **Identify current issues in which the Supreme Court has, or will likely play a role in, developing rights and liberties.**

   c. **Describe the effects, or lack of effects, on society after these Supreme Court decisions.**

   d. **Explain the role of the Fourteenth Amendment in the expansion of rights and liberties.**

Sample Answers:

a. The Supreme Court has played an important role in developing individual rights and liberties through its interpretation of the laws that are being challenged.

b. Some of the important cases include: *Gideon v. Wainwright*, which holds that indigent criminal defendants are entitled to be represented by counsel in serious cases. *Shelley v. Kraemer* involved a racially restrictive property covenant, and the Court held that those covenants violate the Equal Protection clause of the Fourteenth Amendment. The Civil Rights Act of 1964 was the focus of *Heart of Atlanta Motel Inc. v. U.S.* The Court upheld the Civil Rights Act and the valid exercise of Congressional power under the Commerce Clause. The case holding prohibits private discrimination in public accommodations, such as motels and restaurants. In *Miranda v. Arizona* the Court held that detained criminal suspects must be informed of their constitutional rights prior to police questioning. In 2015, the Court in *Obergefell v. Hodges* granted the constitutional right to marry for LGBT Americans throughout the country.

The significance of these cases is the protection of individual civil liberties and civil rights. The Court has expanded some of the rights over the years, and has done to gradually in most cases. The Court will likely continue to hear cases involving same sex couples, racial minority rights, and women's rights.

c. The effects on society of the Supreme Court holdings are varied. In some cases, the state legislatures must adopt or rewrite legislation that does not violate the Constitution. In other cases, people will accept the expansion of rights differently but the ultimate outcome is that individual rights and civil liberties have been expanded, whether by small steps or giant leaps.

d. The Fourteenth Amendment has been the basis of many of the cases heard by the U.S. Supreme Court. Some have involved freedom of speech, freedom of the press, right to an attorney, cruel and unusual punishment, and desegregation of schools. Although some of the cases have been "landmark" cases, or cases of historic importance, they may not have resulted in gains or wins that could be seen immediately or without continued effort on the part of society to see that the new rulings were implemented. The holding in *Brown v. Board of Education* is an example. Although the Supreme Court said that separate educational facilities are inherently unequal facilities, the integration of schools did not take place overnight.

3. **The framers of the Constitution drew on ideological and philosophical traditions to draft the new organization of American government.**

   a. **Identify the traditions the framers used.**

   b. **How do these traditions relate to the historical situation at the time of the Constitutional convention?**

   c. **Identify specific concerns of the framers.**

   d. **Explain the concerns that existed in determining whether the Constitution should be ratified.**

   e. **Explain why a Bill of Rights was added to the Constitution.**

      • **Identify the rights that were included.**

      • **Describe the reasons for the inclusion of some of those rights.**

Sample Answers:

a. The Framers used the concept of natural law, which John Locke believed was the basis of government. The idea of certain unalienable rights was also evident in the Declaration of Independence. Locke also expressed the idea of the "social contract" by which the people agree to be governed and the government agrees to protect natural rights. The ideas of the Enlightenment were also embodied in the Constitution. Montesquieu had expressed the importance of separation of powers and checks and balances, and these ideas were included in the Constitution.

b. The ideas were fresh in the minds of the Americans because they were not far removed from the American Revolution and the Declaration of Independence where the philosophical thinking of the European philosophers had played an important role in gaining independence.

c. The Framers had specific concerns about the organization of the new form of government they were drafting. Concerns related to the slavery issue, the formation of the legislative branch in regards to population and responsiveness to the people, and the fear that an executive might become too powerful.

d. Once the Constitution had been written, concerns still existed about whether it would be ratified. The Anti-federalists feared that the new government would not protect individual rights without a bill of rights. The Federalists were concerned that the document would not be ratified even though they promised to include a Bill of Rights shortly after the Constitution was ratified.

e. A Bill of Rights was added to the Constitution after the document had been ratified. The purpose of the amendments was to keep the promise to the Anti-Federalists who were concerned about the possible disregard of individual rights.

The first ten amendments to the Constitution are called the Bill of Rights. The first amendment guarantees the freedoms of speech, press, assembly, religion and the right to petition the government for redress of grievances. The right to petition the redress of grievances, for example, was included because when people had petitioned the king of England, their grievances were largely ignored. The Second Amendment guarantees the right to bear arms and the Third Amendment guarantees that the militia will not be quartered in people's homes during the time of peace. Soldiers had been quartered in homes at times during England's rule.

The Fourth Amendment protected people from unreasonable search and seizure, and the Fifth Amendment guaranteed citizens that they would not lose life, liberty, or property without due process of law. The "process" was not identified, but the amendment guaranteed there would be a process and that there would not be arbitrary decisions to deprive people of life, liberty, and property. This amendment also provides that there shall be a grand jury in certain kinds of cases. In addition, this amendment guarantees that a person does not have to incriminate himself / herself by testifying against himself / herself.

The Sixth Amendment guarantees criminal defendants certain rights: trial by jury, right to confront witnesses, right to an attorney; and the Seventh Amendment guarantees a jury trial at the federal level in civil cases where a certain amount of money is involved. The Eighth Amendment guarantees against cruel and unusual punishment; and the Ninth Amendment states that the listing of rights in the Constitution does not mean that the public does not have other rights. The Tenth Amendment states "the powers not delegated to the United States by the Constitution, nor prohibited by it to the states, are reserved to the states respectively, or to the people." This amendment describes the basic concept of federalism.

Many of these amendments were included because they were rights that the citizens felt had been denied to them as colonists.

4. **Interest groups and the media play a role in politics.**

   a. **Define the term interest group.**

   b. **Define the term media.**

   c. **Explain the role of each in politics.**
   - **How does each group function?**
   - **How do the activities of each group affect the process of government?**
   - **How do the activities of each group affect public policy?**

Sample Answers:

a. Interest groups are organized groups that have a specific goal of influencing public policy or public opinion.

b. Media is the method of transmitting news and information to the public through organized means, such as television, the Internet, and written materials. It also refers to the people communicating the news.

c. The media has a role in politics by communicating the platforms of candidates and parties. It also interprets the statements of candidates. The media and interest groups can have a great deal of influence on the process of government because the media's interpretation of events can shift public opinion; and interest groups shape public opinion through advertisements, litigation, and conversations with legislators. Both groups affect public policy through communications and promoting their views, whether through newscasts, documentaries, litigation, or communications.

APPENDIX:
US Government and Politics Time Line

This XAMonline time line is an outline of the evolution of the Constitution, balance of powers resolutions, public policy reforms, and the progression of civil liberties in the history of the United States government. It is to be used as a supplement to the study guide and is not meant as a comprehensive list of material covered in the AP U.S. Government and Politics Course.

SECTION 7:
Title

1775 ☐ **First U.S. Currency,** known as "continentals," issued by the Continental Congress.

1776 ☐ **Declaration of Independence**

1778 ☐ The **Treasury System** reorganized.

1787 ☐ **Northwest Ordinance** established how Northwest Territory was to be organized and eventually organized into states.

1789 ☐ **George Washington** inaugurated first President.

U.S. Constitution approved, replacing the Articles of Confederation and establishing a stronger federal government.

Judiciary Act established the U.S. district courts to serve as the federal trial courts for admiralty and maritime cases, as well as for some minor criminal cases and minor civil suits brought by the United States.

First U.S. Veterans Pension Law approved during the first session of the U.S. Congress for invalid Revolutionary War soldiers on September 29, 1789.

The Fifth Act of Congress established the United States Customs Service.

Department of the Treasury established.

Postal Service established.

The Department of War established.

1791 ☐ **The Bill of Rights** approved and became Amendments One through Ten of the Constitution.

1791 ☐ **First Bank of the United States** established.

The Revenue Act of 1791, the first system of internal taxation in the United States was established. It imposed an excise tax on distilled liquors and was called the "whiskey tax."

1796 ☐ Seat of Government established in **Washington, DC.**

John Adams (Federalist) elected President.

(left margin) George Washington

(right sidebar)

Constitutional Evolution
U.S. Constitution approved
The Bill of Rights

Balance of Powers Resolutions
Judiciary Act

Constitutional Evolution

Twelfth Amendment

Balance of Powers Resolutions

Marbury v. Madison

Fletcher v. Peck

McCulloch v. Maryland

John Adams

1798 ☐ **Alien and Sedition Acts** passed, establishing more stringent citizenship requirements, allowing deportation of non-citizens from an enemy nation or those deemed dangerous and criminalized making false statements critical of the government.

1800 ☐ **Thomas Jefferson** (Democratic Republican) elected president.

Thomas Jefferson

1803 ☐ *Marbury v. Madison* established the principle of judicial review.

Louisiana Purchase Treaty doubled the size of the United States.

1804 ☐ **Twelfth Amendment** establishes separate ballots for President and Vice President.

1808 ☐ **African Slave Trade** ends.

James Madison elected president.

James Madison

1809 ☐ **Non-Intercourse Act** lifted embargoes on American shipping except for those bound for British or French ports.

1810 ☐ *Fletcher v. Peck* establishes that action of a state can be declared unconstitutional.

1816 ☐ National Bank rechartered.

National Road expanded.

James Monroe (Democratic Republican) elected president.

James Monroe

1819 ☐ *McCulloch v. Maryland* established the principle that federal law takes precedence over state law.

1820 ☐ **Missouri Compromise** admitted Maine as free state and Missouri as a slave state but allowed no slave states north of Missouri.

1823 ☐ **Monroe Doctrine** warned European nations against further involvement in and colonization of territories in the Western Hemisphere.

1824 ☐ *Gibbons v. Ogden* established that federal courts control interstate trade.

J. Monroe	**1824** ☐ Election of **John Quincy Adams** (Democratic Republican) Contested election, Jackson calls it a "corrupt bargain."
	1828 ☐ **Andrew Jackson** (Democrat) elected president.
Andrew Jackson	**1833** ☐ *Barron v. Baltimore* established that each American is separately a citizen of the national government and of the state government.
	1834 ☐ The **Indian Department** established within the War Department.
W.H. Harrison	**1840** ☐ **William Henry Harrison** (Whig) elected president.
John Tyler	**1841** ☐ After one month in office, Harrison dies and Vice President **John Tyler** (Independent) becomes president.
	1844 ☐ **James K. Polk** (Democrat) elected president.
James K. Polk	**1846** ☐ **Oregon Treaty** stipulated that the United States gained territory in the northwest that would become the states of Oregon, Washington, Idaho, and parts of Wyoming and Montana.
	1848 ☐ **Treaty of Guadalupe Hidalgo** ends the Mexican-American War and the United States gained California and territories in the Southwest.
	Zachary Taylor (Whig) elected president.
Zachary Taylor	**1849** ☐ **Department of the Interior** established.
	1850 ☐ Vice President **Millard Fillmore** becomes president upon President Taylor's death.
Millard Fillmore	**Compromise of 1850** regulated slavery in California, Utah Territory, New Mexico Territory and The District of Columbia.
	Treaty of Fort Laramie sets precedent for Native Americans to be moved to certain territories.
	1856 ☐ **James Buchanan** (Democrat) elected president.
James Buchanan	**1857** ☐ *Dred Scott v. Sanford* established that slaves were not citizens, Scott did not have a right to sue in federal court, and that the Missouri Compromise was unconstitutional.

Public Policy Reforms

Alien and Sedition Acts

Civil Liberties Progression

Gibbons v. Ogden

Dred Scott v. Sanford

Constitutional Evolution

Thirteenth Amendment

Fourteenth Amendment

Fifteenth Amendment

Balance of Powers Resolutions

Evarts Act

Abraham Lincoln

1860 ☐ **Abraham Lincoln** (Republican) elected president.

1861 ☐ Southern states seceded to form the **Confederate States of America**.

Ex Parte Merryman ruled that the authority to suspend habeas corpus lay exclusively with Congress.

1862 ☐ **Homestead Act** allowed anyone over the age of 21 who had not "taken up arms" against the United States and who was the head of a household, to acquire 160 acres of land if he lived on the land for five years and improved it.

Department of Agriculture established.

Morrill Act allotted federal land to townships for public schools, and provided the first public aid to education.

Army Medal of Honor established.

1863 ☐ **Habeas Corpus Suspension Act** authorized President Lincoln to suspend the writ of habeas corpus during the civil war, allowing the arrest and imprisonment without trial of anyone who threatened public safety.

Emancipation Proclamation announced the freedom of slaves in areas still in rebellion.

National Banking Act allowed nationally chartered banks to circulate notes backed by government securities, in effect establishing a national currency.

1865 ☐ **Thirteenth Amendment** abolished slavery and involuntary servitude, except as punishment for a crime.

President Lincoln assassinated by John Wilkes Booth and Vice President **Andrew Johnson** becomes president.

Andrew Johnson

1867 ☐ **Purchase of the Alaska Territory** from the Russian Empire.

Tenure of Office Act prohibited President from removing cabinet members without Senate approval.

A. Johnson

1868 ☐ **Impeachment trial of President Andrew Johnson** for violating the Tenure of Office Act

Fourteenth Amendment guaranteed citizenship rights and equal protection of the laws, especially in reference to the newly emancipated African Americans after the Civil War.

Ulysses S. Grant (Republican) elected.

Ulysses S. Grant

1870 ☐ **Attorney General** becomes the head of Department of Justice.

Fifteenth Amendment prohibits denial of the right to vote to any citizen based on that citizen's "race, color, or previous condition of servitude."

1876 ☐ *U.S. v. Reese* allowed voting qualifications like literacy tests and poll taxes.

1877 ☐ *Munn v. Illinois* upheld power of federal government to regulate private industries.

Compromise of 1877: **Rutherford B. Hayes** (Republican) becomes president, reconstruction ends.

R.B. Hayes

James Garfield

1880 ☐ **James Garfield** (Republican) elected president, six months later Garfield dies and Vice President **Chester Arthur** becomes president.

Chester Arthur

1882 ☐ **Chinese Exclusion Act** suspended immigration of Chinese laborers, and prohibited Chinese immigrants from becoming citizens for ten years.

Grover Cleveland

1884 ☐ **Grover Cleveland** (Democrat) elected president.

1887 ☐ **Interstate Commerce Act** regulated railroad monopolies.

1888 ☐ **Benjamin Harrison** (Republican) elected president.

Benjamin Harrison

1890 ☐ **Sherman Antitrust Act** outlawed practices deemed monopolistic and thus harmful to consumers and the market economy.

1891 ☐ **Evarts Act** gave the U.S. courts of appeals jurisdiction over the great majority of appeals from the U.S. district and circuit courts.

Public Policy Reforms

Munn v. Illinois

Chinese Exclusion Act

Sherman Antitrust Act

Interstate Commerce Act

Civil Liberties Progression

Habeas Corpus Suspension Act

Emancipation Proclamation

U.S. v. Reese

Constitutional Evolution

Sixteenth Amendment

Eighteenth Amendment.

Nineteenth Amendment

Balance of Powers Resolutions

Wabash, St. Louis & Pacific Railway Company v. Illinois

Grover Cleveland

1892 ☐ **Grover Cleveland** (Republican) elected president.

1893 ☐ **Court of Appeals of the District of Columbia** established to hear appeals from the Supreme Court of the District of Columbia.

1895 ☐ *U.S. v. E. C. Knight Company* established that the Anti-Trust Act regulates commerce but not manufacturing.

Pollack v. Farmers' Loan and Trust Co established that income tax is unconstitutional.

1896 ☐ *Plessy v. Ferguson* upheld racial segregation in public facilities under the doctrine of "separate but equal."

Wabash, St. Louis & Pacific Railway Company v. Illinois (Wabash Case) denied states rights to regulate interstate railroads.

William McKinley (Republican) elected president

William McKinley

1901 ☐ **Platt Amendment** ends the Spanish-American war.

Insular Cases establish that full constitutional rights do not automatically extend to all places under American control.

President McKinley assassinated, **Theodore Roosevelt** (Republican) becomes president.

Theodore Roosevelt

1903 ☐ First wildlife refuge established at **Pelican Island National Bird Reservation** by President Theodore Roosevelt

1906 ☐ **Pure Food and Drugs Act** outlawed the adulteration and misbranding of food and drug products moving in interstate commerce and required active ingredients to be listed on labels.

1908 ☐ *Muller v. Oregon* upheld restrictions on the working hours of women as justified by the need to protect women's health.

William Howard Taft (Republican) elected president.

W. H. Taft

1911 □ The Judicial Code of 1911 **abolished the U.S. circuit courts,** transferring their jurisdiction to the U.S. district courts.

Standard Oil Co. v. U.S. broke up Standard Oil Company.

1912 □ **Woodrow Wilson** (Democrat) elected president.

Woodrow Wilson

1913 □ **Sixteenth Amendment** established the first constitutionally mandated income tax.

Federal Reserve Act established the Federal Reserve.

1914 □ **Clayton Antitrust Act** enabled the federal government to outlaw practices that it foresaw as potentially damaging to consumers and the competitive market.

1915 □ **Federal Trade Commission** established to protect consumers and promote competition.

1916 □ **National Park Service** created.

1919 □ *Schenck v. U.S.* determined that there is no freedom of speech when it presents a "clear and present" danger.

Treaty of Versailles ended World War I

Volstead Act implemented the prohibition of production, sale, and transport of "intoxicating liquors," enforcing the **Eighteenth Amendment.**

1920 □ **Nineteenth Amendment** gave women the right to vote.

Warren G. Harding (Republican) elected president.

W. G. Harding

1921 □ **United States Veterans Bureau** established to consolidate federal veterans programs.

1923 □ President Warren G. Harding died and **Calvin Coolidge** (Republican) became president.

1924 □ **Immigration Act of 1924** and **Chinese Exclusion Act** limited the total number of immigrants of each nationality and excluded all immigrants from Asia.

Calvin Coolidge

1925 □ *Gitlow v. New York* established that state laws cannot impair the freedom of speech or freedom of the press protected by the due process clause of the Fourteenth Amendment.

1928 □ **Herbert Hoover** (Republican) elected president.

Public Policy Reforms

U.S. v. E. C. Knight Company

Pure Food and Drugs Act

Clayton Antitrust Act

Immigration Act of 1924 and Chinese Exclusion Act

Civil Liberties Progression

Plessy v. Ferguson

Insular Cases

Muller v. Oregon

Schenck v. U.S.

Gitlow v. New York

Constitutional Evolution

Twenty-first Amendment

Herbert Hoover

1929 ☐ **Wall Street Crash**, or Black Tuesday, began ten-year Great Depression.

1932 ☐ **Federal Home Loan Bank Act** lowered the cost of home ownership.

Franklin D. Roosevelt (Democrat) is elected president.

Franklin D. Roosevelt

1933 ☐ **Twenty-first Amendment** repealed the Eighteenth Amendment, ending Prohibition.

Roosevelt's **New Deal** programs developed, including:

- WPA – Works Progress Administration
- CCC – Civilian Conservation Corps
- NIRA – National Industrial Recovery Act
- SEC – Securities and Exchange Commission
- AAA – Agricultural Adjustment Association
- TVA – Tennessee Valley Authority
- CWA – Civil Works Administration
- NYA – National Youth Administration
- HOLC – Home Owners Loan Corp.
- **Glass-Steagall Banking Act**, which established the FDIC and limited affiliations between commercial banks and investment banks.

1935 ☐ **Social Security Act** created social security system.

1938 ☐ **Food, Drug, and Cosmetic Act** required all new drugs to be reviewed by the Food and Drug Administration to ensure that they are safe.

1941 ☐ **U.S. Army Air Forces** was established.

1944 ☐ *Korematsu v. United States* ruled that it was not unconstitutional to impose legal restrictions on persons with "foreign enemy ancestry," allowing the government to send Japanese-Americans to internment camps during World War II.

The "**G.I. Bill**" or Serviceman's Readjustment Act of 1944 provided new education, training, housing, and rehabilitation benefits for veterans.

1945 ☐ Upon the death of Franklin Delano Roosevelt, **Harry Truman** (Democrat) becomes president.

United States dropped atomic bombs on Japanese cities of **Hiroshima and Nagasaki**.

Japan and Germany surrender, **ending WWII**.

United Nations (UN) organization created.

1946 ☐ **Atomic Energy Act** (McMahon Act) transferred control of atomic energy from military to civilian hands.

1947 ☐ **National Security Act** ordered major reorganization of U.S. military establishments and federal offices that planned and executed foreign policy, creating the National Security Council (NSC) and the Central Intelligence Agency (CIA).

Truman Doctrine established financial commitment to nations fighting communism, particularly in Turkey and Greece.

Taft-Hartley Act placed restrictions on the power of labor unions.

1948 ☐ **Marshall Plan** (European Recovery Act) provided large-scale aid to rebuild Europe and protect it from communism.

President Truman's Executive Order 9981 **abolished racial discrimination in the Armed Forces** ending segregation in the services.

1949 ☐ **North American Treaty Organization** (NATO) established.

Geneva Conventions defined the basic rights of wartime prisoners, protected wounded, and established protections for civilians in and around a war zone.

Fairness Doctrine required broadcast news to present controversial issues of public importance in an honest, equitable, and balanced.

1951 ☐ *Roth v. United States* established that obscenity is not protected by the First Amendment and created a test that would more accurately and strictly define "obscene materials."

Public Policy Reforms

Federal Home Loan Bank Act

New Deal

Social Security Act

G.I. Bill

Taft-Hartley Act

Roth v. United States

Civil Liberties Progression

Korematsu v. United States

Executive Order 9981

Constitutional Evolution

Twenty-second
Amendment

Twenty-fourth
Amendment

Harry Truman

1951 ☐ **Twenty-second Amendment** establishes that no president can be elected more than twice or act as president more than ten years.

1952 ☐ **National Security Agency** (NSA) established.

Dwight D. Eisenhower (Republican) elected president.

Dwight D. Eisenhower

1954 ☐ *Brown v. Board of Education of Topeka* determined "separate but equal" does not apply to educational facilities.

Atomic Energy Act created **Atomic Energy Commission** (AEC) foster and control the peacetime development of atomic science and technology.

1956 ☐ **Bank Holding Company Act** makes the Federal Reserve the regulator of bank holding companies that own more than one bank.

Interstate Highway Act began construction of the Interstate Highway System.

1957 ☐ **Civil Rights Act of 1957** establishes the Civil Rights Commission

1958 ☐ **National Defense Education Act** passed to increase the technological sophistication and power of the United States.

National Aeronautics and Space Administration (NASA) established by Congress.

Federal Aviation Act establishes **Federal Aviation Agency** (FAA).

1960 ☐ **Civil Rights Act of 1960 begins** federal government registration of black voters.

First televised presidential debate.

John F. Kennedy (Democrat) elected president.

John F. Kennedy

1961 ☐ *Mapp v. Ohio* declared that evidence obtained through unreasonable search and seizure, banned by the Fourth Amendment, cannot be used in trial.

1962 ☐ *Baker v. Carr* ends gerrymandering, forcing reapportionment of federal, state, and local election districts.

John F. Kennedy

1962 ☐ *Engel v. Vitale* banned prayer in public schools on basis of First Amendment.

Kefauver-Harris Drug Amendments to the 1938 Food, Drug, and Cosmetic Act required all new drugs to be proven both safe and effective prior to marketing.

1963 ☐ *Gideon v. Wainwright* established that defendants in criminal cases must be appointed counsel if they cannot afford their own attorneys.

President Kennedy assassinated by Lee Harvey Oswald and **Lyndon Johnson** (Democrat) becomes President

1964 ☐ *New York Times v. Sullivan* established that a news story cannot be deemed libelous unless it resulted from "actual malice" or "reckless disregard" for the truth.

The Civil Rights Act of 1964 outlawed discrimination based on race, color, religion, sex, or national origin.

Twenty-fourth Amendment outlaws poll tax.

Wilderness Act created legal definition of wilderness and protected 9.1 million acres of federal land.

Indian Reorganization Act restored tribal ownership of lands, recognized tribal constitutions and government, and provided loans for economic development.

Lyndon B. Johnson

1965 ☐ *Griswold v. Connecticut* established that state laws restricting circulation of birth control information and married couples' use of contraceptives violated the right to privacy.

Social Security Act of 1965 establishes Medicare and Medicaid programs.

Higher Education Act increased federal money given to universities, created scholarships, gave low-interest loans for students, and established a National Teachers Corps.

The Voting Rights Act of 1965, amended and extended in 1960s and 1970s, prohibited racial discrimination in voting.

Immigration and Nationality Act abolished the national origins quota system and replaced it with a preference system that focused on immigrants' skills and family relationships with citizens or U.S. residents.

Public Policy Reforms

National Defense Education Act

Mapp v. Ohio

Indian Reorganization Act

Social Security Act of 1965

Higher Education Act

Immigration and Nationality Act

Civil Liberties Progression

Brown v. Board of Education of Topeka

Civil Rights Act of 1957

Civil Rights Act of 1960

Engel v. Vitale

Gideon v. Wainwright

The Civil Rights Act of 1964

Griswold v. Connecticut

The Voting Rights Act of 1965

Constitutional Evolution

Twenty-fifth Amendment

Twenty-sixth Amendment

Balance of Powers Resolutions

The War Powers Resolution

United States v. Nixon

Foreign Intelligence Surveillance Act

Lyndon B. Johnson

1966 *Miranda v. Arizona* established that detained criminal suspects must be informed of their rights before being questioned.

Department of Housing and Urban Development (HUD) established to create strong, sustainable, inclusive communities and quality affordable homes.

Department of Transportation Act combined 31 previously scattered federal elements under one Cabinet Department, including The Federal Aviation Agency.

Freedom of Information Act (FOIA) identified the kinds of executive branch agency records that can be disclosed and described mandatory disclosure procedures.

1967 **Twenty-fifth Amendment** allows a Vice President to appoint a new Vice President if he becomes President.

1968 **Civil Rights Act of 1968** attempts to provide African Americans with equal-opportunity housing.

Richard M. Nixon (Republican) elected president.

Richard Nixon

1969 **National Environmental Policy Act** (NEPA) passed to help assess the impacts of major federal development projects on fish and wildlife.

1970 **Clean Air Act** established to control air quality, administered by the U.S. Environmental Protection Agency (EPA), which was established to protect human health and the environment by writing and enforcing regulations based on laws passed by Congress.

1971 *Reed v. Reed* established that the Fourteenth Amendment applies to a law that discriminated against women.

New York Times Co. v. U.S. established that the government could not prevent publication by the *New York Times* of the Pentagon Papers.

Twenty-sixth Amendment prohibited the denial of the right of U.S. citizens, eighteen years of age or older, to vote on account of age.

1972 **Equal Rights Amendment (ERA)** passed but not ratified by all states.

1973 ☐ *Roe v. Wade* established a woman's right to have an abortion after the second trimester.

Gideon v. Wainwright decided state and local courts must provide counsel for defendants in felony cases.

The **War Powers Resolution** established that the President cannot order the military into action without a declaration of war by Congress.

Endangered Species Act passed to protect critically imperiled species from extinction.

1974 ☐ *United States v. Nixon* established that executive privilege does not extend to the use of data in presidential files or tapes for evidence in a criminal prosecution.

Richard Nixon resigns presidency and **Gerald Ford** (Republican) becomes president.

President Ford pardons Richard Nixon.

1974 ☐ **The Federal Election Campaign Act** regulated political campaign spending and fundraising, limiting the size of contributions.

The Budget and Impoundment Control Act of 1974 created standing budget committees in the House and the Senate and established the Congressional Budget Office.

1975 ☐ **Nuclear Regulatory Commission** established and Atomic Energy Commission dissolved.

1976 ☐ *Buckley v. Valeo* declared limits on freedom of individuals to contribute their own money to election campaigns to be unconstitutional.

Medical Devices Amendment to the 1938 Food, Drug and Cosmetic Act made it necessary to consider a premarket approval process for medical devices.

James Earl "Jimmy" Carter, Jr. (Democrat) elected president.

1977 ☐ President Carter creates **Department of Energy.**

1978 ☐ **Foreign Intelligence Surveillance Act** (FISA) established process of judicial review of applications for warrants related to national security investigations.

Public Policy Reforms

Department of Housing and Urban Development established

National Environmental Policy Act

Clean Air Act

Endangered Species Act

Department of Energy created

Civil Liberties Progression

Miranda v. Arizona

Civil Rights Act of 1968

Reed v. Reed

New York Times Co. v. U.S.

Roe v. Wade

Gideon v. Wainwright

Jimmy Carter

1978 □ *Regents of the University of California v. Bakke* established that universities could consider minority status in admissions to help contribute to a "diverse student body."

Humphrey-Hawkins Act required The Federal Reserve chairman to report to Congress twice annually on monetary policy goals and objectives.

1979 □ **Department of Energy** created to oversee energy policy and ensure safety in handling nuclear material.

1980 □ **Monetary Control Act** established reforms to the Federal Reserve including the establishment of reserve requirements for all eligible financial institutions.

Ronald Reagan (Republican) elected president.

1987 □ The FCC eliminated the Fairness Doctrine, the requirement for equal coverage of controversial issues on public airwaves, on the basis that it violated broadcasters' freedom of speech. (Officially repealed in 2011)

Ronald Reagan

1988 □ Veterans Administration elevated to Cabinet-level department and renamed the **Department of Veterans Affairs.**

Civil Liberties Act granted reparations to Japanese Americans who had been interned by the United States government during World War II.

George H. W. Bush (Republican) elected president.

1990 □ **Americans with Disabilities Act** established protection against discrimination based on disability, requires employers to provide reasonable accommodations to employees with disabilities and requires public places to adhere to accessibility accommodations.

Nutrition Labeling and Education Act required packaged food products to bear nutrition labeling in a standardized format labeled "Nutrition Facts."

George H. W. Bush

1992 □ *Roe v. Wade* upheld by Supreme Court.

William Jefferson "Bill" Clinton (Democrat) elected president.

1993 ☐ **Brady Handgun Violence Prevention Act** mandated federal background checks on firearm purchasers in the United States, and imposed a five-day waiting period on purchases.

1996 ☐ **Personal Responsibility and Work Opportunity Act** (Welfare Reform Act) established welfare eligibility requirements including work in exchange for time-limited assistance, child support enforcement, and increased child care funding assistance.

Telecommunications Act deregulated segments of the electronic media, leading to consolidation of major media corporations.

1998 ☐ **President Clinton is impeached** by the United States House of Representatives.

1999 ☐ **President Clinton is acquitted** by the United States Senate.

Gramm-Leach-Bliley Act replaced the Glass-Steagall Act of 1933 allowing banks to offer financial services, including investment banking and insurance.

2000 ☐ *Bush v. Gore* prevented recount of presidential election ballots in several Florida counties, leading to the presidency of George W. Bush.

2001 ☐ **Education Reform Bill** (No Child Left Behind Act) enacted to improve education performance by tying annual standardized performance testing to amount of federal education funds provided to states.

Terrorist attack on the World Trade Center and the Pentagon. A third highjacked plane downed near Shanksville, Pennsylvania.

USA Patriot Act passed to deter and punish terrorist acts in the United States and around the world and to enhance law enforcement investigatory tools by expanding surveillance authority.

George W. Bush

Public Policy Reforms

Nutrition Labeling and Education Act

Brady Handgun Violence Prevention Act

Personal Responsibility and Work Opportunity Act

Telecommunications Act

Education Reform Bill

USA Patriot Act

Civil Liberties Progression

Regents of the University of California v. Bakke

Civil Liberties Act

Americans with Disabilities Act

USA Patriot Act

George W. Bush

2002 ☐ **Homeland Security Act** established to prevent terrorist attacks, minimize damage and assist in recovery from attacks that do occur, and to unify organizations such as FEMA, U.S. Coast Guard, U.S. Secret Service and the Transportation Security Administration under the U.S. Department of Homeland Security.

2003 ☐ *Grutter v. Bollinger* established the legality of affirmative action policy of the University of Michigan Law School.

Lawrence v. Texas struck down sodomy laws and established the legality of homosexual sexual activity in the United States.

McConnell v. Federal Election Commission ruled that campaign contributions from minors could not be banned, and that a party committee cannot make independent and coordinated expenditures for a candidate after that candidate's nomination.

U.S. Customs and Border Patrol established to prevent terrorists and those with a criminal record from entering the U.S. illegally, and to stem the flow of illegal drugs, protect agricultural and economic interests from importation of harmful pests and diseases, and protect American businesses from intellectual property theft.

2004 ☐ **Intelligence Reform and Terrorism Prevention Act** established the position of Director of National Intelligence (DNI), the National Counter Terrorism Center (NCTC), and the Privacy and Civil Liberties Oversight Board.

2008 ☐ **Global Financial Crisis** results in bankruptcy of Lehman Brothers and national governments bail out banks to prevent further collapses.

Barack Hussein Obama (Democrat) elected first African American president.

Barack Obama

2009 ☐ **American Recovery and Reinvestment Act** passed as a stimulus package to save and create jobs, to provide temporary relief programs and invest in infrastructure, education, health, and renewable energy.

Barack Obama

2010   *Citizens United v. Federal Election Commission* establishes that the First Amendment prohibits the restriction of independent political expenditures by corporations, labor unions, and other associations.

Patient Protection and Affordable Care Act passed to improve quality and lower healthcare costs, increase access to healthcare, and define new consumer protections

Dodd-Frank Wall Street Reform and Consumer Protection Act establishes the Consumer Financial Protection Bureau.

Don't Ask, Don't Tell Repeal Act passed to allow gay, lesbian, and bisexual individuals to serve openly in the United States Armed Forces.

2013   *Shelby County v. Holder* establishes that Section 4 of the Voting Rights Act is unconstitutional; effectively repealing the requirement that certain jurisdictions prove that any proposed voting change is not discriminatory before implementation.

2015   *Obergefell v. Hodges* established legality of gay marriage.

Public Policy Reforms

McConnell v. Federal Election Commission

American Recovery and Reinvestment Act

Dodd-Frank Wall Street Reform and Consumer Protection Act

Patient Protection and Affordable Care Act

Civil Liberties Progression

Grutter v. Bollinger

Lawrence v. Texas

Citizens United v. Federal Election Commission

Don't Ask, Don't Tell Repeal Act

Shelby County v. Holder

Obergefell v. Hodges

AP

The Advanced Placement® program is designed to offer students college credit while still in high school. The more than 30 AP courses culminate in an intensive final exam given every year in May.

Successful completion of a course and a passing score on the exam not only provides students with a deep sense of accomplishment, but also gives them a jumpstart on their college careers. AP credit is almost universally accepted by post-secondary schools, however each school has different guidelines as to what scores they will accept.

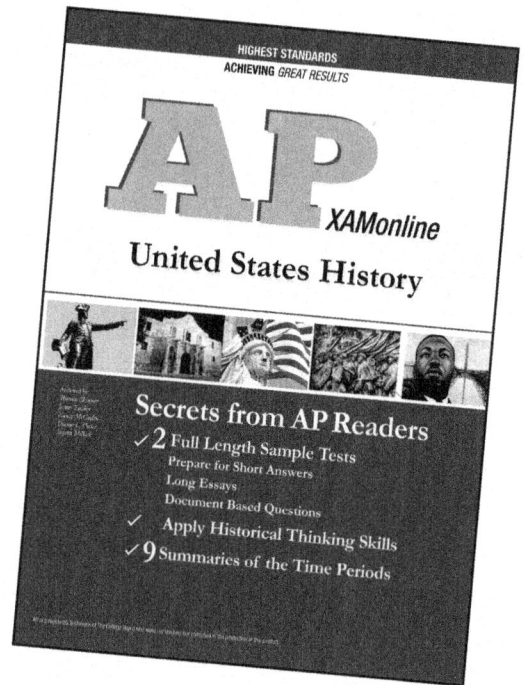

AP US History
ISBN 978-1-60787-552-9 $18.99

AP Government and Politics
ISBN 978-1-60787-600-7 $18.99

AP Biology
ISBN 978-1-60787-553-6 $18.99

AP Calculus
ISBN 978-1-60787-555-0 $18.99

AP Chemistry
ISBN 978-1-60787-554-3 $18.99

AP Psychology
ISBN 978-1-60787-556-7 $18.99

AP English
ISBN 978-1-60787-557-4 $18.99

AP Spanish
ISBN 978-1-60787-558-1 $18.99

AP Microeconomics/Macroeconomics
ISBN 978-1-60787-545-7 $18.99

TO ORDER ➤ These titles are available from **amazon** or **BARNES & NOBLE BOOKSELLERS**

CPSIA information can be obtained
at www.ICGtesting.com
Printed in the USA
BVOW04s1204250817
493105BV00017B/322/P

9 781607 876359